County Court Practice Handbook

County Court Practice Handbook

Ninth edition

Robert Blackford, LL B

Longman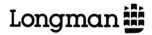

Longman

©Longman Group UK Limited 1967, 1989

Published by
Longman Group Ltd 1989
21–27 Lamb's Conduit Street
London WC1N 3NJ

Associated Offices
Australia, Hong Kong, Malaysia, Singapore, USA

Notes on County Court Practice and Procedure

First published 1967 (Author: Hugh Collins)
Second edition 1972 (Author: Hugh Collins)
Third edition 1974 (Author: Hugh Collins)
Fourth edition 1976 (Author: Hugh Collins)
Fifth edition 1978 (Author: Hugh Collins)
Sixth edition 1982 (Authors: Robert Blackford and David Price)
Revised reprint 1983 (Authors: Robert Blackford and David Price)

County Court Practice Handbook

Seventh edition 1984 (Authors: Robert Blackford and David Price)
Eighth edition 1987 (Authors: Robert Blackford and David Price)
Ninth edition 1989 (Author: Robert Blackford)

A CIP Catalogue record for this book is available
from the British Library.

ISBN 085121 4401

Printed in Great Britain by
Mackays of Chatham Ltd., Kent

Contents

Preface

The *County Court Practice Handbook* started out as *Notes on County Court Practice and Procedure* by Hugh Collins, LLB, who was for many years, until his retirement, Chief Clerk at Birmingham County Court, but the basis of this and the last two editions was conceived largely by Mr Registrar David Price of Wandsworth County Court. The basis of this new edition and its structure have been maintained, and Mr Registrar Price has provided as usual much material. This apart, he has given his penetrating comments on the rules and their practical application. Nonetheless, I wish to make it clear that for this new edition I am entirely responsible for any and every error.

ROBERT BLACKFORD

14 November 1988

Table of Statutory Instruments

Introduction

County courts came into existence under the County Courts Act 1846 and were originally brought into existence to deal with small civil claims within their designated areas. A local solicitor as part time registrar would keep the registers and supervise enforcement. Jurisdiction over the years since 1846 has continually increased and recent statistics show that 90 per cent of all civil litigation throughout the country is now undertaken in county courts.

The general jurisdiction of the county courts is derived from the County Courts Act 1984, and special jurisdiction from a variety of statutes and statutory instruments some of which confer jurisdiction on the county court exclusively.

Wide powers are given to the High Court to refer cases to the county court and there are costs penalties for cases brought initially in the High Court which were within the jurisdiction of the county court.

The Courts Act 1971 instituted the circuit judges whose judicial functions include sitting as judges in the county court and Crown Court. The registrar is the assistant judge of the county court.

Administration is carried out or directed by the county court chief clerk who is one of the court's officers.

Procedure is governed by the County Court Rules 1981 (SI 1981 No 1687 (L 20), as amended).

The County Courts Act 1984, s 37 provides that any judge of a county court may exercise any jurisdiction or power conferred by any Act on 'a county court or on a judge of a county court' whether such jurisdiction or powers are conferred on all county courts and all judges, or conferred only on a particular county court or judge. The rules prescribe what jurisdiction and powers of the court or of the judge may be exercised by the registrar, with a proviso that some such powers may be exercised only with the judge's leave. The rules,

Chapter 1

Officers of the Court: Jurisdiction and Powers

The officers of the county court are: judge and registrar comprising the judicial officers, and chief clerk and staff who are the administrative officers.

Judges

Circuit judges are assigned by s 5 of the 1984 Act to sit in county courts. Section 37 of the 1984 Act, set out below, vests them with their powers, and gives them authority of jurisdiction:

37 – (1) Any jurisdiction and powers conferred by this or any other Act—
    (a) on a county court or
    (b) on the judge of a county court, may be exercised by any judge of the court.
    (2) Subsection (1) applies to jurisdiction and powers conferred on all county courts or judges of county courts or on any particular county court or the judge of any particular county court.

The jurisdiction and powers conferred by the 1984 Act are contained in a number of sections. For a treatment of these sections, and of jurisdiction conferred by other Acts, see heading 'Limits of County Court Jurisdiction' below. The judges also have a general ancillary jurisdiction as provided in ss 38 and 39 of the 1984 Act, set out below:

38 – (1) Every county court, as regards any cause of action for the time being within its jurisdiction, shall:
    (a) grant such relief, redress or remedy or combination of remedies, either absolute or conditional; and
    (b) give such and the like effect to every ground of defence or counterclaim equitable or legal as ought to be granted or given in the like case by the High Court and in as full and ample a manner.

1

(3) *to hear an action referred to arbitration.*
Registrars have authority to hear actions referred to arbitration under Ord 19, r 2(3) (the amount(s) in dispute being £500 or less).

(4) *to grant an order for an injunction in certain limited cases.*
Generally, an application for an injunction before or after the trial or hearing can be made only to the judge (Ord 13, r 6(1), (2)), save that under s 35(3) of the Hire-Purchase Act 1965, in the case of an agreement dated 18 May 1985 or earlier, an order may be made by the registrar for the interim protection of goods (Ord 49, r 6(4)). In the case of a later agreement, the similar power given by s 131 of the Consumer Credit Act 1974 may be exercised by the judge or the registrar (Alternative Ord 49, r 4(6)). The registrar may also make an injunction insofar as it is ancillary or incidental to the appointment of a receiver (Ord 32, r 1(4)). Where the court is a divorce county court, a registrar may make an injunction under s 37(2)(*a*) of the Matrimonial Causes Act 1973 restraining any person from attempting to defeat a claim for financial provision, or otherwise for protecting the claim (Matrimonial Causes Rules 1977, r 84(1)). If an injunction is sought on the trial itself of an action, or on the final hearing of a matter, then the registrar is empowered to grant an injunction (Ord 21, rr 1(1), 5; Ord 50, r 2(1); ss 37 and 38 of the 1984 Act). Additionally, on entering a final judgment on a pre-trial review under Ord 17, rr 6, 7, or 8 when he is considered to be 'determining the action or matter' within Ord 50, r 2(1), the registrar is empowered to grant an injunction. But when the registrar sits as an arbitrator under Ord 19 he is not 'trying an action or hearing a matter' (Ord 50, r 2(1)) and he therefore cannot grant an injunction as part of his award. It may be that where a case has been referred to arbitration under Ord 19, r 2(3) (the amount(s) in dispute being £500 or less) and an injunction is asked for, then the claim for an injunction is part of the 'subject matter' within Ord 19, r 2(4)(*d*) and the registrar if he were to revoke the reference to arbitration and try the case in open court, would then be enabled under Ord 50, r 2(1) to grant the injunction asked for.

(5) *in possession actions.*
The registrar may hear and determine any action for possession where the defendant fails to attend or admits the claim (Ord 21,

5(1)(*a*)). Further, if the judge gives leave under Ord 50, r 3(2) the registrar may hear and determine actions for possessions:

   (*a*)   under the summary procedure laid down in Ord 24, rr 1–4 (Ord 24, r 5(2));
   (*b*)   where the former tenancy was not statutorily protected and has come to an end or where the statutory tenant has died and where a restricted contract created a licence (Protection from Eviction Act 1977, ss 3 and 9(2) and Housing Act 1985, s 85);
   (*c*)   (with the additional consent of the parties) where the tenancy is statutorily protected by the Rent Act 1977 (Ord 21, r 5(1)(*d*));
   (*d*)   (subject to objection by the tenant) where the tenancy is a secure tenancy under the Housing Act 1985: Housing Act 1985, s 111 and the Housing Act 1980 (Registrars' Jurisdiction) Direction 1985.

All such actions are heard in open court.

In addition the registrar may hear and determine actions for possession:

   (*a*)   where a mortgagee seeks possession under a mortgage (Ord 21, r 5(1)(*c*));
   (*b*)   under r 6(2) of the Rent Act (County Court Proceedings) Rules 1981 (SI 1981 No 139).

Mortgage possession actions are heard in chambers, unless the court otherwise directs (Ord 49, r 1). Proceedings under the Rent Act (County Court Proceedings) Rules 1981 are heard in open court or chambers as directed (r 6(2)).

(6) *pursuant to special enactments.*

   For example, to vacate a class F land charge registered under s 2(8) of the Matrimonial Homes Act 1983.

(7) *in general to exercise 'the jurisdiction and powers of a county court or the judge of a county court' wherever the rules so prescribe.*

   See s 75(3)(*d*) of the 1984 Act.

   Notes

   (*a*)   Where jurisdiction may be exercised by either judge or registrar, then the judge may arrange the distribution of business between them (Ord 50, r 3 and note thereunder), and where necessary enquiry at the court office should be made.

(b) Insofar as the rules relate to the judge, they prescribe only procedure, but in relation to the registrar they prescribe not only his procedure, but also his general jurisdiction and powers.

(c) A registrar determining a dispute in his judicial capacity cannot be sued in negligence. (See *Moberly* v *Price*, CA 26 June 1984 (unreported).)

Assistant registrars

Assistant registrars (appointed under s 7 of the 1984 Act) and deputy registrars (appointed under s 8 of the 1984 Act) exercise the full jurisdiction and powers of a registrar.

Chief clerk and 'proper officer'

Section 75(3)(d) of the 1984 Act provides that the rules made thereunder may prescribe cases in which:

(a) the jurisdiction or powers of a county court or the judge of a county court may be exercised by a registrar or *some other officer of the court* or

(b) the jurisdiction or powers of the registrar of a county court may be exercised by *some other officer of the court.*

The 1981 Rules recognise that the chief clerk performs most of the functions assigned by the former rules to the 'registrar' except those of a purely judicial character. Accordingly, except in the judicial context, the term 'registrar' is replaced in the 1981 Rules by 'proper officer' which is defined (Ord 1, r 3) as the registrar, or in relation to any act of a formal or administrative nature, the chief clerk or any other officer of the court, acting on his behalf. There is a saving for acts which are by statute the responsibility of the registrar, such as the keeping of records under s 12 of the 1984 Act. However, in some cases the Rules go beyond allowing officers of the court to perform acts of a formal or administrative nature, for example, under Ord 25, r 3(1) a debtor (or officer of a debtor body corporate) may be ordered to be examined as to means before an officer of the court not below the rank of higher executive officer.

Solicitors

Solicitors advise and represent litigants before the court providing a channel of communication between the court and the parties to the proceedings as well as between the parties themselves.

A solicitor begins to represent his clients when he 'comes on the record' by signing a pleading (Ord 6, r 8; Ord 9, r 19), by filing a notice of change (Ord 50, r 5(1)), or by giving a certificate that he accepts service (Ord 7, r 11).

A solicitor can 'come off the record' only in one or other of three ways:

(a) by an order of the court under Ord 50, r 5(4) following an application by the solicitor made on notice to the represented litigant to be removed from the record (notice is not required to be given to other parties: *Re Creehouse* [1982] 1 WLR 710). The application should normally be supported by an affidavit giving the facts relied on, eg that the client declines or fails to give instructions or that the solicitor is otherwise entitled to terminate his retainer;

(b) when the represented litigant has filed a notice with the court that he is now acting for himself, or where other solicitors file a notice that they are now acting for the litigant; in either case service of such notice on all other parties is required (Ord 50, r 5(1));

(c) where a litigant assisted under the Legal Aid and Advice Act 1974 has had his certificate discharged or revoked and his solicitor has both sent a copy of the notice of discharge or revocation to the court, and given notice thereof to the other parties or to their solicitors if represented (Legal Aid (General) Regulations 1980, regs 83(2), 84(2); Ord 50, r 5(5)).

Whilst he is 'on the record' all documents (unless another mode of service is prescribed) may be served, whether by the court or another party, by delivery or by first class post on the solicitor (Ord 7, r 1(1)(*b*)). A solicitor who fails to observe the rules as to being 'on the record' may himself be ordered to pay costs wasted of any other party. A solicitor is entitled to act for a litigant in person if so appointed, without acting as advocate at the trial (Ord 50, r 5(2)), but this provision applies only when the litigant has himself started the proceedings, or has in person defended the proceedings. It does not apply to arbitrations. A litigant may therefore receive help from a solicitor in the interlocutory proceedings, and subsequently represent himself on the final hearing.

If an order for discovery or for interrogatories is served on a solicitor and he fails without reasonable excuse to give notice to his client, the solicitor himself is liable to committal (Ord 14, rr 10(4), 11(5)).

As a matter of general law relating to solicitors, a solicitor, unless there is an agreement (in writing) to the contrary, undertaking to represent a client in court undertakes a 'whole contract' and is therefore not entitled to terminate his retainer if the client refuses to make payments on account of costs incurred, or to be incurred. For exceptions reference should be made to *In re Romer & Haslam* [1893] 2 QB 286. See also *Chamberlain v Boodle & King* [1982] 1 WLR 1443 at 1446. He may however terminate if the contract of retainer so provides (and it should be in writing or confirmed by letter for the avoidance of doubt), or if the sum requested by the solicitor is a reasonable sum and the client has a reasonable time in which to pay (Solicitors Act 1974), s 65(2)).

It will be seen that it is not sufficient for a solicitor simply to write to the court to say he is not instructed or cannot get instructions, nor for him to purport to file notice that his former client is henceforth acting in person; it is the former client only, and not the former solicitor who may file such notice.

Rights of audience

The 1984 Act, s 60(1) and (2), provides that a barrister, solicitor on the record, solicitor agent, and any other person allowed by leave to appear instead of a party, may address the court, and, in actions brought by local authorities for possession of a house and/or the recovery of rent or other sum claimed in respect of any persons in occupation of such house, then insofar as the proceedings are heard by the registrar, any authorised officer of the authority.

A Lord Chancellor's Practice Direction, dated 27 January 1978, provides that Fellows of the Institute of Legal Executives, employed in giving assistance in the conduct of litigation to solicitors, may address the court where those solicitors are acting in unopposed applications for an adjournment, or to obtain judgment by consent (unless, notwithstanding the consent, a question arises as to the applicant's entitlement to the judgment or its terms).

Solicitors' clerks are usually allowed to address the registrar on applications, and on arbitrations, in chambers.

Chapter 2

County Court Jurisdiction

The court has jurisdiction for the causes of action, the proceedings and the remedies, mentioned below. Special jurisdiction is given under a number of statutes, whereas the court's general jurisdiction derives from the County Courts Act 1984. Its financial limits as are imposed or varied by Order in Council (s 145 and s 147(1) of the 1984 Act). In this chapter and throughout the book, the financial limits given are those presently current.

All references to sections are those contained in the 1984 Act, unless otherwise stated.

Contract and tort

(a) *Actions founded in contract and (excluding libel or slander) in tort* where the amount claimed is not more than £5,000 (s 15(1), (2)).

(b) *Actions to recover (if it not recoverable only in the High Court or summarily) a sum under any enactment* where the amount claimed does not exceed £5,000 (s 16).

(c) *In proceedings for wrongful interference with goods under the Torts (Interference with Goods) Act 1977* where the demand or damage claimed does not exceed £5,000 (s 15(1)).

In arriving at the figure of £5,000 interest payable under any contract or under any statute up to the date of claim is taken into account. (The sum may consist of the balance due to the plaintiff after the admitted sum due to the defendant has been subtracted.) A plaintiff may, in order to give the court jurisdiction, abandon any excess of his claim over £5,000 (s 17(1)), but he cannot thereafter claim the excess (s 17(2)).

Recovery of land

Actions which include those for forfeiture of leases under s 146 of the Law of Property Act 1925 (for practical purposes breach of covenant other than to pay rent) and under s 138 of the 1984 Act (non-payment of rent): where the net annual value for rating does not exceed in Greater London, where the Rent Act 1977 applies, £1,500, and in other cases, £1,000. Where the land does not consist of hereditaments having a separate net annual value for rating, the land is taken to have a net annual value for rating equivalent to its value by the year, but shall not be taken to have a net annual value for rating exceeding that of any hereditament of which it forms part (s 147(2), (3)). Where the net annual value brings proceedings for possession under the Rent Act 1977 within the county court's financial jurisdiction, then such jurisdiction will be unaffected by the fact that the claim for possession is accompanied by a money claim which exceeds £5,000.

The Housing Act 1985, s 110 in giving county courts jurisdiction in proceedings relating to secure tenancies, provides that if such proceedings are taken in the High Court which could have been taken in the county court, the plaintiff shall not be entitled to any costs.

Possession actions by mortgagees

(1) *Jurisdiction in the case of dwelling houses or property including dwelling houses*
(i) *In Greater London*
    (*a*) If the net annual value exceeds £1,500, the Chancery Division of the High Court of Justice has sole jurisdiction.
    (*b*) If not, the Chancery Division and the county court have concurrent jurisdiction.
(ii) *Outside Greater London*
    (*a*) If the net annual value exceeds £1,000, the Chancery Division has exclusive jurisdiction.
    (*b*) If not, the county court has exclusive jurisdiction (s 21(3) of the 1984 Act).

(As to properties other than dwelling houses see under 'Recovery of Land'.)

If, in an action for possession by a mortgagee, the money claim exceeds £5,000, then this will not of itself exclude the county court's jurisdiction, provided the county court has jurisdiction otherwise:

(s 21(5)). Section 21 does not restrict actions in the county court to those criteria to which the county court's financial limits apply where a mortgage on land secures a 'regulated agreement' within the meaning of s 189(1) of the Consumer Credit Act 1974 (and see ss 126 and 189(1) ibid) when whatever is the amount in question the county court has sole and exclusive jurisdiction (presumably even though the maximum amount of a 'regulated agreement' before it becomes exempt is £15,000 from 1985 (SI 1983 No 1878)).

Title to an hereditament

Actions in which such title comes into question, and which would otherwise be within the jurisdiction:

(a) in the case of an easement or licence, if the net annual value for rating of the hereditament in respect of which, or on, through, over or under which, the easement or licence is claimed, does not exceed £1,000; or

(b) in any other case, if the net annual value for rating of the hereditament does not exceed £1,000 (s 21(2)).

Except by consent of the parties, the county court does not have jurisdiction in an action in which the title to any toll, fair, market or franchise is in question (ss 15(2)(b), 18).

Equity

By virtue of s 23 of the 1984 Act, the court has all the jurisdiction of the High Court in proceedings:

(a) for the administration of the estate of a deceased person where the estate does not exceed in amount or value £30,000;

(b) for the execution of any trust or for a declaration that a trust subsists and for variation under the Variation of Trusts Act 1958 where the estate or fund subject, or alleged to be subject, to the trust does not exceed in amount or value £30,000;

(c) for foreclosure or redemption of any mortgage or for enforcing any charge or lien, where the amount outstanding in respect of the mortgage, charge or lien does not exceed £30,000 (with the proviso that there is no financial limit where the mortgage or charge secures a 'regulated agreement' (ss 126, 189(1) of the Consumer Credit Act 1974);

(d) for the specific performance, or for the rectification, delivery-up or cancellation, of any agreement for the sale, purchase or lease of any property, where, in the case of a sale or purchase, the purchase money, or in the case of a lease, the value of the property, does not exceed £30,000; (actions for specific performance of repairing covenants in leases under s 17 of the Landlord and Tenant Act 1985 are in the nature of applications for mandatory injunctions and hence the monetary limit in such actions appears to be £5,000);

(e) for maintenance or advancement of a minor where the property of the minor does not exceed £30,000;

(f) for the dissolution or winding-up of any partnership (whether or not the existence of the partnership is in dispute) where the whole assets of the partnership do not exceed in amount or value £30,000;

(g) for relief against fraud or mistake where the damage sustained or the estate or fund in respect of which relief is sought does not exceed £30,000.

Admiralty

Certain county courts have by order jurisdiction in admiralty under ss 26–31 of the 1984 Act. These courts are listed at the end of *The County Court Practice*. Order 40 applies to such proceedings and *The County Court Practice* itself should be referred to.

Disputes as to grant and revocation of probate and administration

Where an application for the grant or revocation of probate or administration has been made through the principal registry of the Family Division or a district probate registry and a county court is satisfied that the net value of the deceased's estate at death does not exceed £30,000, the county court has jurisdiction in any contentious matter connected with the grant or revocation. 'Net estate' is the estate less property the deceased held as trustee, funeral expenses, debts and liabilities (s 32 of the 1984 Act). Order 41 applies and *The County Court Practice* should be consulted. As to venue, see Ord 4, r 4.

Counterclaims

A defendant bringing a counterclaim is not limited to the same *type* of claim as would be a plaintiff in bringing an action; for example, unlike a plaintiff in a claim, a defendant may counterclaim for libel or slander: *Hardwicke* v *Gilroy* [1944] KB 460; [1944] 1 All ER 521, CA. Besides being quite uninhibited as to the type of claim for which he may counterclaim, a defendant counterclaiming, or raising a set-off, is not limited as to any financial maximum, and may bring his counter-claim, or claim his set-off in any amount: s 43 of the 1984 Act.

Declarations and injunctions

In general, declarations and injunctions may be granted only if claimed or applied for as ancillary to a claim which is within the court's jurisdiction, or if some enactment specifically empowers the granting of an injunction or the making of a declaration. The ancillary claim may be for an amount which is nominal, see *Hatt & Co (Bath)* v *Pearce* [1978] 1 WLR 885; [1978] 2 All ER 474. Exceptions, outside of the general rule, are:

(*a*) injunctions or declarations in respect of land which may be granted where the net annual value for rating is within the court's jurisdiction: s 22(1) of the 1984 Act;

(*b*) injunctions restraining a party to a marriage from molesting the other or from molesting a child living with the applicant (Domestic Violence and Matrimonial Proceedings Act 1976, s 1). The Act applies also to a man and woman living with each other in the same household s 1(2);

(*c*) declarations under Pt II of the Landlord and Tenant Act 1954;

(*d*) declarations and injunctions in proceedings under the Sex Discrimination Act 1975 and the Race Relations Act 1976;

(*e*) ouster orders under the Domestic Violence and Matrimonial Proceedings Act 1976 and ouster orders, and orders regulating occupation, under the Matrimonial Homes Act 1983.

Specific delivery of goods

Orders may be made by a county court where the amount or value of the goods is within its monetary jurisdiction.

Replevin

Section 144 and Sched 1 of the 1984 Act apply. Replevin is a judicial redelivery to the owner or bailee of chattels alleged to be wrongfully seized. If an owner or bailee of goods alleges that goods have been wrongfully seized under execution by the county court, his proper course is to file a claim in writing with the bailiff or court, and if the creditor does not admit the claim, to have the matter dealt with by way of interpleader (Ord 33, see below). Where an owner or bailee of goods alleges they have been wrongfully distrained otherwise than under execution by the court, he may apply as replevisor to the registrar of the appropriate county court for redelivery of the goods. He will be required to give security with the condition that he commences an action of replevin in the High Court within one week or in a county court within one month from the date of giving the security. If the goods are not returned to the replevisor after giving security, a warrant for their recovery may be issued; but whether the goods are returned or not the owner must commence his action against the seizor in compliance with the condition. The county court registrar has exclusive jurisdiction to grant replevin whatever the value of the goods seized.

Hire-purchase

(1) Agreements dated 18 May 1985 or earlier

Where goods have been let on a hire-purchase agreement or have been agreed to be sold under a conditional sale agreement, and the hirer or buyer is not a body corporate, and the total hire-purchase or purchase price does not exceed £7,500, and one-third of such price has been paid, the owner or seller may recover possession of the goods only by order of the appropriate county court and subject to the powers of the court (Hire-Purchase Act 1965, as amended by the Hire-Purchase (Increase of Limit of Value (Great Britain)) Order 1983 (SI 1983 No 611).

(2) Agreements dated 19 May 1985 or later

In these cases the Consumer Credit Act 1974 gives similar powers in the county court but the upper credit limit is £15,000 in place of £7,500. (See Chapter 27 as to jurisdiction.)

Consent or agreement

In any action which could have been assigned to the Queen's Bench Division, if the parties agree by a memorandum signed by them or their solicitors that a county court specified in the memorandum shall have jurisdiction, then the court will have power to hear and determine the action (s 18 of the 1984 Act). Similarly, in 'equity' proceedings, if a county court would have jurisdiction but for the limitations of amount imposed by the various enactments (which include among others the Settled Land Act 1925, the Trustee Act 1925 and the Law of Property Act 1925) listed in s 24(2) of the 1984 Act, the parties may agree by a memorandum signed by them or their solicitors or agents that a specified county court shall have jurisdiction (s 24(1)). Increased jurisdiction by consent cannot (s 24(3)) be obtained under the Variation of Trusts Act 1958 and application in the county court under that Act is therefore limited to £30,000.

Special jurisdiction

Besides general jurisdiction under the 1984 Act, the Matrimonial Causes Act 1973 and the Insolvency Act 1986, county courts have special jurisdiction under a variety of statutes, among others, the Adoption Act 1958, the Inheritance (Provision for Family and Dependants) Act 1975, the Guardianship of Minors Act 1971, the Guardianship Act 1973, the Landlord and Tenant Act 1954 and the Race Relations Act 1976.

The financial limits specific to proceedings under certain enactments are specified in sections inserted in each of such enactments by Sched 2 of the 1984 Act. Enactments concerned are, among others, the Trustee Act 1925, the Law of Property Act 1925, the Administration of Estates Act 1925, the Land Changes Act 1972, the Settled Land Act 1925, the Arbitration Act 1950, the Housing Act 1964, the Taxes Management Act 1970, and the Administration of Justice Act 1970 (Sched 2 of the 1984 Act should be referred to).

Note

Under Ord 5, r 1 a plaintiff may in the one action claim relief against the same defendant in respect of more than one cause of action if the plaintiff claims and the defendant is alleged to be liable in the same capacity in respect of all the causes of action, or in the capacity of executor or administrator in respect of one or more of the causes of action and sues or is sued in his personal capacity in respect of the same estate as to the other causes of action, or in any other case with leave of the court.

For separate trials, misjoinder and nonjoinder: see Ord 5, rr 3, 4.

Proceedings begun without jurisdiction

A list of county courts showing admiralty, bankruptcy and divorce jurisdiction and addresses and telephone numbers is given at the back of *The County Court Practice* published annually and commonly referred to as '*The Green Book*'.

Should proceedings have been commenced inadvertently without the court having jurisdiction, and should this not have been discovered until the hearing, the action may proceed at the hearing on the parties signing a memorandum of consent. Apart from this provision, should proceedings have been commenced for which the county court does not have jurisdiction, the court shall order the proceedings to be transferred to the High Court. However, where, on the representation of any defendant, it appears to the court that the plaintiff or one of the plaintiffs knew or ought to have known that the court had no jurisdiction, the court may, instead of transferring the proceedings, order that they be struck out (s 34).

Where the question of jurisdiction is one of venue alone, that is, when proceedings are commenced in the wrong county court, Ord 16, r 2 applies and in the absence of agreement the court may either transfer the proceedings to the correct court, or order the proceedings to continue in the court in which they were commenced, or order them to be struck out. Former Ord 16, r 4 was discussed in *Faulkner* v *Love* [1977] 1 All ER 791.

Sharma v *Knight* [1986] WLR 757 is authority for the proposition that jurisdiction conferred on county courts by statute is a general one and is not restricted to the district in which proceedings should have been brought in accordance with Ord 4, r 8, and if proceedings have been brought in 'the wrong county court', that is not in accordance with Ord 4 r 8, then nevertheless the court has jurisdiction to deal with the matter.

Whether or not any address is within the district of any particular county court can usually only be reliably ascertained by enquiry at the court office where a directory is held. Early enquiry should obviously be made where an application, eg under s 29(3) of the Landlord and Tenant Act 1954, is required to be made within strict time limits.

Chapter 3

Nature of Proceedings; Joinder; Venue

All proceedings where the object is relief against any person, or where it is to compel any person to do or abstain from doing any act, are brought by 'action', and on the filing of the required documents and payment of the fee, a 'plaint' is entered (Ord 3, rr 1 and 3(2)(*a*)). Any proceedings not required by any act or rule to be brought otherwise may be brought by 'originating application', and on the filing of the documents and payment of the fee, the proceedings are entered (Ord 3, r 4(1) and 4(4)). Where there is a choice between 'action' and 'originating application', practical considerations are as follows: the originating application will set out the prayer often with reference to a specific statute and will be accompanied by an affidavit presenting the facts surrounding and supporting the plaintiff's case. Thus the evidence is on record prior to any substantive hearing, formal pleadings are eliminated, and in many instances the matter is disposed of in chambers. Particulars of claim are appropriate when there is likely to be contention on the facts, as thereby the court is better enabled to contrast these and identify the issues.

Actions classified

Actions are classified as default actions, in which the only relief claimed is payment of money whether that sum be liquidated or not, fixed date actions in which relief other than payment of money is claimed, admiralty actions, and rent actions.

Matters

All proceedings brought otherwise than by plaint are referred to as 'Matters' (s 147(1) of the 1984 Act). They may consist of:

17

(a) originating applications (Ord 3, r 4);
(b) petitions (Ord 3, r 5);
(c) appeals to county courts (Ord 3, r 6); and
(d) other proceedings specially provided for.

Joinder of causes of action and parties

Order 5, rr 1–4 deals with joinder of causes of action and parties. A plaintiff may in the same action claim relief in respect of more than one cause of action where the parties' capacities are the same for each cause of action or where the matter arises entirely in the administration of an estate but where one party is alleged to be liable in a personal capacity (Ord 5, r 1(a) and (b)), or where leave has been given by the court (Ord 5, r 1(c)). Two or more persons may be joined together in one action as plaintiffs or as defendants, where all rights to relief claimed (joint, several or alternative) arise out of the same transactions and, if separate actions were brought, some common questions of law or fact would arise, or by leave of the court (Ord 5, r 2). In all cases involving joinder, the court may order separate trials (Ord 5, r 3).

Venue

Order 4 sets out the general rules as to venue. An *action* may be commenced in the court for the district in which the defendant or one of the defendants resides or carries on business or in the court for the district in which the cause of action wholly or in part arose (Ord 4, r 2(1)).

In proceedings for the recovery of *income tax*, the cause of action is deemed to have arisen in part at the office of the collector of taxes by whom the demand of the sum claimed was made (Ord 42, r 3).

An assignee must sue in the court in which the assignor would have had to sue (Ord 4, r 2(2)).

Where the defendant does not reside or carry on business in England or Wales and the claim is founded in *tort*, the action may be brought in the court for the district in which the plaintiff or one of the plaintiffs resides or carries on business (Ord 4, r 2(4)). Leave would be required to serve the defendant out of England and Wales (Ord 8).

In the case of an action arising out of:

(a) a *hire-purchaser or conditional sale agreement* (but not claiming delivery of goods) or

(b) a contract for the sale or hire of goods under which the purchase price or rental is payable otherwise than in one sum (whether or not claiming delivery of goods),

the action shall be brought in the court for the district in which the defendant or one of the defendants resides or carries on business, or in the court for the district in which the defendant or one of the defendants resided or carried on business when the contract was made (Ord 4, r 2(3) and Ord 1, r 11). In the case of an action arising out of a hire-purchase agreement or a conditional sale agreement, to which the Hire Purchase Act 1965 applies (see Chapter 2), an action for the delivery of goods must be brought in the court for the district in which the hirer or buyer resides or carries on business, or in the court for the district in which the hirer or buyer resided or carried on business at the date on which he last made a payment under the agreement (s 49 of the HPA 1965).

Where the agreement was made on 19 May, 1985 or later, in all the cases referred to in the preceding paragraph, the action should be commenced in the court for the district in which the defendants or one of the defendants resides or carries on business, or resided or carried on business at the date when he last made a payment under the contract. In the case where delivery of the goods is sought 'the payment' is limited to that made by the person receiving credit under the agreement. (Ord 1, r 11; Ord 4, r 2(3) as amended by [and Ord 49, r 4(2) as alternatively inserted by] rr 4, 7 and 10 of the County Court (Amendment) Rules 1985.)

In proceedings against the *Crown*, the action must be commenced in the court for the district in which the cause of action wholly or in part arose. If there is any reasonable doubt as to the court in which an action against the Crown should be brought, it may be commenced in the court for the district in which the plaintiff or one of the plaintiffs resides or carries on business (Ord 42, r 2).

Proceedings for *recovery of land*, for foreclosure or redemption of a mortgage, for enforcing a charge or lien on land (other than a charging order made under the Charging Orders Act 1979), or for the recovery of moneys secured by a mortgage or charge on land, must be started in the court where the land or part of it is situated (Ord 4, r 3).

Proceedings for enforcing a *charging order on land* or other property by sale if the charging order was made by a county court shall be commenced in that county court, and in any other case shall be commenced in the court in whose district the debtor resides or carries on business or, if there is no such district, the court in whose district the judgment creditor resides or carries on business (Ord 31, r 4(2)). It should be noted that only a legal mortgage, or a charge having the effect of a legal mortgage, entitles the mortgagee or chargee to claim possession of land. A charging order on land made under the Charging Orders Act 1979 has effect as an equitable charge under hand (s 3(4)). The remedy in this instance is sale or appointment of a receiver: *The Supreme Court Practice* at 50/1–9/23.

Proceedings under the Settled Land Act 1925, the Trustee Act 1925 and for the *administration of the estate of a deceased person*, may be commenced in the court which the plaintiff regards as most convenient having regard to the residences or places of business of the parties or to the subject matter of the proceedings (Ord 4, r 4), but payment into court under s 63 of the Trustee Act 1925 shall be made to the court in whose district the person (or any of them) making the payment resides (Ord 49, r 20(2)).

Proceedings for the *dissolution or winding up of a partnership* are commenced in the court for the district in which the partnership business was or is carried on (Ord 4, r 5).

Originating applications and petitions may be subject to specific enactments or rules, but otherwise they may be commenced in the court for the district in which the respondent or one of the respondents resides or carries on business or in which the subject matter of the application is situated, or if no respondent is named, in the court for the district in which the applicant or petitioner or one of them resides or carries on business (Ord 4, r 8). If the application is urgent eg for a non-molestation injunction under the Domestic Violence and Matrimonial Proceedings Act 1976 and there is no judge sitting, the court office will say at what court there is a judge and the application may be made and heard at that court but the more usual practice is for the application itself to be made in the court which would otherwise have been appropriate, and to that court the papers and order are sent back after the hearing.

In the case of an originating application against the Crown, the proceedings must be commenced in the court for the district in which the subject matter of the application is situated (Ord 42, r 2(1)).

Appeals to county courts are commenced in the court for the district in which the order, decision, or award appealed against was made or given (Ord 4, r 9).

A judge or registrar may sue or be sued in accordance with the rules, but if the court in which the action would be commenced is a court of which he is judge or registrar, then the action may be commenced in the nearest court or most convenient one of which he is not the judge or registrar (Ord 4, r 7).

For venue in *other types of proceedings*, see separate headings.

Chapter 4

Parties

Limited companies

A plaintiff limited company's registered office must be given in the request for issue of a summons. No other address need be shown unless to give an address for service in England and Wales.

The registered office of a defendant limited company must also be given. If this is outside England and Wales see, the Civil Jurisdiction and Judgment Act 1982, s 42 and Sched 1 Arts 2–6 and Chapter 7 below.

The head office is not of course, necessarily the registered office and a company search may be necessary. As to where a company resides which may be relevant for some purposes, a company or corporation resides where it carries on business and it can reside in more places than one (*Davies* v *British Geon Ltd* [1956] 3 All ER 389).

It is of course important, in the interests of later enforcement, for a plaintiff instituting proceedings to distinguish between a defendant firm (or partnership), a single person trading under a business name, and a defendant limited company.

Companies in liquidation

The words 'in liquidation' should follow the name and after the address there should be added: 'by the liquidator AB of [address and description]'.

The Crown

The title of the department suing or being sued should be precisely stated in accordance with the list of Crown departments published under s 17 of the Crown Proceedings Act 1947. This list appears in *The County Court Practice.*

The particulars of claim in actions against the Crown must specify the circumstances in which the Crown's liability is said to have arisen and 'as to the government department and officers of the Crown concerned' (Ord 42, r 4).

If the Crown does not consider the particulars of claim give sufficient information as to the government department and officers concerned under Ord 42, r 4, it may, before the time for filing a defence has expired, file with the court two copies of a request for such information, one of which is sent to the plaintiff. The time for defence is then extended to four days after either the Crown gives notice to the court and to the plaintiff that it is satisfied with the information given, or the court decides that no further information is required. Such a decision may be given on the plaintiff's application on seven days' notice to the Crown (Ord 42, r 5(1), (2)). No default judgment can be entered against the Crown save by leave of the court on application on seven days' notice (Ord 42, r 5(4)), nor can summary judgment be given against the Crown under Ord 9, r 14 (Ord 42, r 5(5)).

Fixed date action against the Crown

On issue, the court does not fix a return day but serves on the Crown copy of the particulars of claim, and a notice (N 390) of entry of plaint, and of the effect of paragraphs (3) and (5) of Ord 42, r 6, namely the rights of the Crown if it considers that the particulars of claim do not contain sufficient information and the action itself is stayed. The Crown may then seek further information within 21 days as in the case of a default action. If it does not, or when it files and gives notice that it is satisfied, or the court on application decides it needs no further information, then only is a return day fixed by the court.

Partners and business names

Any one of two or more partners carrying on business in England or Wales may sue and be sued in the name of the firm in which he was a partner when the cause of action arose (Ord 5, r 9(1)). This is the situation even if one of the partners is under a disability, such as minority. A person carrying on business in a name other than his own whether or not he is within the jurisdiction may be sued in his own name, followed by 'trading as AB', or in his business name followed by the words 'a trading name' (Ord 5, r 10). He may not sue in his business name, although this may properly be recited in the particulars of claim to avoid confusion.

Where partners sue or are sued in a firm name, the partners shall on demand in writing by any other party, forthwith deliver, and file a statement, of the names and places of residence of all the persons who were partners when the cause of action arose (Ord 5, r 9(2)). An order may be made staying an action, until a request for particulars has been completed, or, in the case of defendants, barring them from defending (see Ord 5, r 9(3) and (4)).

Persons under disability

The procedure is contained in Ord 10. 'A person under disability' is either 'a minor' or 'a mental patient'. The latter is a person who, by reason of mental disorder within the meaning of the Mental Health Act 1983, is incapable of managing and administering his property and affairs (Ord 1, r 3). A minor may sue for wages, piece work or for work as a servant (s 47 of the 1984 Act), but apart from this a person under disability may not bring or defend proceedings, or counter-claim, except if a plaintiff by his next friend or if a defendant by a guardian ad litem (Ord 10, r 1(1), (2)).

Where the person under disability wishes to be a plaintiff or applicant, before commencing proceedings, if he is a mental patient and a person is authorised by order of the Court of Protection to conduct the proceedings, then that person must file in the court office a sealed office copy of the Court of Protection's order (Ord 10, r 2(a)).

In the case of a minor, or of a mental patient where no person is authorised to act for him by the Court of Protection, then the 'next friend' must file a written undertaking (N 235), attested as would be an affidavit, to be responsible for costs (Ord 10, r 2(b)).

Should proceedings be commenced by a person under disability without a 'next friend', the court may on application appoint the authorised person, or person who gives an undertaking (N 235) as to costs, as next friend, or may strike out the proceedings (Ord 10, r 3). Where the person under disability is a defendant or respondent, and a person proposes to act as 'guardian ad litem', he should deliver to the court office a defence, answer, counterclaim or admission, and if he is appointed to act by order of the Court of Protection a sealed copy of the order. If he has not been appointed to act, he should deliver a certificate that he is a fit and proper person to act as guardian ad litem and has no interest adverse to the defendant. Thereupon such person shall be the guardian ad litem (Ord 10, rr 5, 8(2)). A guardian ad litem has no personal liability for costs unless occasioned by his personal negligence or misconduct (Ord 10, r 9). If a counterclaim is delivered in addition to a defence or admission, the appointment as guardian ad litem is still automatic under Ord 10, r 5. Where a defendant or respondent under disability has no guardian ad litem acting for him under rr 5 or 8(2), the plaintiff (or applicant) shall, after the time for delivering a defence (or answer) has expired and before taking any further steps, apply to the court without fee on not less than three days' notice to the person on whom the summons was served under Ord 10, r 4 for the appointment of a guardian ad litem (Ord 10, r 6). The application shall be supported by an affidavit (N 237) showing that the proposed guardian is a fit and proper person, has no interest contrary to the defendant (or respondent), and consents to act. A copy is served with the notice of application (N 238).

At the hearing, the court may appoint (N 239) the person proposed, any other person willing to act, or in default the registrar (Ord 10, rr 6, 8(2)). However, it is not generally considered practicable, if no suitable person can be found, to appoint a registrar, and in practice the Official Solicitor should be approached.

Where a defendant/respondent minor attends a hearing at court and he has no guardian ad litem, the court may appoint (N 240) any person the defendant/respondent names who is willing to act; otherwise the court may appoint (N 241) any person present who is willing to act, or again may appoint the registrar.

Where a person appearing to be a mental patient attends court without a guardian ad litem, the court may give the necessary directions under Ord 13, r 2(1) of its own motion.

Where a minor is sued for a liquidated sum, which includes the cost of repairs to a vehicle or to any property in, on, or abutting a highway (Ord 1, r 10), the court may on the plaintiff's application dispense with the appointment under Ord 10, rr 6 or 7 of a guardian (Ord 10, r 8(1)).

If a judgment has been obtained without the appointment of a guardian ad litem (save where an order has been made under

Ord 10, r 8(1) see above) the judgment may be set aside by the court under Ord 37, r 5.

Where a money claim is made on behalf of a person under disability, the approval of the court is required to any settlement, compromise, or payment into court. If the sole purpose of bringing an action for a money claim is to obtain such consent, the particulars of claim need state the case only briefly and ask for approval (Ord 10, r 10). For further detail see Chapter 10. The registrar may give approval, whatever the sum involved (Ord 10, r 10(3)).

Unless the court otherwise directs, money received or paid into court in respect of persons under disability shall remain in court and be invested or dealt with as the court thinks fit, which in many cases may be its transfer to the High Court (Ord 10, r 11(1)–(3)). For form of order see N 292. Solicitors should consider whether a charge arises on such moneys under s 9(6) of the Legal Aid and Advice Act 1974. No investment rule applies to a claim under s 47 of the 1984 Act, that is, minors suing for wages.

Bankruptcy of the plaintiff

The bankruptcy of the plaintiff in an action which the trustee might maintain for the benefit of the creditors does not cause the action to abate if, within such reasonable time as the court orders, the trustee elects to continue the action and to give security. The hearing of the action may be adjourned until an election is made. When the trustee does not elect to continue the action and to give security, the defendant may use the bankruptcy as a defence (s 49 of the 1984 Act).

Where a defendant has a bankruptcy order made against him, or being a limited company is subject to a winding-up order, the plaintiff in a simple money claim should consider whether it is not best to ask for the action to be adjourned generally and lodge a proof of debt. (*Williams on Bankruptcy* should be consulted.)

A trustee in bankruptcy should sue or be sued as 'Trustee of the Estate of AB a bankrupt' without adding his own name (s 305 (4) of the Insolvency Act 1986; *Pooley's Trustee* v *Whetham* (1884) 28 Ch D 38). A trustee to a bankrupt mortgagor may be in possession actually or constructively and should be made a party.

Death

Where a plaintiff or defendant dies and the cause of action survives but no person is substituted for the deceased under Ord 5, r 7, the defendant (or his personal representatives) may apply for an order directing the plaintiff (or other person entitled) to proceed within such time as may be ordered, and in default, the action may be struck out (Ord 5, r 12). A like order may be made on a counterclaim.

An action purporting to have been commenced against a person who is dead at its commencement is treated as if it had been commenced against his estate, whether or not a grant of representation had been issued at its commencement (Ord 5, r 8(3)).

Change of parties by transmission of interest

Where at any stage of proceedings by assignment, transmission, or devolution the interest or liability of any party devolves on some other person, the court may order ex parte that other person to be made a party 'to carry on' the proceedings (Ord 5, r 11).

The requirements are:

(*a*) application (N 213) with as many copies of notices as there are parties to be served;

(*b*) affidavit of truth of facts.

The court sends the order (N 214) and a copy of the application (N 213) to all existing, former or new parties, and if to new parties, a copy of the originating process.

The rule has no application if a plaintiff becomes bankrupt (Ord 5, r 14), when s 49 of the 1984 Act will apply enabling the trustee to elect to continue and give security for the costs.

Persons having the same interest

In such circumstances, one or more persons may be appointed to sue or be sued in a representative capacity as having a common interest with all other persons (Ord 5, r 5 (1)). A plaintiff or a defendant sued in a representative capacity may apply for the appointment of one defendant to represent all, or all those named, and a plaintiff suing in a representative capacity may apply to be similarly appointed (Ord 5, r 2). A judgment in such 'representative proceedings' may not be enforced against a non party without the leave of the court (Ord 5, r 5 (5)).

Proprietary clubs are often limited companies, and if so, they of course sue or are sued in their corporate name.

Change in parties after judgment

Order 26, r 5 applies where any change has taken place after judgment by death, assignment or otherwise, in the parties entitled to enforce a judgment or order or in the parties liable under a judgment or order. A party entitled to enforce the judgment or order may apply on affidavit to issue the necessary process.

The requirements are as for an application applying for leave to issue enforcement process (ex parte unless court orders) with supporting affidavit. (Application in form N 213).

If the application affects more than one judgment, one application may be made specifying judgments in a schedule.

Order 5, r 13 applies where there is money in court (N 213 (1)).

In an action for recovery of land, any person in possession (by himself or by his tenant) and not named as a defendant may by leave be made a defendant on filing an ex parte application showing that he is in possession, by himself or by his tenant, and giving grounds for the application. If the applicant is added as a defendant the court sends the order to all parties, annexing to it a copy of the application (Ord 15, r 3). In the case of summary proceedings for recovery of land, Ord 24, r 4, any person not named as a respondent may apply to be joined at any stage of the proceedings on the question whether an order for possession should be made.

Chapter 5

Commencement of Proceedings: Security

The originating process is described as an action or a matter. Actions are fixed date actions, rent actions, default or admiralty actions. All actions are commenced by plaint, that is, by summons (Ord 3, r 1). Matters are those proceedings which are initiated by an originating process other than by action. (See Chapter 3, 'Nature of Proceedings; Joinder; Venue'.)

In actions, the parties are described as 'plaintiff' and 'defendant' and in matters as 'applicant' or 'petitioner' or 'appellant', as the case may be, and 'respondent'.

Where the proceedings are brought by way of action then, unless the plaintiff is preparing a 'multiple summons' (see below), the court prepares and issues a summons for each of the defendants and where brought by way of originating application, it prepares a notice to each respondent.

The title of the action or matter must refer to any Act (if other than the 1984 Act) which is relied on to give the court jurisdiction (Ord 3, r 7(2)). On issue of the originating process, the court office allots a distinguishing number (Ord 3, r 7(1)). Every document of whatsoever kind filed, issued or served thereafter shall bear the title of the action or matter and the 'case' number (Ord 3, r 7(1)). It is important that the case number be quoted in all communications with the court, particularly as the court office keeps few alphabetical indices and unless a case number is given it will be difficult to link with the court papers or file. A letter sent for the court should generally be addressed to 'The Chief Clerk'.

The court may be reluctant to act on a letter of which a party with opposing interests is unaware, and so where appropriate, a copy should be sent to all other parties, whether represented or not.

29

When a defendant or respondent becomes an assisted person, his solicitor must forthwith serve all other parties with notice of the issue of the certificate for legal aid, and file the certificate by prepaid post at the court (Legal Aid (General) Regulations 1980, reg 51). He must similarly serve notice of all amendments, and must file the amendments with the court (reg 55).

Payment of fees and other payments

Payment at a court office

Hours 10.00 am to 4.00 pm Monday to Friday except in vacation.

Payment may be made by cash, banker's or giro draft, cheque supported by a cheque card (present limit £50) or by other cheques, subject to clearance and the Chief Clerk's consent. (Solicitors' cheques are usually accepted.)

The payer (unless issuing a summons) should produce the plaint note or summons to enable the court to identify the plaint number of the case.

Payment by post

Payment may be made to the court office by postal order, banker's or giro draft or cheques (subject to clearance and the Chief Clerk's consent). (Solicitors' cheques are usually accepted.)

The payer must send the payment in a properly stamped envelope, enclosing the plaint note or summons (or otherwise clearly identifying the plaint number) and enclosing also a self addressed envelope so the court can return a receipt with the plaint note or summons (if sent).

Cheques, postal orders and drafts must be made payable to 'HM Paymaster General' and crossed.

The court cannot accept stamps or payments by bank and giro credit transfers.

Fixed date actions

Order 3 applies.

In a fixed date action the summons issued gives a date of hearing, called the return day (N 3–4). A fixed date action is one in which relief, other than payment of money, is claimed (Ord 3, r 2(1)). It includes an action for the purpose of approving a compromise or settlement on behalf of a person under disability, when a date is normally given for hearing before a registrar (Ord 10, r 10(3)).

On the issue of a summons in a fixed date action in proceedings against the Crown a return day is not fixed; in such cases a return day is given later.

Except in an action for recovery of land (N 5–6), arrears of rent and mesne profits, the return day must, unless the court otherwise directs, be a day fixed for a pre-trial review under Ord 17 (Ord 3, r 3(3)). In an action for recovery of land a claim joined with a claim for some relief other than arrears of rent or mesne profits or for moneys secured by a mortgage or charge, a return day for a pre-trial review is given (Ord 3, r 3(3), (4)), but in an action by a mortgagee for possession of a dwellinghouse a return day for a hearing in chambers, unless the court otherwise orders, will be given (Ord 49, r 1). Forms of admission, defence and counterclaim will be annexed by the court to the summons as appropriate (N 9–11).

Rent actions

Order 24, rr 8–11 apply.

Where a landlord claims arrears of rent from a tenant or former tenant who is still in occupation, the claim may be brought by a 'rent action'.

A rent action must be brought in the court for the district in which the land is situated and the request (N 203) must contain a statement that the plaintiff requires a summons under Ord 24, Pt II. The summons (N 7) with a copy of the particulars of claim attached may be served personally or by pre-paid post, in attendance with Ord 7, r 1, but must be served not less than seven clear days before the return in accordance with Ord 7, r 1.

Order 9, which provides for the delivery of an admission, defence or counterclaim, relates to default and fixed date actions only. There is no provision in the rules for the filing or delivery of admissions, defences or counterclaims in rent actions (Ord 24, r 11(11)), and forms for such admissions etc are not annexed to summonses in rent actions. However, the court may give directions on application or on its own motion under Ord 13, r 2, and may at any time direct that the proceedings continue as a fixed date action (Ord 24, r 11(2)). A pre-trial review may then be ordered under Ord 17, r 10. Payment may be made into court by the defendant under Ord 11, r 1, and r 4(2) then applies.

Default actions

A default action is one in which the only relief claimed is payment of money (Ord 3, r 2). In a default action, a summons N 1 (fixed amount) and N 2 (amount not fixed) is issued; a date of hearing is not fixed unless the defendant files a defence or makes an offer of payment not accepted (whether as to part of the claim or as to the mode of payment) by the plaintiff. Forms of admission, defence and counterclaim are annexed by the court to the summons as appropriate (N 9). Plaint notes are not issued unless specifically asked for in the case of multiple users who provide schedules.

When a default action is brought against the Crown, judgment may be entered by default only by leave of the court on application on seven days' notice (Ord 42, r 5(3), (4)).

The lay-out of these forms provides space for the proper officer to include on the face of the summons N1 or N2 what the claim if for and particulars of the nature of the claim, the plaintiff having done so as his form of Request for Default Summons (N 201). The space is sufficient really only where the claim arises out of a simple debt.

Where, however, plaintiffs prepare their own summonses, there is no need for the Request for Default Summons to be in form N 201 and it is unnecessary for such plaintiffs to lodge separate requests for each proceeding; a single request to the court to serve the summonses, enclosing the prescribed fees and the copy documentation required by CCR Ord 6 and CCR Ord 3, r 3(1A) will be acceptable. In these cases the request should list the names of the defendants against whom the plaintiff requests the issue of default summonses.

Multiple summons

Where the circumstances are that a plaintiff (such as a mail order company) wishes to bring separate proceedings in one county court against a great number of defendants, provision is made for a combined request and particulars of claims by the Lord Chancellor's Practice Directions made on 1 March, 1979 and 17 March, 1987 setting out full instructions; these are given under Ord 3, r 3 in *The County Court Practice*.

Admiralty actions

See *The County Court Practice.*

Requirements on issue of summonses

Fixed date and default actions
Order 3, r 3(1) and (1A) apply.
The requirements are:
(*a*) appropriate form of request for the issue of a summons (N 201–204);
(*b*) particulars of claim and a copy for each defendant;
(*c*) if allowed by the court, the summons prepared by the plaintiff with a copy for each defendant: (no request for the issue of a summons is required in this case);
(*d*) plaint fee and fee for service by bailiff where applicable (see Table of Fees);
(*e*) addressed envelope if issued by post (Ord 2, r 5(1);
(*f*) where the plaintiff is under a disability an undertaking by next friend as to costs (N 235) or a sealed office copy order of the Court of Protection (Ord 10, r 2);
(*g*) Civil aid certificate, if any, and notice of certificate for service on the defendant (Legal Aid (General) Regulations, 1980, reg 51).

Forms of particulars of claim are supplied by the court office to parties in person. Particulars of claim may be dispensed with if a form of request in N 202 is used and the proper officer allows (Ord 6, r 1(2), (4)). A plaint note (N 205 or 206) is issued to the plaintiff which, in the case of a fixed date summons, shows the return day. A plaint note in N 207 is issued in adoption applications.

On the request for issue of a summons, or any other originating process, the full first names of the plaintiff must be given. The registered office of limited companies must be given and so described. Solicitor's costs to be entered on summonses are given in Costs Appendix B, Pt I. If service is to be by solicitor or plaintiff or his agent, this should be stated on the request. The summons itself, unless prepared by the plaintiff, is prepared by the court. If service is not by an officer of the court, an affidavit of service must be filed in N 215 (Ord 7, r 6(1)(*b*).

If service is to be effected on a solicitor acting on behalf of the defendant, this should be indicated clearly either by separate letter or below the defendant's name and address on the form of request.

Requirements on issue of originating processes other than actions

Originating applications
Order 3, r 4 applies.
An originating application is the form of originating process where no other form of proceeding is specified. Requirements on issue of an originating application are:
 (*a*) a request for the issue of the originating application (no prescribed general form);
 (*b*) originating application with a copy for each respondent to be served;
 (*c*) fee for issue and for service by bailiff where appropriate (see Table of Fees);
 (*d*) addressed envelope, if issued by post;
 (*e*) if applicant under disability, undertaking by next friend as to costs or sealed office copy order of the Court of Protection (Ord 10, r 2);
 (*f*) civil aid certificate, if any, and notice of certificate for service on respondent.
The court issues a plaint note (N 206). The return day may be a hearing day or, if the court so directs, a day for a pre-trial review (Ord 3, r 4(4), (5)).
A limited company may issue proceedings without a solicitor. (See *Chas P Kinnell and Co Ltd* v *Harding Wall and Co* [1918] 1 KB 405.)

Summary proceedings for recovery of land
Order 24, rr 1–7 apply.
Where a person claims possession of land he alleges is occupied solely by a person or persons (not a tenant or tenants holding over) who entered into or remained in occupation without his licence or consent or that of his predecessor, the proceedings may be brought by originating application. These proceedings apply to a trespasser, following the determination of a licence to occupy the premises (*Greater London Council* v *Jenkins* [1975] 1 All ER 354) and to an unlawful subtenant (*Moore Properties (Ilford) Ltd* v *McKeon* [1977] 1 All ER 262).
The requirements are:
 (*a*) originating application (N 312) and copy for each named respondent and two further copies;

(*b*)   affidavit in support with the same number of copies for service; the affidavit should state:

     (i)   the plaintiff's interest in the land;

    (ii)   the circumstances in which the land has been occupied without licence or consent and in which the claim to possession arises, and

   (iii)   if it be that the name of any person occupying the land is not stated in the originating application the affidavit should state that the plaintiff does not know the name of such person.

(*c*)   fee for issue and for service by bailiff (see Table of Fees);

(*d*)   addressed envelope if issued by post.

If there is a person or persons in occupation whose name or names are not known to the plaintiff, they should be referred to in the application and in the title to the proceedings as 'other occupiers'. This is preferable to describing them as 'persons unknown', for the purposes of the warrant.

The court prepares notice of the return day (N 8(1)), (Ord 3, r 4(4)(*b*)). Such notice shall contain notice to the effect that any person who, being in occupation of the land but not named as a respondent, wishes to be heard, may apply *at any stage of the proceedings* to be joined as a respondent (Ord 24, r 4).

Service of the originating application, notice of the return day and service of a copy of the affidavit must be effected on each named respondent not less than five clear days before the day fixed for hearing, in the case of residential premises, and otherwise two days. Shorter notice may be permitted in cases of urgency, and by leave of the court. Such service may be personal, or may be effected by an officer of the court leaving the documents to be served, or sending them to the respondent, at the premises; service may also be on a solicitor who accepts service, or in such manner as the court may direct (Ord 24, r 3(1)). Unless the court otherwise directs, service may also be effected:

(*a*)   by affixing copies of all documents to the main door or other conspicuous part of the premises, and

(*b*)   if practicable, by inserting copies through the letter-box at the premises in a sealed transparent envelope addressed to 'the occupiers' (Ord 24, r 3(2)), or

(*c*)   by placing stakes in the ground and affixing thereto transparent envelopes containing copies of all the documents.

The order for possession must be made by a judge or, with

the leave of the judge, by a registrar (Ord 24, r 5(2)). The order may be for possession forthwith or, by virtue of Ord 24, r 5(4), for possession on 'a specified date'.

Jury trials

Jury trials have slightly increased in number, though still a rarity, in the main confined to malicious prosecution or false imprisonment. For information thereon, see the Law Society's Gazette for 24 February, 1988 at pp 19–20. Application is made under Ord 13, r 10.

Petitions

Order 3, r 5 applies.

Requirements on issue are as for originating applications, save that 'petitioner' and 'petition' are substituted for 'applicant' and 'application'.

Appeals to county courts

Order 3, r 6 applies.

The requirements on issue are:

(*a*) request for entry of appeal N 209) stating the names and addresses of the persons intended to be served ('the respondents') and the appellant's address for service, and a copy for each respondent to be served;

(*b*) a copy of the order or decision or award appealed against;

(*c*) where the enactment under which the appeal lies requires the appellant to give to the other parties notice in writing of his intention to appeal and of the grounds of his appeal, a copy of such notice; in any other case, the request for entry of appeal must include the grounds of the appeal;

(*d*) fees for issue and for service by bailiff if appropriate (see Table of Fees);

(*e*) addressed envelope if issued by post.

An appeal must be filed within 21 days after the date of the order, decision or award appealed from. The procedure follows that for originating applications.

Proceedings in wrong form

If proceedings are commenced by action when they should have been commenced by originating application or vice versa, such a breach of the rules is not necessarily fatal; the court may set the proceedings aside or it may allow them to be amended and give such directions as it thinks fit (Ord 37, r 5).

Photographic copies

The Lord Chancellor's Practice Direction of 17 March 1987 provides that clear photographic copies (of all documents) will be accepted as if printed or typed.

Security

Plaintiff residing out of England and Wales

Where it appears that the plaintiff is ordinarily resident out of England and Wales, on the defendant's application, the court may order the plaintiff to give security for costs (Ord 13, r 8(1)).

The plaintiff may make a similar application against a defendant who counterclaims (Ord 13, r 8(2)).

Limited company

Where it appears that a plaintiff limited company, wheresoever registered, may be unable to pay a successful defendant's costs, security may be ordered (s 726 of the Companies Act, 1985). An affidavit should be filed to support the application exhibiting, if appropriate, copies of the company's last filed accounts, though impecuniosity is only one factor and the court must take all circumstances into account: *Aquila Design (GRP Products)* v *Cornhill Insurance* (1987) 9 CL 274. Applications may not be favoured if considered oppressive or made late in the proceedings.

Terms

The court may say on what terms security is to be ordered and has discretion as to the manner in which it is to be given (Ord 50, r 9).

Chapter 6

Particulars of Claim

Order 6 deals with particulars of claim. Particulars of claim are signed by the plaintiff or by solicitors acting for the plaintiff giving an address for service (Ord 6, r 8). Where solicitors are acting, the following or similar wording should appear on the particulars of claim below their signature: 'AB (& Co) of . . . [address] solicitor(s) for the plaintiff, who at this address will accept service of all documents on his behalf'. The signature should be legible or repeated in type because it is from this signature that notices and orders are addressed. If settled by counsel, his draft pleading will have been signed by him, and the particulars of claim should show his name, in capital letters for preference, as having signed them (Ord 50, r 6). Except in the shortest of particulars of claim, allegations should be divided into paragraphs and numbered consecutively.

In the case of debts, a copy of or repetition of the plaintiff's bill or account is accepted, but the particulars of claim should show the consideration such as 'for goods sold and delivered', or 'for work done and materials supplied'; to say 'account rendered' is not sufficient.

The date of the bill or account, or the date from when the cause of action arises, must be given. Where in an action for a debt the particulars of claim can conveniently be incorporated in the form of request for a summons (N 202) this may be done if the proper officer allows (Ord 6, r 1(2)); otherwise, a copy of the particulars of claim is to be filed for each defendant (Ord 6, r 1(4)). A claim for debt or liquidated demand may be expressed in a foreign currency (*Miliangos* v *George Frank (Textiles) Ltd* [1975] 3 All ER 801). High Court Practice Direction of 18 December 1975 [1976] 1 All ER 669 should be followed so that the particulars of claim will state: 'The rate current in London for the purchase of [state unit

38

of foreign currency] at the close of business on the [state date next or most nearly preceding the date of issue of summons] was . . . to the £ sterling and at this rate the amount claimed, namely [state the sum of foreign currency claimed] amounts to £ . . .'.

If a plaintiff abandons the excess of his claim over £5,000 to bring it within the jurisdiction of the county court, the abandonment must be stated at the end of the particulars (Ord 6, r 1(3)). Where a plaintiff in the first instance desires to have *an account taken*, the particulars must state the amount which the plaintiff claims subject to the taking of the account, and if no such amount is stated, the plaintiff will be deemed to claim £5,000 (Ord 6, r 2).

Where there are issues which require pleading, it is said in the White Book that this is 'a task fitted only for counsel'; but solicitors will be likely to have precedents available to them for common types of cases. Nonetheless, if counsel is to be briefed for the hearing he should settle the pleading, and for that matter, the letter before action.

Further particulars

The delivery of a request for further and better particulars is not a condition precedent to the making of an order for them, but the failure to make a prior request is a ground for refusing the order: Ord 6, r 7. Particulars delivered pursuant to an order, or to a request, must incorporate the text of the order, or of the request.

Recovery of land

Order 6, r 3 applies.

In an action for recovery of land, the particulars must give:

(a) a full description of the land;

(b) the net annual value for rating, or, if the land does not consist of one or more hereditaments having a separate net annual value for rating:

(i) where the land forms part of a hereditament having a net annual value not exceeding the county court limit (see under 'Limits of County Court Jurisdiction'), the net annual value of that hereditament, or

(ii) in any other case, the value of the land by the year;

(c)   the rent, if any, of the land;

(d)   the grounds on which possession is claimed;

(e)   in a case under s 138 of the 1984 Act (proceedings to enforce a right of re-entry or forfeiture for non-payment of rent), the daily rate at which the rent in arrear or mesne profits are to be calculated;

(f)   in proceedings for forfeiture the name and address of any underlessee or mortgagee entitled to claim relief against forfeiture and a copy of the particulars of claim for that person (Ord 6, r 3(2));

(g)   a claim for arrears of rent and mesne profits should be included if applicable (see Chapter 16).

The landlord must notify any person entitled to relief of whom he is aware (r 2 of the County Court (Amendment No 2) Rules 1986, (SI 1986, No 1189).

Injunctions and declarations relating to land

Where the plaintiff claims an injunction or declaration unaccompanied by any other claim for relief under s 22 of the 1984 Act, the particulars of claim must give a full description of the land and the annual value for rating (Ord 6, r 4).

Mortgagee possession actions

Order 6, r 5 provides that in mortgagee possession actions—that is where the plaintiff claims payment of money secured or possession of the property mortgaged—the particulars of claim must state:

(a)   the date of the mortgage;

(b)   the state of the account, giving particulars of the amount of the advance, the periodic payments required, the amount of any interest in arrear, the amount of the unpaid instalments, the amount of any costs or fines or insurance unpaid; the daily rate of interest and the amount remaining due under [and required to redeem] the mortgage;

(c)   what proceedings (if any) the plaintiff has taken against the defendant in respect of the money secured by the mortgage or the mortgaged property and, where payment of such money only is claimed, whether the plaintiff has obtained possession of the property;

(*d*) where the plaintiff claims possession of the property, whether or not the property consists of or includes a dwellinghouse within the meaning of Part IV of the Administration of Justice Act 1970;

(*e*) where a plaintiff claims as mortgagee possession of land which consists of or includes a dwellinghouse, he shall state, in his particulars of claim, whether there is any person on whom notice of the action is required to be served in accordance with section 8(3) of the Matrimonial Homes Act 1983 and, if so, he shall state the name and address of that person and shall file a copy of the particulars of claim for service on that person (Ord 6, r 5(1A)).

At the hearing there should be handed to the registrar an affidavit verifying the particulars of claim, in particular the arrears of instalments and the amount required to redeem, sworn say some seven days before, the charge certificate and a completed search on Form 106 (registered land) or on Form K15 (unregistered land). If the search reveals an existing land charge Class F or a caution, notice shall be given by the mortgagee (s 8(3) of the Matrimonial Homes Act, 1983).

Notes

(i) 'Mortgage' includes a legal or equitable mortgage or charge (Ord 6, r 5(2)). An equitable *mortgagee* seeking possession is in precisely the same position as a legal mortgagee (*Barclays Bank Ltd* v *Bird* [1954] Ch 274 at p 280), but the remedy of an equitable *chargee* is only by way of sale (see *The Supreme Court Practice* Vol 1 at 50/1–9/23). A charging order has the same effect and is enforceable in the courts in the same manner as an equitable charge (s 3(4) of the Charging Orders Act 1979).

(ii) Until a transfer of mortgage is registered the transferor is deemed to be the mortgagee (s 33(2) of the Land Registration Act 1925) and the transferee is unable to bring proceedings.

(iii) Part IV of the Administration of Justice Act, 1970 gives exclusive jurisdiction to County Courts, save if in Greater London, wheresoever the mortgage includes a dwellinghouse (s 37) and invests the court with its powers (s 36). See Chapter 16.

(iv) 'Dwellinghouse' includes any building or part thereof used as a dwelling.

Landlord and Tenant Act 1954

The county court has jurisdiction in proceedings under the Landlord and Tenant Act 1954 Pt II relating to a new lease or tenancy. These may be heard in the county court if the net annual value does not exceed £5,000 per annum. Proceedings wrongly commenced in the High Court or county court will be transferred without the proceedings being invalidated (Landlord and Tenant Act 1954, s 53(4)). Proceedings by a tenant for a new tenancy must be commenced within four calendar months of the date of the original notice or the tenant will lose his rights under the Act, and this limitation of time is absolute. In the main, notices to be given under the Act can only be given in the prescribed form: see the Landlord and Tenant (Notices) Regulations 1957 (SI 1957, No 1157). The procedure on application for a new lease is similar to that to be followed in the Chancery Division (see *Chancery Practice Handbook*, Blackford and Jaque, (Oyez Longman, 1983)).

Section 38 of the 1954 Act as amended by s 5 of the Law of Property Act, 1969 provides for application to the court for the court's approval to an agreement excluding the provisions of the Landlord and Tenant Act 1954. Such applications are made by way of joint application of the landlord and tenant, one of the parties issuing on behalf of both, supported by an affidavit exhibiting the proposed lease. These applications are not regarded as a mere formality by most courts which may require the originating application to state the grounds in proper detail, for example that the lessor may require to occupy at the expiration of the lease; that the premises are temporarily surplus to the needs of the lessor; that the lessee has indicated that he only requires the premises for a limited period; that there is to be development at the expiration of the term; that the lessor is only prepared to grant if the section is excluded; that exclusion of the section has been taken into consideration in negotiations for the rent, or possibly that the premises form part of other premises which brings the provisions of management of the whole into question if the section is not excluded. The tenant and the landlord should each be represented on the hearing which will be before the Registrar. Early appointments may usually be obtained, as a matter of practice, for such applications. For procedure for application see Chapter 28.

Hire-purchase actions

Agreements dated 18 May, 1985 or earlier

Order 6, r 6 applies.

The 1981 Rules so far as they relate to hire-purchase agreements apply also to conditional sale agreements (Ord 1, r 11). In hire-purchase cases, where a plaintiff claims *the delivery of goods* let under a hire-purchase agreement to a person other than a body corporate, he must state consecutively in the particulars of claim, in the same order as below, the following:

(*a*) date of the agreement and the parties thereto;

(*b*) place where the agreement was signed by the hirer;

(*c*) goods claimed;

(*d*) amount of the hire-purchase price;

(*e*) amount paid by or on behalf of the hirer;

(*f*) amount of the unpaid balance of the hire-purchase price;

(*g*) whether a notice of default within the meaning of the Hire-Purchase Act 1965, s 25, has been served on the hirer, and if it has, the date on which it was so served;

(*h*) date when the right to demand delivery of the goods accrued;

(*i*) amount, if any, claimed as an alternative to the delivery of the goods; and

(*j*) amounts, if any, claimed in addition to the delivery of the goods or any claim under sub-para (i), stating the cause of action in respect of which each claim is made (Ord 6, r 6(1)).

Where a plaintiff's claim arises out of a hire-purchase agreement but is *not* for the delivery of goods he must state consecutively in the particulars of claim in the same order as below, the following:

(*a*) date of the agreement and the parties thereto;

(*b*) goods let under the agreement;

(*c*) amount of the hire-purchase price;

(*d*) amount paid by or on behalf of the hirer;

(*e*) amount, if any, claimed as being due and unpaid in respect of any instalment or instalments of the hire-purchase price;

(*f*) amount of any other claim and the circumstances in which it arises (Ord 6, r 6(2)).

Agreements dated 19 May, 1985 or later

Where a plaintiff claims the delivery of goods let under a hire-purchase agreement to a person other than a body corporate, he shall in his particulars state in the following order:

(*a*)   the date of the agreement and the parties to it, with the number of the agreement or sufficient particulars to enable the debtor to identify the agreement;

(*b*)   where the plaintiff was not one of the original parties to the agreement, the means by which the rights and duties of the creditor under the agreement passed to him;

(*c*)   whether the agreement is a regulated agreement and, if it is not a regulated agreement, the reason why;

(*d*)   the place where the agreement was signed by the debtor (if known);

(*e*)   the goods claimed;

(*f*)   the total price of the goods;

(*g*)   the paid-up sum;

(*h*)   the unpaid balance of the total price;

(*i*)   whether a default notice or a notice under s 76(1) or s 98(1) of the Consumer Credit Act 1974 has been served on the debtor and if it has, the date on which and the manner in which it was so served;

(*j*)   the date when the right to demand delivery of the goods accrued;

(*k*)   the amount (if any) claimed as an alternative to the delivery of the goods; and

(*l*)   the amount (if any) claimed in addition to the delivery of the goods or any claim under sub-paragraph (*k*), stating the cause of action in respect of which each such claim is made.

Where a plaintiff's claim arises out of a hire-purchase agreement, but *is not for the delivery of goods*, he shall in his particulars state in the following order:

(*a*)   the date of the agreement and the parties to it with the number of the agreement or sufficient particulars to enable the debtor to identify the agreement;

(*b*)   where the plaintiff was not one of the original parties to the agreement, the means by which the rights and duties of the creditor under the agreement passed to him;

(*c*)   whether the agreement is a regulated agreement and, if it is not a regulated agreement, the reason why;

(*d*) the place where the agreement was signed by the debtor (if known);

(*e*) the goods let under the agreement;

(*f*) the amount of the total price;

(*g*) the paid-up sum;

(*h*) the amount (if any) claimed as being due and unpaid in respect of any instalment or instalments of the total price; and

(*i*) the nature and amount of any other claim and the circumstances in which it arises.

Notes

As to 'regulated agreement' see s 189(1) of the Consumer Credit Act 1974. 'Total price' (as to which see s 189(1) is, broadly, the same as 'hire-purchase price' under the Hire-Purchase Act, 1965.

Actions against the Crown

The particulars of claim must contain information as to the circumstances in which it is alleged that the liability of the Crown has arisen and as to the government departments and officers of the Crown concerned (Ord 42, r 4). (See also the section on 'The Crown' in Chapter 4.)

Interest

This must be specifically claimed (Ord 6, r 1A) and reference could usefully be made to Practice Note (Claims for Interest) (No 2), [1983] 1 WLR 377 issued for the Queen's Bench Division of the High Court which specifies the particulars required to be pleaded in the Queen's Bench in claims for interest on debt or damages made under s 15 of the Administration of Justice Act 1982, the empowering Act. For county court purposes interest should be claimed pursuant to s 69 of the County Courts Act, 1984:

Interest may be given for all or any part of the period between the date when the cause of action arose and: (a) in the case of any sum paid before judgment, the date of the payment; and (b) in the case of the sum for which judgment is given, the date of judgment.

Interest is not payable under this section for any period during which, for whatever reason, interest on the debt already runs (69(4)). Interest, if given under the section, may be calculated at different rates in respect of different periods (69(5)).

Where there is a judgment for personal injuries (or death) which exceeds £200 the court has no discretion but must give interest under (a) above unless the court is satisfied that there are special reasons to the contrary (see *Jefford* v *Gee* [1970] All ER 1202 and *Birkett* v *Hayes* [1982] 2 All ER 710).

Precedent of claim to be inserted at the foot of the Particulars of Claim

(The example assumes the date of the application as 5 November 1986)

And the Plaintiff claims the said sum of [£250.00] together with interest pursuant to s 69 of the County Courts Act 1984 at the rate of 15 per cent per annum from the [First day of October 1986] [the date upon which payment became due] to the date hereof [£3.70] and continuing hereafter at the daily rate of [£0.1027] until the date of judgment or sooner payment.

The plaintiff therefore claims the said sum of [£253.70] continuing interest and costs.

Chapter 7

Service

Generally

Subject to the requirements of any act or particular rule (as to which see below) any document may be served, if the person to be served is acting in person, by delivering it to him personally or by delivering it at, or sending it by first class post to, the address he has given for service.

A party in person may give his place of residence or business, or if he resides outside England or Wales any address in England or Wales (Ord 1, r 3). If he has given no address for service, service may be effected by delivering the document at his residence or by sending it by first class post to his last known residence, or in the case of a proprietor of a business, by delivering the document at his place of business or sending it by first class post to his last known place of business (Ord 7, r 1).

If the person to be served is represented by a solicitor, the document may be served by delivering the document at, or sending it by first class post to, the solicitor's address for service (Ord 7, r 1(*b*)). See below.

Service by post of documents, other than of originating process (as to which, see below) is deemed to have been effected at the time the letter would have been delivered in the ordinary course of post (s 7 of the Interpretation Act 1978).

Where *personal* service of a document is required, it may be served by a court bailiff, or if the person to be served attends and is present at court, or in the court office, by any other officer of the court.

Following service, the bailiff or other officer of the court files a certificate of the manner, place and date of service (N 12). If a court bailiff fails to effect service, a notice of non-service (N 216) is sent by the court of which he is bailiff to the plaintiff or other party issuing the process (Ord 7, rr 2–6). If the bailiff knows or ascertains before notice of non-service is sent that the defendant is at another address within the district, he should attempt to serve the summons there and state the new address in his certificate of service (Ord 7, r 17(3)).

If the address for service by the bailiff is not within the district of the court issuing the summons, or within five hundred yards thereof, the issuing court must send the summons to the court within the district for which the address for service is situated for personal service to be effected by that court (Ord 7, r 7). The judge or registrar of the issuing court may order process to be served by their own bailiff out of area (Ord 7, r 4(2)).

Where it is a party, his agent or his solicitor who effects personal service, this is proved by filing an affidavit of service (N 215) (Ord 7, rr 2, 6). Until it is filed, judgment cannot be entered nor the action or matter proceed unless the defendant has filed a defence, admission or counterclaim (Ord 7, r 12). Personal service may not be effected by anyone under sixteen years of age (Ord 7, r 2).

No process, except in an admiralty action, may be served or executed within England or Wales on a Sunday, Christmas Day or Good Friday, except in case of urgency with leave of the court (Ord 7, r 3).

Service by post of documents, other than of originating process (see below), is deemed to have been effected at the time the letter would have been delivered in the ordinary course of post. All documents sent by post for service, whether originating process or otherwise and whether to companies or to persons, should be sent by prepaid letter post, not registered or recorded; only documents other than originating process can be sent by second class post. By s 7 of the Interpretation Act 1978, proof of prepaid posting to the proper address raises a statutory presumption of delivery (provided that the document has not been returned through the Post Office as undelivered). If a document other than originating process (as to which, see below) is sent by first class post, it is presumed to arrive on the second working day after posting (working days being Monday to Friday and excluding Bank Holidays). (See Practice Direction [1985] 1WLR 489.) Affidavits should therefore specify whether first or second class mail has been used.

Substituted service

If it appears to the court that it is impracticable for any reason to serve a document in any manner prescribed by the rules, the court may, upon an affidavit showing grounds, make an order for substituted service (N 217) giving leave for such steps to be taken as the court directs to bring the document to the notice of the person to be served (Ord 7, r 8(1)). Although an order of substituted service may be made in committal proceedings, the judge may decide to exercise his discretion not to commit until personal service has been effected. If the defendant's address can be proved, but he is denied there, an order for substituted service 'by first class prepaid post in a plain white or blue (but not buff) handwritten envelope on which is to be affixed an ordinary postage stamp' may be sought, and some county court registrars are familiar with an order in these terms knowing of the antipathy to buff envelopes when received by some defendants, particularly debtors. Once the envelope is known to have been slit open, an explanation from the recipient may be required. For subsequent service, different coloured envelopes and different handwriting may be desirable. Substituted service may be made at a defendant's place of employment or his bank or his former solicitor (see Supreme Court Practice, Vol 1, 65/4/16). If via his former solicitor, it is perhaps desirable for the court to send a covering letter making clear that the solicitor is not himself being asked to accept service.

If substituted service by advertisement is required, a draft of the advertisement must be submitted to the registrar to settle. The expense is to be borne by such party as the court may direct (Ord 50, r 8), and on a taxation reasonable costs may be allowed (Ord 38, r 12).

Where a document is to be served by a bailiff, the proper officer of the bailiff's court shall, if so requested, take such steps as may be necessary to provide evidence on which an order for substituted service may be made (Ord 7, r 8(2)).

Service of summons or other originating process

Unless the plaintiff requests that he (the plaintiff) serve personally, service is effected in the first instance by the court by first class postal service to the address given for the defendant in the request for summons (N 201–4, 208 or 209).

Where the summons has been so sent by post and returned to the court office undelivered, notice of non-service (N 216) is sent to the plaintiff saying that he may request bailiff service. If such service is requested, the bailiff then serves by inserting the summons etc through the letter-box or handing it to a person (apparently not less than sixteen years old) at the address given in the request for summons. Alternatively he serves the defendant personally (Ord 7, r 10(1), (2) and Ord 3, rr 4(6), 5 and 6(6)).

Time as relating to service of originating process

A fixed date summons, originating application, petition or appeal should be served not less than twenty-one clear days before the return day, but on the plaintiff satisfying the registrar by affidavit that a defendant is about to remove, it may be served at any time before the return day (Ord 7, r 10(5), Ord 3, rr 4–6). Furthermore, if the originating process is served late, the court may allow the hearing or pre-trial review to proceed even in the defendant's absence, or it may adjourn the hearing (Ord 7, r 16). Notice of service (N 222) is to be sent by the court office to the plaintiff when a default summons is served by the court (Ord 7, r 21).

Where an originating process is sent by post (first class as required), the date of service is deemed to be seven days thereafter unless the contrary is proved (Ord 7, r 10(3); Ord 3 rr 4–6). Thus in calculating the date to be given for a hearing (Ord 7, r 10(5)), an additional seven days must always be allowed where postal service is effected.

Service on solicitor

(a) Summons or originating process

The defendant's solicitor endorses on the copy summons a certificate duly accepting service and giving an address for service. The copy summons so endorsed will be sent by the solicitor to the court office or else retained by the person who has effected service. Where the solicitor accepts service, no affidavit of service is required.

(b)   Documents other than originating process

Service is deemed to have been effected on the date of the certificate (Ord 7, r 11):

(i)   by delivering the document at, or sending it by first-class post to the solicitor's address for service. Service by post is deemed to have been effected at the time the letter would have been delivered in the ordinary course of post (s 7 of the Interpretations Act 1978): or

(ii)   where the solicitor's address for service includes a numbered box at a document exchange in a county court, by leaving the document at that exchange or at an exchange which transmits daily to the first exchange. The document is then deemed to have been served on the second day after the day on which it was left, but any day on which the court office in which one or both exchanges is situated is shut shall not be taken into account (Ord 1, r 3; Ord 2, r 5(1A); Ord 7, rr 1(1)(*b*), 1(3), and (4)).

Crown and government departments

Service must be effected on one of the persons acting or deemed to be acting as solicitor for the department. A list of authorised government departments and their solicitors and addresses is published by the Treasury for the Civil Service, and is reproduced in *The County Court Practice*. Service is to be effected by posting the process or document in a prepaid registered envelope, or by personal delivery.

Minors and mental patients

If a defendant is a minor, a summons must be served (if he is not also a mental patient) on a parent or guardian, or if he has no parent or guardian, then on the person with whom he resides or in whose care he is (Ord 10, r 4). If, however, the defendant is a mental patient, the summons must be served on the person, if any, who is authorised under the Mental Health Act 1983, Pt VII to conduct proceedings on the defendant's behalf or if there is no such person, then on the person with whom he resides or in whose care he is (Ord 10, r 4(1)).

If a summons is purported to be served otherwise on a person under disability, the court is empowered to order that the summons be deemed duly served (Ord 10, r 4(2)).

Partners

Where partners are sued in the name of their firm, unless the plaintiff requests that he (the plaintiff) serve a partner personally, service is effected in the first instance by the court by first class postal service to the address given for the firm in the request for summons (N 201–4).

Where the summons has been so served by post and returned to the court office undelivered, notice of non-service is sent to the plaintiff (N 216). If he then requires bailiff service the bailiff serves the summons by delivering it at the said address and by delivering it to the person having, or appearing to have, control or management there alternatively to a partner personally. (The above applies even if any of the partners are out of England or Wales.)

If the firm has been dissolved to the knowledge of the plaintiff before the commencement of the action, the summons must be served upon every person within England and Wales sought to be made liable (Ord 7, r 13).

Limited companies

A summons must be served on a limited company by leaving it at, or by sending it by post to, the registered office pursuant to s 725(1) of the Companies Act, 1985. The expression 'by post' includes ordinary post, though it may be preferable to use first class. Order 7, r 10(4) which provides that the date of service is deemed to be the seventh day after posting does not apply, and the summons is in this case deemed, by virtue of s 7 of the Interpretation Act 1978, to be received in the time it would be delivered 'in the ordinary course of post'. The fact that the limited company has vacated its registered office and/or made no arrangements for forwarding post does not affect the validity of service. If, however, the summons is returned by the post office, the registrar will normally require proof that the address was the up-to-date registered office on the date of service before deeming service to have been effected.

Where a company is registered in Scotland a summons may be served on it by leaving it at, or by sending it by post to, its principal place of business in England or Wales addressed to the manager or head officer and by further posting a copy to the registered office. (s 725(2) and (3) Companies Act 1985).

Corporations aggregate

Service may be effected on the mayor, chairman or president, or on the chief executive, clerk, treasurer or secretary, in the absence of any statutory provision (Ord 7, r 14).

Members of the armed forces

Reference should be made to the Memorandum issued by the Lord Chancellor's office on 26 July, 1979 entitled 'Memorandum on service of legal process on members of HM Forces'. This requires a letter of inquiry to be addressed to the Ministry of Defence, for example.

Service of summonses for recovery of land

If in the opinion of the court a summons for recovery of land cannot be served in accordance with Ord 7, rr 4–10, an order may be made on request in N 220 for service on the husband or wife of the defendant, a person living with but not married to the defendant, or upon anyone who is or appears to be authorised by the defendant to reside or carry on business in the premises, to manage them or to safeguard or deal with the premises or contents thereof (Ord 7, r 15(1)–(3)). Notice in N 220(1) is to be served on the 'representative' of the defendant. Such service must be effected twenty-one days before the return day (Ord 7, rr 15(2), 10(5)).

In an action for recovery of land, if there is no one in occupation, or where the property is occupied only by virtue of the presence of furniture or other goods, the summons may be served on request (N 220) and if so ordered by the court, by affixing it to a conspicuous part of the property (Ord 7, r 15(4)).

If the summons for recovery of land has been served under Ord 10, r 15 and a money claim is joined, the court must, unless it thinks it just to do otherwise, mark the summons 'not served' as to the money claim (Ord 10, r 15(5)).

Where a mortgagee claims possession a person who has registered a land charge, notice or caution under s 2(7) of the Matrimonial Homes Act 1967 or a notice under s 2(8) of the Matrimonial Homes Act 1983 must be served with a copy of the particulars of claim (Ord 6, r 5(1A)).

Note the special rules for service under Ord 24, r 3 (see Chapter 6).

Services of notices under the Law of Property Act 1925 eg 's 146 notices' may be served by registered letter post (s 196(3) and (4)) and also by recorded delivery (Recorded Delivery Service Act 1962).

Service relating to the Landlord and Tenant Act 1954, Part 2

The plaintiff will be the tenant and the landlord the defendant, but if head lessors or mortgagees are likely to be affected they should be added as defendants and served, or else notice should be given to them that they may apply to be joined if desired. Mortgagees in possession must be joined as defendants. Section 137 of the 1984 Act provides that 'every lessee to whom there is delivered any summons issued from a county court for the recovery of land held by him . . . shall forthwith give notice to his lessor . . . if a lessee fails to give notice he shall be liable to forfeit to the person of whom he hold the land an amount equal to three years improved rent of the land'.

Doubtful service

Where a summons has been served in accordance with Ord 7, r 10(4)(b) by delivering the summons to a person not under sixteen years of age, if it is doubtful from the endorsement whether the summons will come to the knowledge of the defendant in sufficient time, notice of doubtful service (N 221) is sent by the court. Where such a notice has been served, then unless the court receives from the defendant a defence, admission or counterclaim, the plaintiff will have to satisfy the court that the defendant received the summons in 'sufficient time' (Ord 7, r 18(2). For default summonses, 'sufficient time' means sufficient time for the defendant to deliver a defence, admission or counterclaim within fourteen days after delivery of the summons, and sufficient time in the case of fixed date summonses for him to attend on the return day (Ord 7, r 18(3)). If the court is unable to effect service, notice of non-service (N 216) is sent to the plaintiff or his solicitor (Ord 7 r 6(2)). If the defendant files a defence, admission or counterclaim, service is presumed on the date of such filing (Ord 7, r 12).

Alteration in summons or request

If a summons has not been served, it may be amended if the plaintiff files an amended request 'notwithstanding that the amendment consists of the addition or substitution of a defendant'. However, the court may disallow such amendment (Ord 7, r 17(2)).

The requirements are:
(*a*)   amended request;
(*b*)   plaint note;
(*c*)   addressed envelope, if requested by post. No fee.

If the defendant was wrongly shown in the request as residing or carrying on business in the court's district, the address may only be amended on the plaintiff filing a fresh request showing that the court has jurisdiction (Ord 7, r 17(4)).

If, on amendment, it is found that the court does not have jurisdiction by virtue of the change in address, an application can be made to transfer it to the appropriate court (Ord 16, r 2). No fee.

Successive fixed date summonses

Where a fixed date summons has not been served on *every* defendant before the return day, successive summonses may be reissued with fresh return days (Ord 7, r 19(1)).

The requirements are:
(*a*)   amendment request;
(*b*)   plaint note, to show amended return day;
(*c*)   addressed envelope, if requested by post. No fee.

Where such a summons has not been served because the defendant has left the district after issue, successive summonses may be issued for service in any district to which he has moved (Ord 7, r 19(2)). Successive summonses bear the same number and date as the original and are deemed to be a continuance of the original fixed date summons (Ord 7, r 19(3)).

Duration and renewal of default and fixed date summonses

A summons may, unless extended, only be served within twelve months from the date of the issue of the original summons (Ord 7, r 20(1)). A note of the extension is made by the court on the summons and copy.

A successive fixed date summons is deemed to have been issued on the date of the original summons (Ord 7, r 19(3)).

The registrar may extend the period of twelve months for a further period or periods each not exceeding twelve months, if reasonable efforts have been made to serve the summons and provided that the application has been made before the preceding twelve months expire, or if later, in the court's discretion (Ord 7, r 20(2)). The application, setting out the facts, may be made by letter. It is made ex parte and usually without attendance. The plaint note should be produced. There is no fee. A note of the extension is made by the court on the summons and copy.

Service of matters

An originating application, petition or an appeal to the county court is served in accordance with the rules for a fixed date summons unless an enactment or rule otherwise provides (Ord 3, rr 4(6), 5 and 6(6)). The rules as to renewing summonses apply to matters.

Originating applications for new tenancies under s 24 of the Landlord and Tenant Act 1954

Such applications must be served within two months of issue unless the period is extended. The time for service may be extended by two months at a time, before the two months expire, or even afterwards in the court's discretion (Ord 43, r 6(3) applying and modifying Ord 7, r 20).

Service out of England and Wales

Order 8 applies.

Service of an originating process out of England and Wales is permissible without the leave of the court provided that each claim made is either:

(a) a claim which, by virtue of the Civil Jurisdiction and Judgments Act 1982, the court has power to hear and determine, made in proceedings to which the following conditions apply:

(i) no proceedings between the parties concerning the same cause of action are pending in the courts of

any other part of the United Kingdom or of any
other Convention territory, and

(ii) either:

(1) the defendant is domiciled in any part of the
United Kingdom or in any other Convention
territory, or the proceedings begun by the
originating process are proceedings to which
art 16 of Sched 1 or of Sched 4 to the 1982
Act refers, or

(2) the defendant is a party to an agreement
conferring jurisdiction to which art 17 of the
said Sched 1 or Sched 4 applies.

[The request for summons *and* the particulars of claim must
contain the certificates required by Ord 3, r 3(5)–(8) or r 4(7).
The rules themselves should be consulted for detail.]
or,

(*b*) a claim which by virtue of any other enactment the
court has power to hear and determine notwithstanding
that the person against whom the claim is made is not
within England and Wales or that the wrongful act, neglect
or default giving rise to the claim did not take place within
England and Wales.

In other cases, service outside England and Wales requires
the court's leave. The following are the principal cases where
that leave would be forthcoming:

(*a*) relief is sought against any person domiciled in England
or Wales;

(*b*) an injunction is sought ordering the defendant to do
an act or refrain from doing anything (whether or not
damages are also claimed in respect of a failure to do
something or for the doing of that thing);

(*c*) the claim is brought against any person duly served within
or out of England and Wales and a person out of England
and Wales is a necessary or proper party thereto;

(*d*) the claim is founded on any breach or alleged breach
of any contract wherever made, which:

(i) according to its terms ought to be performed
in England and Wales, or

(ii) is by its terms, or by implication, governed by
English law, or

        (iii) contains a term to the effect that a court in England or Wales shall have jurisdiction to hear and determine any action in respect of the contract;

(*e*)   the claim is founded on a tort and the damage was sustained or resulted from an act committed, within England and Wales;

(*f*)   the whole subject-matter of the proceedings is land (with or without rent or profits) or the perpetuation of testimony relating to land;

(*g*)   the claim is brought to construe, rectify, set aside or enforce an act, deed, will, contract, obligation or liability affecting land;

(*h*)   the claim is made for a debt secured on immovable property or is made to assert, declare or determine proprietary or possessory rights, or rights of security, in or over movable property, or to obtain authority to dispose of movable property;

(*i*)   the claim is brought to execute the trusts of a written instrument, being trusts that ought to be executed according to English law and of which the person to be served with the originating process is a trustee, or for any relief or remedy which might be obtained when such a claim is brought;

(*j*)   the claim is made for the administration of the estate of a person who died domiciled in England or Wales or for any relief or remedy which might be obtained when such a claim is made;

(*k*)   the claim is brought in a probate action within the meaning of Ord 41;

(*l*)   the claim is brought to enforce any judgment or arbitral award;

(*m*)   the claim is brought against a defendant not domiciled in Scotland or Northern Ireland in respect of a claim by the Commissioners of Inland Revenue for or in relation to any of the duties of taxes which have been, or are for the time being, placed under their care and management;

(*n*)   the claim is brought in respect of contributions under the Social Security Act 1975;

(*o*)   the claim is made for a sum to which the Directive of the Council of the European Communities dated 15 March 1976 No 76/308/EEC applies, and service is to be effected in a country which is a member of the European Economic Community.

When serving out of England and Wales, the court fixes in the case of a default summons the time for delivering an admission or defence or for paying the total claim and costs into court, and in any other case a return day (Ord 8, rr 2(3) and 7). The table in Vol 2 of *The Supreme Court Practice*, para 902 should be used by the court to fix the time allowed for service of admission, defence etc.

Where service is to be effected outside the jurisdiction, the request for service (N 201–204 or N 224) must contain the details required by Ord 3, rr 3(5) and (6). The order is in Form N 223. When jurisdiction is claimed under the Civil Jurisdiction and Judgments Act 1982, the particulars of claim must contain the statement required by Ord 3, r 3(7).

Service of an interlocutory process out of England and Wales is permissible with the leave of the court on a person who is already a party to the proceedings and who in the case of a defendant, respondent or third party, has been served with the originating process but leave shall not be required for such service in any proceedings in which the originating process may by these rules or under any Act be served out of England and Wales without leave, (Ord 8, rr 1 and 4).

The Civil Jurisdiction and Judgments Act 1982, in force from 1 January 1987, waives the need to obtain leave to serve abroad where defendants are resident in the EEC, Scotland or Northern Ireland.

Where service is requested in Scotland or Northern Ireland see Ord 8, r 5.

In the case of a limited company with a registered office in Scotland carrying on business in England and Wales, service can be effected without leave by post or by delivering the process at the address in England and Wales and at the same time sending a copy of the process to the registered office (s 725(2) and (3) of the Companies Act 1985). As to overseas companies which establish a place of business in Great Britain, reference should be made to s 695 of the Companies Act 1985, and to *The Supreme Court Practice*, notes 65/3/7–65/3/15).

The procedure for service out of jurisdiction is complex and Table 3 of the Procedural Tables at the back of Part 1 of *The County Court Practice* should be referred to before any application is made and where the jurisdiction of the court is involved under the Civil Jurisdiction Act 1982. See Ord 3, r 3(5)–(8).

Special note should be made of:

(a) the definitions of 'domicile' of individuals on the one hand and of corporations (including limited companies) and associations on the other, in ss 41 to 46 of the 1982 Act, and

(b) the provisions in Scheds 1 and 4 (ibid) which give the Court jurisdiction to hear and determine claims.

Chapter 8

Admissions, Defences, Counterclaims and Answers

Originating applications

An *obligation* to file an answer to an originating application only arises if there is some specific provision in the rules relating to that particular application, or if the court so orders.

Actions

The provisions are contained in Ord 9 which applies to both default and fixed date summonses.

A defendant who wishes to admit the claim or part of it, or who desires time for payment, or who disputes the whole or part of the claim, or who wants to counterclaim, must within fourteen days of service (exclusive of the day of service) either file the form annexed to the summons or else his own admission, defence or counterclaim in duplicate (Ord 9, r 2(1) and Ord 1, r 9).

The defendant's admission, defence or counterclaim must be signed by him if acting in person, or else by his solicitor in the solicitor's own or firm's name. It must give an address for service (Ord 9, r 19).

The defendant's request for time for payment must contain a specific proposal as to the time or rate of payment (Ord 9, r 2 as amended).

If the defendant is a person under disability he may not defend or counterclaim except by his guardian ad litem (Ord 10, r 1(2)), see Chapter 4.

The court may allow a defendant to withdraw or amend a first admission at any time on such terms as may be just (Ord 9, r 2(3)).

If the admission etc is delivered late but in a default action before judgment is entered or in a fixed date action before the return day, then the court proceeds as if the admission etc had been filed in time, as far as possible. The defendant may defend on the return day even if he has failed to file a defence (Ord 9, r 9(2)). He may be penalised in costs (Ord 9, r 9(3)).

A copy of the admission etc is sent to the plaintiff, with instructions, in default and hire-purchase actions, as to what to do where part is admitted and/or time to pay the whole or part is sought (N 225, 226 and 228).

Where a party cannot protect his position by a payment into court, he may make the other party a written offer filing a copy with the court, but not to be brought to the attention of the court until costs fall to be decided (Ord 12, r 10) and similarly, where contribution arises a party may make a written offer to contribute (Ord 12, r 7).

Admissions in fixed date actions

Recovery of land

If the defendant admits the plaintiff's right to recovery of land, notice is sent to the plaintiff (N 229). No costs are allowed after receipt of such notice of proving anything the admission renders it unnecessary to prove (Ord 9, r 16).

Early judgment in other fixed date actions

If the defendant files an admission of the whole or part of the claim within fourteen days of service, notice is sent in N 227 to the plaintiff, who may then apply, on notice to the defendant before the return day, for judgment for the whole, or that part of the claim, which the defendant admits, without waiting for any other issues to be resolved. The court may make such order as is just (Ord 9, r 4).

Admissions in actions for delivery of goods

Where goods, in hire-purchase and conditional sale cases, are protected under s 33 of the Hire-Purchase Act 1965, or under s 90 of the Consumer Credit Act 1974, if the defendant makes an offer to pay the whole or part of the outstanding balance by instalments, the plaintiff must notify the proper officer within fourteen days of notice whether he accepts or not. If he does, the registrar will enter judgment (N 32(2)) as soon as practicable. Where there is a guarantor or where the offer is not accepted, judgment cannot be entered before the return day (Ord 9, r 3(1), (2); Ord 49, r 6(5)) (for agreements dated 18 May, 1985 or earlier). For agreements dated 19 May, 1985 or later see Ord 9, r 3(1) and (2) and the alternative Ord 49, r 4(7). There appears to be no difference in substance between the procedures.

Admissions of part, or request for time, in default actions

(1)   The plaintiff should within fourteen days after notice notify the court whether he accepts the amount (of the debt or liquidated damages) which has been admitted by the defendant and as to whether he accepts the proposals made as to payment (Ord 9, r 3(1)).

(2)   If he accepts, judgment is entered for the amount of the debt or liquidated damages admitted (N 30)(Ord 9, r 3(2)).

(3)   If the whole claim is admitted (or the plaintiff accepts the part admitted) but the plaintiff does not accept the proposals as to payment, a 'disposal day' is fixed on not less than eight days' notice (N 230 and 231) to the parties. This is heard by the registrar in court or in chambers (Ord 9, rr 3(3), (5)).

(4)   If the defendant admits part only of the claim, and the plaintiff does not accept, a pre-trial review is given (N 233) or a hearing date is fixed. If the claim or amount involved is for £500 or less the matter is referred to arbitration either immediately (N 232, with Terms of Reference attached) or with a preliminary consideration N 18 (Ord 19, rr 2(3), 5(2); Terms of Reference 1).

(5)   If the claim is for unliquidated damages and the plaintiff accepts a specific sum offered in satisfaction by the defendant, the same provisions apply as if the defendant had admitted part of a plaintiff's claim for debt or liquidated damages (Ord 9, r 3(6)(a)).

(6)   If the claim is for unliquidated damages and liability is admitted but quantum is disputed, the court on the plaintiff's application (N 234) may enter interlocutory judgment for damages to be assessed and costs (N 17) or may make such other order as it thinks just (Ord 9, r 3(6)(b)).

If the disposal under Ord 9, r 3(3) or the pre-trial review could more conveniently be heard in another court the registrar may order the transfer of the action or matter accordingly (N 271)

(Ord 16, r 1(*b*), (*c*)). Notice from the transferee court is given in N 272 or N 275. Where a third party notice has been issued in a default action, judgment on admission or default, cannot be entered without a hearing (Ord 12, r 1(7)). Where the defendant is under disability, a plaintiff may not enter judgment on an admission unless there is a guardian ad litem or steps are taken to appoint a guardian ad litem (Ord 10, r 6(1), but see Ord 10, r 8). If judgment is so entered it may be set aside under Ord 37, r 5. As to proceedings against persons under disability, see Chapter 4.

Defence or counterclaim delivered in default actions

If a defence without part admission (see above) or a counterclaim is delivered to the court before judgment is entered, a pre-trial review is fixed (N 233) or a hearing date given (N 232) or, if the claim and/or counterclaim do not exceed £500, the matter is referred to arbitration either forthwith (N 232, with Terms of Reference attached) or with a preliminary consideration (N 18)(Ord 9, rr 5, 9; Ord 19, rr 2(3), 5(2); Term No 1).

Judgment in default or on unqualified admissions in default actions

(*a*) Where the defendant fails in time to pay the full claim and costs or deliver an admission etc, or else delivers an admission of the *whole* claim without counterclaiming or requesting time to pay, judgment may be entered for payment forthwith or at such time or times as the plaintiff requests (Ord 9, r 6(1)). The request for judgment is in Form N 14 and to this may now be added: 'Interest (if any) Period . . . Rate . . . ', per r 2 of the County Court (Forms)(Amendment) Rules 1984 (SI 1984 No 879). The judgment is in N 30.

(*b*) If the claim is for unliquidated damages, judgment is for damages to be assessed and costs (N 17)(Ord 9, r 6(1), (2)).

The requirements are:

(*a*) request for judgment (N 14, noting the sum, interest and costs claimed, see Costs Appendix B below; or N 234 if for interlocutory judgment);

(*b*) plaint note;

(*c*) stamped addressed envelope (if application by post).

Notes

(a) If the claim is for money secured by a mortgage or charge, legal or equitable, judgment may be entered only on application to the registrar on notice to the defendant (Ord 9, r 7).

(b) Except with leave, no judgment can be entered in default against the Crown (Ord 42, r 5(3)).

(c) In addition to the sum claimed, judgment for interest to *date of judgment* or payment if earlier, may be given (i) at the contractual or statutory rate specified in the particulars of claim or (ii) if no *rate* is specified, at the rate allowed in the High Court (when the summons is issued), assessed without appointment (Ord 9, r 8). (See Chapter 6 under 'Interest')

(d) Where the defendant is an individual or a company who has been served outside the jurisdiction under Ord 8, r 2(2) (9), *or*, within the jurisdiction but is 'domiciled' in Scotland, Northern Ireland, Belgium, Denmark, France, the Federal Republic of Germany (West Germany), Italy, Luxembourg or the Netherlands, judgment may be entered in default of defence only by leave of the Registrars. This may be given ex parte on affidavit and the order giving leave must be attached to the judgment (Ord 9, r 6(4), RSC Ord 13, r 7B and Queens Bench Masters Practice Note of 17 December 1986). (NB 'Domicile' is defined specifically for these purposes by ss 41–46 of the Civil Jurisdiction and Judgments Act 1982.)

Interlocutory judgment

When this has been entered (unless a date has been given for the assessment) the plaintiff should, when ready to prove his figures, apply for an appointment before the registrar (N 244). The court gives seven days' notice to the parties (Ord 22, r 6(1)). Judgment cannot be entered merely on an affidavit lodged by the plaintiff.

Interim payment of damages

Application for such payment can be made where more than £500 is claimed or involved (Ord 13, r 12).

Inactivity in a default action

Should twelve months have expired from date of service, without judgment having been entered by the plaintiff on an admission, the action is struck out and cannot be revived. The same applies where neither plaintiff nor defendant have, after service, taken any action at all (Ord 9, r 10).

Defence of tender before action

This is valid only if the sum in question is paid into court (Ord 9, r 12).

Irregularities

Delivery of a defence is not waiver of an irregularity, but the defendant must promptly apply to set aside the proceedings and take no other step meanwhile (Ord 9, r 13).

Letters and documents purporting to dispute or admit

The court shall treat *any document* which shows a desire to dispute, admit, ask time to pay, or counterclaim as prima facie admission, defence etc (Ord 9, r 17) provided that it is properly signed (Ord 9, r 19).

Plaintiffs (and their solicitors) should not write to the court ex parte asking for judgment to be entered 'because there is no real (or proper) defence'. Such submissions must be made at the pretrial review or preliminary consideration, or on application under Ord 9, r 14 where more than £500 is claimed.

Counterclaims

If the sum counterclaimed exceeds the sum claimed a fee is payable on the difference (See Table of Fees.)

Originating applications

Where an answer is required to be filed of which notice must have been given to the respondent (Ord 9, r 18(5)), the answer shall be filed within fourteen days inclusive of the day of service, unless another period is prescribed, and shall be accompanied by sufficient copies for all other parties, including other respondents separately represented. These are sent to the other parties by the court (Ord 9, r 18).

Chapter 9

Payment into and out of Court before Judgment

Order 11 contains the provisions which apply.

Money may be paid into court at any time before judgment (Ord 11, r 1).

The requirements are:

(*a*)   the summons;

(*b*)   addressed envelope if by post;

(*c*)   if payment of claim and costs is not made in full, a notice or letter identifying the nature of the payment(s) made, unless payment is made simply on account of the sum or sums claimed and admitted to be due (Ord 11, r 1(1)(*b*), (2)).

Payment should be made in the manner described in Chapter 5 under 'Fees'.

Action by court office

A receipt is issued. Notice of payment in is prepared and sent by the court office to all parties (N 242 or 243) (Ord 11, r 1(10)).

Form of notice of payment in satisfaction

(*a*)   If in satisfaction of the only or all the causes of action, the notice should simply state that the payment is 'in satisfaction of the plaintiff's claim' (Ord 11, r 1(5)).

(*b*)   If there are two or more causes of action and a payment in satisfaction is made for each separately, the notice must in respect of each cause of action identify it and give the figure applicable to it—stating 'nil' if such be the case (Ord 11, r 1(5)).

If one (or more) only of several defendants makes payment, this also must be stated (Ord 11, r 1(3)). Payment in shall not be mentioned in the pleadings and the notice must not be with the pleadings or documents for the use of the court at the trial or arbitration until after its decision, except in the case of a defence of tender, or the filing of a plea under the Libel Acts (Ord 11, r 7). Defendants in person unfortunately often mention payment in, in their defences. This can be corrected at the pre-trial review or preliminary arbitration hearing.

A sum paid into court 'to abide order'

A sum paid into court 'to abide order' may be appropriated as a payment into court in satisfaction under Ord 11, r 9. Notice must be given by the defendant not only under this rule, but to the Accountant-General (The Court Funds Rules 1987, rr 25(2) and 31).

Payment of whole sum

(*a*) Where the whole amount is paid into court (including interest to payment in if claimed) the action is stayed save as to costs, or where an order for payment out is required, or where hospital expenses are claimed (Ord 11, rr 2(1), 1(8)).

(*b*) Where the action is for a *debt or liquidated demand* (including interest to payment in, if claimed) and the defendant pays the claim and interest into court *within fourteen days* of service exclusive of the day of service, together with summons costs, then the action is stayed and the defendant is liable to no further costs unless the court otherwise orders or unless the plaintiff is under disability (Ord 11, r 2(1), (2), (4); Ord 10, r 1). In the latter case it seems that the court must approve the payment in pursuant to Ord 10, r 10, though it is difficult to see to what approval a debt or liquidated sum can be subject.

(*c*) In cases where payment in is made *later* than within fourteen days of service, or without summons costs, the action is stayed but the defendant is liable for the plaintiff's costs up to the date when the plaintiff receives notice of payment in, but not for costs thereafter (Ord 11, r 2(3)).

On receiving notice of payment in, the plaintiff may either (i) lodge his bill of costs for taxation, or (ii) if he so opts or in any event where the amount recovered does not exceed £100 but exceeds £25, ask for his costs to be assessed under costs Appendix C to the 1981 Rules (see Costs Appendix C) to which will be added the plaint fee (Ord 38, r 19).

If the costs are not paid then, except where a defence to costs has been filed, the plaintiff may enter judgment in default for them. However if an order for payment out is required under Ord 11, r 4(2), or if a legal aid certificate is in force in favour of the defendant, then the plaintiff must apply for his judgment and order for costs (Ord 11, r 2(3)(*b*); s 8(1)(*e*) of the Legal Aid and Advice Act 1974 and reg 117 of the Legal Aid (General) Regulations 1980).

Where payment in is made of the whole or on account of the sum or sums claimed, the court pays out automatically to the plaintiff's solicitor or to the plaintiff if acting in person, subject to Ord 11, r 4(2) and Ord 10, rr 10, 11 (Ord 11, r 4(1)).

Acceptance of a 'lesser sum'

The provisions below apply to cases where a claim other than one for money is made (Ord 11, r 3(1)) and since unliquidated damages cannot be the 'whole sum' to which Ord 11, r 2 (above) applies they appear to apply as well where unliquidated damages are claimed.

Whether the payment is made within or after fourteen days of service, if the plaintiff elects to accept the sum he must within twenty-one days after receipt by him of the notice of payment into court or, if the notice is received less than three days before the return day, then before the hearing of the action begins, give notice of his acceptance to the court and to every other party (Ord 11, r 3(1)). If the hearing of the action has begun and thereafter money is paid into court in satisfaction (or the amount paid in is increased) the plaintiff may accept within fourteen days of notice provided that the court has not commenced delivering judgment (Ord 11, r 3(2)). The cause(s) of action in respect of which the payment is made is/are then stayed (Ord 11, r 3(3)). Except in a case to which Ord 11, r 4(2) applies, the plaintiff is entitled to have the accepted sum paid out to him without any order of the court, if he accepts it within the time limited by the rule (Ord

11, r 4(1)). Further (i) he may apply for an order for the costs incurred by him before the receipt of the notice of payment into court where the defendant has legal aid or where Ord 11, r 4(2) (see below) applies, or (ii) in any other case provided he abandons all other claims, he may lodge a bill of costs for taxation, or have costs assessed and if the costs allowed are not paid within fourteen days, he may have judgment entered for them (Ord 11, r 3(5)). However, where payment in was made in the case of a liquidated claim within fourteen days of service together with appropriate summons costs (Ord 38, r 4) the defendant is under no further liability for costs unless the court so orders (Ord 11, r 3(4)).

If payment in, 'in satisfaction' is not accepted within the time prescribed (see above) the proper officer sends a remittance and notice to the Accountant-General, twenty-two days after payment in (The Court Fund Rules 1987, r 31(2)). If payment is made into court 'to abide issue', a remittance and notice is sent to the Accountant-General immediately (ibid r 31(3)).

Late acceptance

If the plaintiff fails to give notice of acceptance within the time limited by the rules, he may still give notice at any time before the hearing of the action begins, but an order for payment out of court is then required, and the court may order the plaintiff to pay the defendant's costs reasonably incurred since the date of payment into court (Ord 11, r 5).

Payment out requiring an order

Where payment into court is made:
(*a*) by one or more of several defendants sued jointly or in the alternative (unless the matter is settled by acceptance and the claims against the other defendants are abandoned and they agree in writing);
(*b*) with a defence of tender before action;
(*c*) in admiralty actions;
(*d*) where the plaintiff is a person under disability;
(*e*) where more than one person is entitled to the money in claims under the Fatal Accident Act 1976 and/or the Law Reform (Miscellaneous Provisions) Act 1934 (Ord 11, r 1(7) and Ord 11, r 4(2), (3));

(*f*) or, where the plaintiff has given 'late acceptance' (see above).

Payment out of court to the plaintiff is made automatically unless an order is required.

Interest

Money paid into court to abide the event, whether in satisfaction under Ord 11, r 1(1) or as a condition of obtaining relief, is placed by the court in a deposit account (in case of payment in satisfaction after the time for acceptance expires). Therefore, on payment out, the court must direct what is to happen to the accrued interest. If an order is made the judge should be asked to include a direction therein as to the interest. If no such direction is made the registrar will order payment of any interest accruing between payment in and its acceptance (or the judgment or order for payment out) to the party making the payment.

Legally-aided parties

Money in court for the benefit of a person who has legal aid must be paid out only to his solicitor or, if he is no longer represented by a solicitor, to the Law Society (Ord 11, r 4(4)).

Hospital expenses

As to such expenses under s 154(1) of the Road Traffic Act 1972, see Ord 11, r 6.

Forfeiture for non-payment of rent

The effect of early payment into court in actions for possession on the ground of non-payment of rent is specifically dealt with in s 138 of the 1984 Act. If the rent in arrear to the date of service (*Canas Property Co Ltd* v *KL Television Services Ltd* [1970] 2 QB 433; [1970] 2 All ER 795) and summons costs are paid into court five clear days before the hearing, the action ceases. The court has no power to award further costs. In contrast to the High Court's requirements, in the county court the defendant need not pay in such mesne profits as might have accrued after service.

See also Chapter 16.

Counterclaims

Where payment is made into court by a defendant who makes a counterclaim, it must be accompanied by a notice to show how the counterclaim has been taken into account (Ord 11, r 1(9)). (See Ord 11, r 3(6) as to 'stays on acceptance'.) A plaintiff or other person made defendant to a counterclaim may pay money into court as if he were a defendant (Ord 11, r 8). If the plaintiff accepts a sum which takes a counterclaim into account, he must say so (Ord 11, r 3(6)).

Payment in by trustees – See Chapter 26.

Costs on payment in

If assessed or taxed costs under Ord 11, rr 2(3)(a) or 3(5)(a) are not paid, the plaintiff may obtain judgment for them on filing a request (Ord 22, r 5(3)). The court should not enter these on the court record card before such request is lodged.

If an order for costs or additional costs is required to be made, the time for applying is when an application is made for payment out of court. Application for payment out may be made on the return day, or it may be made earlier by application on notice. Some courts will make an order ex parte on production of a consent signed by the other parties (Ord 11, rr 8(3), 9(c)).

No costs (save the plaint fee) are allowable where £25 or less is recovered save by special order (Ord 38, r 3(4)). Where a claim has been automatically referred to arbitration (when £500 or less was claimed or in dispute, Ord 19, r 2(3)), costs are limited to the summons costs, save by special order (Ord 19, r 6).

Where it is desired to make an offer to settle a claim other than one for a sum of money by making a written offer 'without prejudice save as to costs', the offer should be filed with the court; it is not brought to the attention of the court until the question of costs falls to be decided: Ord 11, r 10.

Chapter 10

Applications

The basic procedure is set out in Ord 13, r 1.

All applications must be made on written notice unless otherwise directed.

The following items are required:

(a) Notice of application and copy for each respondent to application, unless ex parte (N 244).

(b) Fee (see Table of Fees) if any. Subject to a special fee being prescribed for some applications, the plaint fee includes all other interlocutory applications (see Appendix II to County Court Fees Order 1982 as amended—at back of book).

(c) Affidavit, if any, but an affidavit is not necessary on the hearing of applications unless an enactment or rule specifically requires.

(d) Plaint note or originating process, to be receipted with any fee paid.

(e) Addressed envelope, if by post.

On issue the place, date and time of hearing are completed by the court and, unless service is to be effected by the court, a copy of the application duly sealed will be available for service to be effected by the party issuing the application. Applications are heard in chambers unless otherwise directed. If made ex parte, the application must be filed a reasonable time before the hearing subject to the power of the court to hear applications at any time. All applications, unless the judge otherwise directs or unless it be an 'excepted application', shall be made to the registrar. Excepted applications are most applications for injunctions, and all applications to commit. Excepted applications must be made to the judge.

Where applications are made on notice: (a) notice is to be

served on the opposite party and filed in the court not less than two days before the hearing, unless the court gives leave for short notice; and (b) the party making the application is responsible for ascertaining that the court will be available to hear the application and that sufficient time will be available.

The court may authorise notice to be given orally (Ord 50, r 4). This may be useful in emergency but leave is given sparingly.

Where the application is made to the registrar he may, if in doubt as to the proper order to be made, refer the application to the judge forthwith or at the next convenient opportunity, and the judge may hear the application and make such order as may be just or may refer it back to the registrar with directions.

Appeals from orders of registrars made on applications are made to the judge on notice to be filed and served within five days after the order is made unless additional time is allowed by the judge. Such appeals are heard in chambers unless the judge otherwise directs.

Copy documents on applications

In Chambers, copy documents are not required: RSC Ord 32/21.

Costs on applications

The costs of an interlocutory application are not taxed until the general taxation of the costs of the action or matter, unless the judge or registrar otherwise orders.

Applications by letter are now generally accepted in cases where no appointment is required. Certain ex parte applications are required to be made by affidavit, in which case the affidavit itself suffices as the application.

The court as a condition of granting any application may impose such terms and conditions as it thinks fit, including the giving of security, the giving of an undertaking, payment of money into court, payment of all or any part of the costs of the proceedings, or the giving of a power of re-entry (Ord 13, r 1(8)). A condition of payment into court is often imposed where a judgment is to be set aside but other terms and conditions are imposed sparingly.

The court may decide applications in the applicant's absence. Some courts allow attendance on simple or agreed applications by letter, but this is not as of right. Enquiry should be made at the court office as to a particular court's practice.

Adjournment or advancement of hearing

The court may upon application or of its own motion adjourn or advance the date of hearing of any proceeding. Notice of such adjournment or advancement is given by the registrar to all parties who were not present when the order was made (Ord 13, r 3(2)); it is common practice to send notice also to those parties who were present (N 232).

Many applications for adjournment are made ex parte on filing written consent of all parties but a reason for the adjournment is usually expected to be given, and the court may not necessarily grant it even if all parties consent. If the application is late, the party may have to apply to the court which is to hear the action. Individual practice in granting adjournments varies, and enquiry should be made at the court office.

An application to restore an action to the list for hearing after being adjourned generally ('sine die' is synonymous) is usually made by letter of which a copy should be sent to all other parties. An estimate of the time required is helpful to the court. Notice of the new hearing is sent by the court (N 232). If an action is not restored within twelve months, it will be struck out after a warning notice sent out by the court (Ord 13, r 3(4)).

Directions for trial

All necessary and desirable directions for disposing of the proceedings should be given at the pre-trial review, and the parties should as far as practicable ask for all the directions they need at the pre-trial review, giving prior notice to all interested parties (Ord 17, rr 1 and 3). As well as the procedure of giving directions on the pre-trial review, the court may on the application on notice of any party, or of its own motion, give directions at any time (Ord 13, r 2(2)). However, it should rarely be necessary to apply to the court for directions before the pre-trial review or preliminary arbitration appointment (Ord 19, r 5; Term No 2).

The court may treat the hearing of an application where no pre-trial date has been fixed as a pre-trial review (Ord 13, r 2(4)), and can be requested to do so.

Further particulars of claim

If a defendant requires further particulars, he should first send a written request to the plaintiff. If the particulars are not supplied, he may apply to the court, which will only order particulars before defence for good reason (Ord 6, r 7(2)).

The further particulars given must incorporate the request or order. They must be filed with the court and a copy must be sent to the defendant (Ord 6, r 7(4)).

Defence and further particulars

If the defendant in a fixed date action fails to deliver a defence in time, the court may order a defence to be filed at any time before the trial (Ord 9, r 11(1)). The procedure for the obtaining and giving of further particulars of defence is the same as appertains in relation to further particulars of claim.

Pleadings and particulars in general

The court has general powers to order a pleading or particulars to be filed and delivered and these may be exercised by the court on applications or, if the court wishes the issue to be defined, on the court's own motion (Ord 6, r 7(1), Ord 9, r 11(2) and (3) and Ord 13, r 2(1) and (2)).

Dismissal of proceedings and striking out

Dismissal and striking out (save for want of prosecution) are conditional on the court first having made an 'unless' order, that is an order which sets a time limit for compliance after which an order for dismissal and striking out may be made (Ord 22, r 3). An order for delivery of particulars may direct that in default the proceedings be dismissed, or that the defendant or respondent be debarred from defending, or that part of a pleading be struck out (Ord 13, r 2(2)). The order must make clear whether the time runs from the date of the order or from service thereof *Van Houten* v *Foodsafe* (1980) 12SJ 277. For the form of wording to be used in 'unless' and peremptory orders, see Chapter 16 under 'Form of peremptory orders'.

Application for dismissal for want of prosecution may be brought on grounds of default in complying with an order, or

for inordinate delay prejudicing the opposing party in having a
fair trial. The loci classici are *Allen* v *McAlpine* [1968] 2 QB 299
and *Birkett* v *James* [1978] AC 297; the principles are given at
25/1/4, 25/1/5, and 25/1/6 in *The Supreme Court Practice
1988*. 'A fresh action started on the same grounds as one struck
out for failure to obey an "unless" order may be struck out as
an abuse of the process of the court' (see *Bailey* v *Bailey* [1983]
1 WLR 1129 at 1133).

Judgment where defendant debarred

Where a defendant is debarred from defending altogether
or the whole of his defence is struck out, the plaintiff may
have judgment entered for his claim and costs (N 30) (Ord 22,
r 5).

A request for judgment for the claim and costs, on grounds
that the defendant has not complied with the 'unless' order,
must be lodged. If the claim is for unliquidated damages the
request (N 234) is for an interlocutory judgment for damages to
be assessed and costs. An application for assessment of damages is
made on notice under the procedure for interlocutory applications
under Ord 22, r 6. The judgment will be in N 34.

Summary judgment

Application may be made only in default actions and where the
claim exceeds £500 and the defendant has delivered at the court
office a document purporting to be a defence; the application is
for judgment on the grounds that notwithstanding the delivery of
that document, the defendant has no defence (Ord 9, r 14(1).

Discovery

Sections 52 and 53 of the 1984 Act and Ord 14, rr 1–10 apply.

Any party requiring general discovery may give notice in
writing to any other party requiring him to make discovery by
list of the documents, relating to any question in the proceedings,
which may be or have been in his possession or power. The list
(N 265) shall state where, within seven days of service, the
documents may be inspected (Ord 14, r 3). [It should be noted
that the rule does not make clear that the form incorporates the

notice.] A party may now require his opponent to supply copies of documents which he is entitled to inspect (rr 3 to 6 of County Court (Amendment) Rules 1988); the notice requiring the copy document must be served at or before the time when inspection takes place and must contain an undertaking to pay the proper charge, which charges are set out in Appendix A item 4 (Ord 14, r 5A).

If the party against whom discovery is sought does not comply with the notice, application may be made to the registrar for an order by lodging an application with copy for service, but application is more frequently made during the pre-trial review under Ord 17, or at the preliminary arbitration hearing. Where a party fails to supply a copy of any document the court may make such order as it thinks fit.

The court may make an order for discovery (N 264) notwithstanding that prior notice has not been given, where it is satisfied that there were reasonable grounds for not giving such notice.

Discovery will not be ordered if unnecessary (Ord 14, r 8). For example, in a claim for cost of repair to a car, the court may think it sufficient merely to order the claimant to send copies of the repair estimates and paid bills to the other party without making any order for discovery.

Limited discovery can be ordered (Ord 14, r 1(3)). For example, in many cases it may be considered sufficient to order the parties to file and deliver lists only of the documents they actually possess. There may well be such an order in the case of litigants in person. Section 53 contains powers of disclosure special to proceedings for personal injuries and death. The section is invoked under Ord 13, r 7(1) which applies the Rules of the Supreme Court.

N 265(1) is the affidavit verifying a list of documents.

Inspection of documents referred to in affidavits and pleadings may be required by a party (Ord 14, r 4). If the request is not complied with, the court may order it (Ord 14, r 5).

If there is a claim or likely claim in respect of personal injuries or death, the Rules of the Supreme Court Ord 24, r 7A(1) is applied to the county court by Ord 13, r (1)(g) and this enables an application for discovery to be made before the action is commenced against a person 'likely to be a party'. See also s 52(1) of the 1984 Act.

In actions for such claims, discovery can also be ordered against non-parties (Ord 13, r 7(1)(g) applying the Rules of the

Supreme Court, Ord 24, r 7A(2)). (See also s 53(1) and (2) of the Act.)

Interrogatories

Interrogatories cannot be administered without leave. Order 14, r 11 applies the provisions of the Rules of Supreme Court Ord 26. Interrogatories can be administerd with leave, application to be made on notice in Form N 244. A copy of the proposed interrogatories must be served with the notice (RSC Ord 26, r 1(2)). The Order in Form N 269, if leave be granted, will require the other party to answer the interrogatories on affidavit within such period as may be specified.

The court only gives leave to serve interrogatories if necessary for disposing fairly of the action, or for saving costs, and before giving leave will consider whether particulars, admissions, or production of documents have been offered (RSC Ord 26, r 1(3)). The principle is to not allow interrogatories as to the evidence of the party interrogated, nor any 'fishing' and there is wide discretionary power. A form of application for leave to deliver interrogatories is given in *Atkin's Court Forms*, second edn., 1980, vol 22 p 492 and examples illustrating the principles are given in the *The Supreme Court Practice* at 26/1/4 et seq.

Enforcement

Orders for discovery, inspection and supply of documents, and for answering interrogatories, may be enforced by committal (Ord 14, rr 10,11).

No reasonable cause of action

The court may order the whole or part of any pleading to be amended or struck out on the ground that (a) it discloses no reasonable cause of action or defence, or (b) it is scandalous, frivolous or vexatious, or (c) it may prejudice, embarrass or delay the fair trial, or (d) it is otherwise an abuse of the process of the court. The court may order that the action be stayed or dismissed or that judgment be entered for plaintiff or defendant. The application for such an order is to be made on notice (Ord 13, r 5). It is not of course sufficient to obtain an order to say that the facts alleged are wrong, as is sometimes done, because that is a matter to be decided on a hearing.

Inspection, detention or preservation of property

Section 52(1) of the 1984 Act gives the court power to make any order for inspection, preservation and detention of property which is the subject matter of proceedings or to which any question may arise in any such proceedings and Ord 13, r 7(*b*) again applies the Rules of the Supreme Court.

Injunctions before and at trial

Order 13, r 6 applies.

Application for such injunctions is to be made to a judge, save in excepted cases where application may be made to a registrar, see under 'Registrars', Chapter 1. The application may be made whether or not an injunction was claimed in the particulars of claim. In a case of urgency, an application for an injunction may be made ex parte (Ord 13, r 6(3)). An application may also be made before the issue of proceedings, but in that case any order made must provide for the issue of proceedings (Ord 13, r 6(4)). Generally however the application must be on notice.

Requirements for an application for an injunction filed *at the same time* as the issue of the proceedings are:

(*a*) request;

(*b*) particulars of claim, originating application, or petition, and copy for each defendant;

(*c*) if plaintiff under disability, undertaking by next friend or order of the Court of Protection;

(*d*) legal aid certificate, if any, and notice of certificate for each defendant;

(*e*) application for injunction and copy for service;

(*f*) affidavit in support (applicant will require a copy for service on each defendant);

(*g*) draft order except in cases of urgency (N 16);

(*h*) fees, ie plaint fee and fee for service by bailiff if bailiff serves (see Table of Fees).

A plaint note is issued.

Requirements for an application for an injunction made *after* issue of proceedings are:

(*a*) application and copy for service;

(*b*) affidavit in support (applicant will require a copy for service on each defendant);

(*c*) draft order (N 16);

(*d*) legal aid certificate and notices.

No fee is payable unless bailiff service.

Requirements for an application for an injunction made *before* issue of proceedings are the same as for an application made at the same time as the issue of proceedings save that there will be no request or particulars of claim. The affidavit in support of such an application must show that the court has jurisdiction to hear and determine the proposed action.

Draft particulars of claim (or draft originating application or petition, as the case may be) are not mandatory,but it is advisable to serve drafts on any opponents and to have them ready to show to the court.

No fee is payable unless for bailiff service.

If an injunction be granted it must be on terms providing for the issue of the action or matter (Ord 13, r 6(4)).

When any application for an injunction is made on notice, the rules do not specifically state that an affidavit is necessary, but an affidavit is generally filed and this follows High Court practice. The notice of application should be served on the opposing parties at least two clear days before the hearing (Ord 13, r 1(2)).

If the notice of application for an interim injunction is filed at the same time as the issue of the summons or originating process, arrangements should be made for the summons to be served prior to or with the notice of application.

Except where the case is one of urgency (and even then if possible) a draft of the order should be prepared beforehand and if the judge grants the application he will settle the order (Ord 13, r 6(6)).

The signed order is delivered to the registrar who issues sealed copies for service. The order must contain or be endorsed with a penal notice (Ord 29, r 1(3)).

The county court's jurisdiction to grant injunctions is dealt with in Chapter 2, and a draft injunction relating to 'domestic violence' is given in Chapter 33. Whilst parties are expected to have draft orders ready, some courts use their own pro-formas.

Some notes on drafting are provided in Chapter 33.

Interim payments

Order 13, r 12 applies the provisions of the Rules of Supreme Court Ord 29, II (Interim Payments) to county courts which are empowered to award interim payments of debt or damages where the sum claimed or amount involved exceeds £500. Application is made on the general form of application (N 244) supported by affidavit which must verify the amount of damages, give the grounds of the application, exhibit any documentary evidence and if under the Fatal Accidents Act 1976 give all particulars (RSC Ord 29, r 10(3)).

Compromise or settlement, persons under disability

Application is for approval of a compromise or settlement on behalf of a minor. Such settlements are regarded as a matter of considerable responsibility for the next friend, solicitors and counsel, and the court will rely heavily upon the latter. Importantly, no settlement figure is given in the application, commonly heard before the registrar, but the facts will be set out in an affidavit, and medical reports, if relevant, and counsel's opinion if taken, should be available to be shown to the court. The extent to which liability can be established can be explained, each party putting his version before the court referring to any police report if a road accident, together with counsel's opinion on liability if such has been obtained. The court will then be in a position to enable it to form its own opinion as to the plaintiff's chances of success. On quantum, the court must decide simply whether the settlement itself is a reasonable one and for the benefit of the minor or other under disability having regard to all the circumstances of the case, including the risk of litigation, desire of the parties to settle, and the disinclination of the plaintiff to go to trial. If the court does not feel entirely satisfied, it may adjourn the application for the parties to be given further opportunity to negotiate. For detail the notes to the Rules of Supreme Court, Ord 80, r 11 at 80/10–11/4 should be carefully consulted.

As to persons under disability generally, see Chapter 4.

Chapter 11

The Pre-Trial Review and Preliminary Consideration

The procedure for a pre-trial review is contained in Ord 17 and applies where a day is fixed for this purpose on the issue of fixed date summonses, or when ordered on the filing of a defence, counterclaim or part-admission in a default or possession action. The same powers are available to the registrar on a preliminary arbitration appointment (Ord 19, r 5(2); Term No 2).

In any proceeding in which no pre-trial review has been fixed, the registrar may nonetheless give notice to the parties requiring them to appear before him on the day named in the notice, so that the question of giving directions may be considered (Ord 17, r 10). Such notice might also be given in an originating application under s 17 of the Married Women's Property Act 1882.

The purposes of a pre-trial review are twofold, viz:

(*a*) if there is no reasonable case in law to be tried (whether on the claim or defence), as far as is possible, to dispose of the case;

(*b*) if there is a case to be tried, to give directions to see that it is properly prepared.

Disposal of case

(*a*) If the defendant *admits* the claim (or such part as the plaintiff accepts in satisfaction) judgment may be entered and the question of payment dealt with (Ord 17, r 6). If liability only is admitted, interlocutory judgment (N 17) may be given and a date fixed for assessment or the plaintiff left to apply under Ord 22, r 6.

(*b*) If the defendant does *not appear* and has delivered *no* admission or defence, then judgment may be entered (or directions given) as the court thinks fit (Ord 17, r 7). If the claim is for unliquidated damages the judgment must be interlocutory (N 17) unless the plaintiff can prove quantum (Ord 17, r 7(2)).

(c) If the defendant *has* delivered a defence but does *not* appear then if the plaintiff so requests and can give evidence of the facts and as to quantum, judgment may be given or alternatively directions (Ord 17, r 8).

(d) At the hearing of a pre-trial review the registrar may exercise any of his interlocutory powers (Ord 17, r 4). In particular if notice of an application for such an order has been given he may:

    (i) strike out the claim or defence if they show no reasonable cause of action or defence and enter judgment (Ord 13, r 5);

    (ii) where £500 or more is claimed, upon submission of affidavit evidence proving the facts (and proof of service of the application, copy affidavit and exhibits seven days before), enter summary judgment where there is no real defence. RSC, Ord 14 applies (Ord 9, r 14). This power may not be exercised against the Crown: Ord 42, r 5(5).

(e) Affidavit evidence may be used at the hearing if notice has been given (Ord 20, rr 5, 7 and 10). However, notice need not be given where the defendant does not appear, or where in a fixed date action he has failed to deliver a defence in time.

(f) The plaintiff may appear by affidavit. If he does not appear the proceedings may be struck out or the registrar may proceed with the review in his absence or may order the action or matter to be struck out (Ord 17, r 5; Ord 21, r 1(2)).

Some courts accept a letter in lieu of attendance, but this is not provided for in the rules. Enquiry should be made of the court as to its particular practice.

Where directions are required

On the pre-trial review the registrar must consider the course of the proceedings and give all necessary or desirable directions. He must endeavour to secure that the parties make such admissions and agreements as are reasonable. Every party should, so far as practicable, apply for any particular direction he may desire on notice to the registrar and the other parties (Ord 17, rr 1–3). At the pre-trial review any interlocutory applications may be made (Ord 17, r 4).

Orders commonly sought are for the delivery of pleadings and particulars, and for discovery, and, as may be appropriate, for the following:

(a) Amendment of pleadings and change of parties where leave is necessary.

(b) Consolidation of proceedings. (*Note:* There is general power to consolidate any action or any matter with another (Ord 13, r 9).)

(c) That the necessary paginated bundles of documents are to be prepared for the hearing. (*Note:* Bundles will be required for the court, the witness and all parties.)

(d) That a sketch plan be prepared (especially in road accident cases; if more than a sketch plan is needed it should be asked for, or there may be a costs penalty in default (Ord 38, r 10)).

(e) Directions as to expert witnesses and any limitations as to number to be called (Ord 20, r 27).

On the pre-trial review applications may be made on notice for reference to arbitration, albeit more than £500 is in issue (Ord 19, r 2(2) and (5)).

As soon as practicable after the pre-trial review, if the action or matter still remains to be heard, the court fixes a date for hearing and gives notice to all parties (Ord 17, r 9).

Notes

(1) (a) If on the pre-trial review the registrar has ordered that the hearing be adjourned generally and certificates of readiness (with an estimate of length of hearing) be lodged by all parties before the matter is set down, then it will not be regarded as practicable by the court to fix a date of hearing until the certificates of readiness are in fact provided.

(b) If a party should be dilatory in providing his certificate of readiness, the correct procedure is not to complain to the court but simply to apply on notice for a hearing date to be fixed.

(2) Many courts have standard forms of orders for directions with which practitioners should make themselves familiar.

Third party contribution and indemnity proceedings

Where a defendant to an action claims against any person *not* already a party, contribution or indemnity, or some relief, remedy, or settlement of an issue connected with the subject matter of the action, he must proceed by way of a third party notice (N 15).

(1) In a default action (where no hearing or pre-trial review date has been fixed) he may issue without leave (Ord 12, r 1(2)).

The requirements are:

(*a*) third party notice for court and copies for third party and plaintiff.

(*b*) addressed envelope if by post; postal service certificate or bailiff's fee (see Table of Fees).

The court then fixes a pre-trial review, giving notice to the plaintiff and defendant and endorsing notice thereof on the third party notice. The third party is served (as in a fixed date action) with the notice, a copy of the summons and any existing pleadings. A copy of the third party notice must be served on the plaintiff (Ord 12, r 1(1), (4), (5), (6). After issue a default judgment cannot be entered against the defendant (Ord 12, r 1(7)).

(2) In a default action where a hearing or pre-trial date has been fixed, or in a fixed date action, the third party notice may issue only with leave of the court (Ord 12, r 1(2)).

The requirements are:

(*a*) form of application and copy for plaintiff;

(*b*) third party notice for filing with court and copy for service with application;

(*c*) addressed envelope if by post.

At the hearing if leave be granted the registrar shall give directions as to service and the further conduct of the case (Ord 12, r 1(3).

The third party notice, accompanied by a copy of the summons and the pleadings, is to be served in accordance with the rules applicable to service of the summons (Ord 12, r 1(6)) but subject to directions, if any, of the registrar. It may well be that the registrar will direct a further pre-trial review for all parties. Where there is a counterclaim, third party notices may be issued by the plaintiff (Ord 12, r 8).

A third party may similarly apply for leave to issue a fourth party notice, and so on (Ord 12, r 6).

Where a defendant makes against any other party in the *same* action a like claim, he may without leave issue and serve on such other party a notice making such a claim (Ord 12, r 5). A copy of the notice must be filed with the court.

The third party should file any defence with copies for delivery to all the other parties within fourteen days of service on him inclusive of the day of service. Judgment against him cannot be obtained by default (Ord 12, r 2); but, if he does not appear at the hearing of the action he is deemed to admit the notice and is bound by any judgment, even if by consent (Ord 12, r 3(3)). After judgment, execution may not be issued against a third party without leave of the court until the defendant has satisfied the judgment against him (Ord 12, r 3(4)).

A party brought in or who has a notice served under these procedures may make an offer of contribution and file a copy with the court. This must not be shown to the court before judgment. No payment in is required (Ord 12, r 7).

It is often unwise of the plaintiff to rely on the defendant sued obtaining an indemnity from a third party if the plaintiff could bring the third party in as a second defendant, eg in road accident cases.

Amendments generally

An amendment on application or notice, or by the court of it's own motion, may be made at any stage of the proceedings (Ord 15, r 1(3)). The items required where no other procedure is prescribed are the application and a copy for service.

Change of parties

Order 15, r 1 provides that the court may at any time allow or direct any person to be added, struck out or substituted as a party to proceedings in accordance with the High Court practice (see RSC, Ord 15, r 6; Ord 20, rr 5, 8). Where a limitation period has expired, see Ord 15, r 1(2). Misjoinder or non-joinder should not defeat an action (Ord 5, r 4). No person may be added as plaintiff without his consent in writing, or in the case of a person under disability without the consent in writing of the next friend (Ord 15, r 1(4)).

Amendment to pleadings

While the court may in any action or matter by order allow or direct the amendment of any originating process or pleading, a party may without an order amend any pleading at any time before the 'return day' by filing the amended pleading and serving a copy on every other party or at any stage in the proceedings the amended pleading if endorsed with the consent of *every* party to the proceeding (Ord 15, r 2). 'Return day' is defined as the day appointed in any summons or proceedings for the appearance of the defendant, or any other day fixed for the hearing of any 'proceedings', that is, for the hearing of an action or matter, or if one had been fixed, for the pre-trial review. The court may disallow an amendment on it's own motion or on application, and shall do so where satisfied that if an application for leave had been applied for under Ord 15, r 1 it would have been refused (Ord 15, r 2(3)). Seemingly, as the rules are at present drafted, if no 'return day' as defined has been fixed, then amendment of a pleading cannot be made without leave (see Ord 7, r 17).

Order 9, r 2(3) provides that admissions may at any time be withdrawn with the consent of the court.

A defendant cannot rely on unpleaded defences or counter-claims, but must if necessary amend his defence. Leave to amend at the trial may be refused (see *Supreme Court Practice* 1988, 20/5–8/1).

The 'slip rule'

Clerical mistakes in judgments or orders or errors arising therein from any accidental slip or omission may be corrected by the court at any time (Ord 15, r 5).

Judgments and orders should be checked on receipt and, if an error is found, a letter written to the court and a copy sent to each other party.

Amendment

Before service, the summons may be amended on the plaintiff filing an amended request (Ord 7, r 17). Any pleading may be amended before the pre-trial review or the date fixed for the hearing without leave (Ord 15, r 2(1)). If an increase in the claim (or counter-claim) results in an increase in the plaint fee this must be paid on filing. A copy of the amended pleading is sent direct by the party filing to the other parties. The copy does not have to be sealed.

In a default action where the plaintiff's claim is amended by adding or substituting a claim which could not have been made in a default action, the action continues as if it had been commenced as a fixed date action (Ord 15, r 2(2)).

A cause of action which did not exist when the summons was issued can be added by amendment only with the consent of the other party (*Chuan Chow Maritime* v *K/S A/S Bulk Transport* (1984) *The Times*, 25 February).

Bankruptcy of the plaintiff

The bankruptcy of the plaintiff in an action which the trustee might maintain for the benefit of the creditors does not cause the action to abate if, within such reasonable time as the court orders, the trustee elects to continue the action and to give security. The hearing of the action may be adjourned until an election is made. When the trustee does not elect to continue the action and to give security, the defendant may use the bankruptcy as a defence (s 49(3) of the 1984 Act).

Where a defendant is adjudicated bankrupt, or being a limited company is liquidated, the plaintiff in a simple money claim should consider whether it is not best to ask for the action to be adjourned generally and lodge a proof of debt. (*Williams on Bankruptcy* should be consulted.)

Non-compliance with the rules

In its discretion, the court may, on application, correct any irregularity, by setting aside proceedings, by amendment or otherwise (Ord 37, r 5).

No party is to be prejudiced by a procedural error of the court (*Aly* v *Aly The Times*, 27 December (1983), CA quoted in *Sharma* v *Knight* [1986] 1 WLR 757).

Chapter 12

Transfers

Transfer to another county court

If the judge or registrar is satisfied that any proceedings can be more conveniently or fairly dealt with in some other court, he may order the action or matter itself to be transferred to that court (Ord 16, r 1).

For this purpose 'proceedings' include the hearing of any action, matter or arbitration (Ord 16, r 4(5)), the disposal of a default action, any pre-trial review or interlocutory application, proceedings for enforcement which can also be transferred under Ord 25, r 2 and payments into court under a judgment or order.

Save for appeals and applications under Ord 37 in cases of transfer for enforcement and payments into court, all further steps after transfer are to be taken in the transferee court (Ord 16, r 4(6)).

Commencement in wrong court

Where proceedings are commenced in the wrong court, the judge or registrar may either:

(*a*) transfer the proceedings to the court in which they ought to have been commenced; or

(*b*) order that they shall continue in the court in which they were commenced; or

(*c*) order them to be struck out (Ord 16, r 2), (but see *Sharma* v *Knight* [1986] 1 WLR 757).

No transfer can be ordered under this rule where an Act or statutory instrument other than the 1981 Rules, eg s 17 of the Married Women's Property Act 1982, requires the matter to be commenced in a particular court (Ord 16, r 3).

An order to transfer may be made by the court on its own

motion, or on the application of any party on not less than two clear days' notice (Ord 16, r 4(1)).

However, where a defendant does not reside or carry on business within the district of the court and he desires the action to be transferred to the court for the district in which he resides or carries on business, he may, after delivering a defence, counterclaim, or request for time for payment, apply ex parte in writing for an order to transfer the action to that court. Before dealing with the application, the judge or registrar may give the plaintiff an opportunity to make representations (Ord 16, r 4(2)).

The transferring court draws the order and notifies all parties (N 271). A certified copy of the entries in the court books is sent to the court to which the proceedings are transferred; so are all other documents, but in enforcement or payment into court cases only if the transferee court so requests (Ord 16, r 4(3), (4)). The court to which the action is transferred sends notice of hearing, (N 272), or pre-trial review, (N 273) (Ord 16, r 4(5)).

Where a judge is the judge for two or more districts the judge or registrar may at any time upon application or upon his own motion direct that the hearing of proceedings pending before the judge in one court shall take place in some other court of which he is the judge. Notice of hearing (N 247) is given by the court (Ord 13, r 2(3)). This procedure is sometimes followed when a 'branch' county court has a long defended action which is more conveniently heard at the judge's main court in some large town.

Infants' funds

The court may, at any time, on application or on its own motion order that any money invested as funds in court under Ord 10, r 11(1) ('infants' settlements') be transferred to another county court (Ord 16, r 5). Application can be made by letter. The court may also transfer such funds to the High Court or to a district registry, and most courts now do so.

All moneys, securities and effects paid or deposited in a county court now vest in the Accountant General; s 38(1) of the Administration of Justice Act 1982. New Rules may be made under s 38(7) and (8) but have not yet been published.

Transfer from the High Court to a county court

Transfer of the whole or any part of proceedings is provided for by s 40 of the 1984 Act. The High Court may transfer the action on the basis that it is suitable for determination by a county court notwithstanding that it is outside the county court's monetary jurisdiction, but the parties must be given notice of the High Court's intention so as to enable them either to consent or be heard (RSC Ord 107, r 2(1)). More actions are transferred than hitherto, including personal injury actions (see Practice Direction, QBD [1984] 2 All ER 672).

As well as transfer of its own motion, the High Court may transfer on application if the parties consent, or if the High Court is satisfied that the claim or balance of claim after allowing for set-off is within the county court's monetary limits, or pursuant to the much used s 40(1) (*d*) of the Act that the High Court considers that the proceedings are not likely to raise any important question of law or fact and are suitable for determination by a county court. The master or district registrar makes these orders.

On a transfer under s 40, the county court may award any relief including any amount of damages which could have been awarded by the High Court: s 40(10).

Interpleader within the county court limit of £5000 may be transferred pursuant to s 44 of the Act and garnishee and leave to issue execution pursuant to s 105.

Setting down in the county court on transfer from the High Court

The Queen's Bench Masters' Practice Direction of 25 March, 1988 states:

Where an order is made transferring an action from the Queen's Bench Division to a county court, the party having carriage of the order by himself or his solicitor shall forthwith produce at the Filing Department of the Central Office the order transferring the action and shall file:

(i) a copy of the order transferring the action;
(ii) a statement of the names and addresses of the parties and of their solicitors;
(iii) copies of any pleadings served;
(iv) if he is the plaintiff and has not served a statement of claim, particulars of his claim together with a copy for each defendant;

(v)   if he is the defendant and only a counterclaim is transferred and no counterclaim has been served, particulars of the counterclaim together with a copy for the plaintiff;

(vi) where money has been paid into court,a copy of the notice of payment into court;

(vii) a statement of the index numbers of any affidavits already filed.

Thereupon the filed documents together with the writ of summons, the acknowledgement of service and any orders made in the High Court shall be sent by post by the Central Office to the registrar of the county court to which the action has been transferred.

These mechanics for transfer are strictly not dealt with through the post but the Filing and Record Department which is at Room 81, Royal Courts of Justice London WC2A 2LL is prepared to make an exception provided there is sent to it by post all of the documents, so far as applicable, set out in the above Practice Direction, and an unofficial proforma provided to solicitors in fact repeats the list; though in lieu of the proforma no doubt a letter referring to the items in the list would equally suffice. If it is necessary to bespeak: (a) affidavits, then their index number, series, by whom sworn, and date of filing, should be provided; (b) other documents, such as writ, appearance, Legal Aid Certificate, Orders (though all of these might already be in the possession of the Solicitor in sealed or photographic copies), filing number and year should be given.

Subject to making such searches as may be required to obtain such affidavits and documents as it has been necessary to bespeak, the Filing and Record Department will send the listed documents to the County named in the Order.

A plaint note (N 206) is issued to a plaintiff or counterclaiming defendant setting down. Notice of hearing (N 272) or pre-trial review (N 273) is sent by post to the parties by the court, the court giving not less than twenty-one clear days' notice (Ord 16, r 6(1)). A copy of the particulars of claim, or counterclaim if any filed, is annexed to the notice sent to the relevant party (Ord 16, r 6(5)).

Where no defence to claim or counterclaim has been served in the High Court, the defendant or plaintiff must, within fourteen days of the receipt of the notice of hearing, deliver at the court office a defence together with a copy for the plaintiff or defendant as the case may be. Any counterclaim must be filed with the defence (Ord 16, r 6(3), (4)).

When a particular issue is directed by the High Court to

be heard by a county court, all of those documents listed above must be lodged. The county court may then either direct a hearing of the issue or a pre-trial review (Ord 16, r 6(1)). Notice of the county court's directions is given by the county court in N 274 or 275.

Interpleader proceedings

For interpleader proceedings transferred from the High Court, Ord 16, r 7 applies, and N 276 and 277.

Transfer to the High Court

The High Court has a general power at any stage of the proceedings (in addition to its powers to make prerogative orders) to order the whole or part of any proceedings commenced in a county court or previously transferred from the High Court to a county court under s 40 to be transferred to the High Court (s 41 of the 1984 Act).

The Supreme Court Practice should be consulted.

The whole or part of any proceedings may also be transferred to the High Court at any stage of the proceedings by the county court under s 42 of the 1984 Act:

(*a*) where the court considers an important question of law or fact is likely to arise;

(*b*) the likely amount recoverable on claim or counterclaim exceeds the county court limits;

(*c*) any counterclaim (or set-off and counterclaim) involves matters beyond the county court jurisdiction.

The court gives notice to all parties (N 278).

Matters previously transferred from the High Court under s 42 may be transferred back to the High Court (s 42(4)). The section applies to all proceedings commenced in a county court other than (a) matrimonial causes, and (b) adoption, custody, access, guardianship and custodianship matters relating to minors (s 42(3)). As to transfer of the latter to the High Court see s 37 of the Matrimonial and Family Proceedings Act 1984 Ord 16, r 12 and *Rayden on Divorce* should be consulted.

Application to transfer (other than Family business)

An application for the transfer of proceedings to the High Court shall be a notice stating the grounds of the application (Ord 16, r 9).

Where a counterclaim (or set-off and counterclaim) are transferred to the High Court but judgment has been given on the claim save for the question of set-off, execution is stayed thereon until the proceedings transferred to the High Court have been concluded, unless the High Court otherwise orders (s 42(2)).

The county court in a case in which it has no jurisdiction must (unless given jurisdiction by consent) either strike it out on the grounds that the plaintiff knew there was no jurisdiction, or else must transfer it to the High Court (s 34 of the 1984 Act). As to jurisdiction to hear a set-off or counterclaim exceeding the county court limit see s 43 of the 1984 Act.

Procedure on transfer to the High Court

In whatever manner a transfer may be ordered, the county court:
(a) gives notice to all parties (N 278);
(b) copies all the court records, has them certified by the registrar, and sends them to the High Court together with:
    (i) all documents filed;
    (ii) the transfer order (if made by the county court) (N 278);
    (iii) (if legitimacy proceedings) a certificate by the registrar showing the state of the proceedings and the steps taken (Ord 16, r 10).

If there is money in court, the county court should transfer the money to the High Court.

Chapter 13

Arbitrations

Section 64 of the 1984 Act applies.

The two main types of arbitration in the county court are those heard by the registrar under the 'small claims' procedure and those heard by outside arbitrators. There is additional power most rarely if at all used to refer an action to be heard by the judge as arbitrator, with the judge's consent (Ord 19, r 2(3), (5)(c)).

'Small claims' procedure

Any proceedings in which the claim or amount involved is £500 or less are automatically referred for hearing by the registrar as arbitrator (N 18) upon the filing of a defence (Ord 19, r 2(3)).

In such cases the registrar may on application rescind the reference if satisfied that:

(a) a difficult question of law or a question of fact of exceptional complexity is involved; or

(b) a charge of fraud is in issue; or

(c) the parties are agreed that the dispute should be tried in open court; or

(d) it would be unreasonable for the claim to proceed to arbitration having regard to (i) its subject matter, for example that an injunction is also claimed (an injunction cannot, so it seems, be granted on the hearing of an arbitration), or (ii) the circumstances of the parties or the interests of any other person likely to be affected by the award (Ord 19, r 2(4)).

Additionally, where sums in excess of £500 are involved, reference to arbitration may be made on application in the request or particulars of claim, the defence or counterclaim, or an application under Ord 13, r 1 (Ord 19, r 2(1), and (2)). In such cases the registrar may, unless the application has at a party's request been referred to the judge (Ord 19, r 2(5)(*b*)), on hearing the application (usually at the pre-trial review) refer the matter to a registrar for arbitration (N 19).

If fraud is in issue the consent is required of the party so charged to the making of an order for arbitration (Ord 19, r 2(5)).

Subject to any directions by the court, the registrar may conduct the hearing at any convenient place or inspect any property or thing involved. The attendance of witnesses may be compelled, and the registrar has the powers of the judge as to discovery and inspection of documents and the conduct of the case but he may not commit for contempt (Ord 19, rr 5(1), 9(*a*)–(*e*), 10).

References to arbitration are on the following numbered Terms unless otherwise directed:

(1) The arbitrator shall appoint a date for the preliminary consideration of the dispute, unless the size or nature of the claim or other circumstances make such a course undesirable or unnecessary. If directions have already been given on pre-trial review, this appointment is not needed.

(2) At or after the preliminary appointment if there be one, the arbitrator shall fix a date for the dispute to be heard (unless the parties consent to his deciding it on the statements and documents submitted to him—an unusual course not usually acceptable to the parties or the registrar) and he shall give such directions regarding the steps to be taken before and at the hearing as may appear to him to be necessary or desirable. A registrar arbitrator shall have the same powers on the preliminary appointment as under Ord 17 on a pre-trial review.

(3) Any hearing shall be informal and the strict rules of evidence shall not apply.

(4) At the hearing the arbitrator may adopt any method of procedure which he may consider to be convenient and to afford a fair and equal opportunity to each party to present his case.

(5) If any party does not appear at the arbitration, the arbitrator may make an award on hearing any other party to the proceedings who may be present.

(6) Where an award has been given in the absence of a party, the arbitrator shall have power on that party's application to set the award aside and to order a fresh hearing as if the award were a judgment and the application were made pursuant to Ord 37, r 2.

(7) With the consent of the parties and at any time before giving his decision and either before or after the hearing, the arbitrator may consult any expert or call for an expert report on any matter in dispute or invite an expert to attend the hearing as assessor.

(8) Subject to the provisions of Ord 19, r 6 in respect of claims involving £500 or less, the costs of the action up to and including the entry of judgment shall be in the discretion of the arbitrator to be exercised in the same manner as the discretion of the court under the provisions of the County Court Rules (Ord 19, r 5(2)).

Additional matters may be included in the reference later, on application to the court (Ord 19, r 3).

Where the reference was automatic (£500 or less only being involved) Ord 19, r 6 provides that no *solicitor's* charges may be awarded except the costs which were stated on the summons or which would have been stated on the summons if the claim had been for a liquidated sum, the costs of enforcing the award, and such further costs as the arbitrator may direct where there has been unreasonable conduct on the part of the opposite party in relation to the proceedings or the claim therein.

A litigant in person for preparation of the case for arbitration, as opposed to the solicitor, *may* claim costs. A copy of a registrar-arbitrator's award is sent by the court to the parties with the judgment. Registrar-arbitrators usually give their reasons orally, the award merely stating the result.

Court fees and witness fees and allowances can be claimed (Ord 38, rr 3(5), 13–16).

Judgment on the award is entered by the court (s 64 of the 1984 Act). While the rules as to admissibility do not apply, the value of any particular evidence, and the weight to be given to it, will be the same in arbitration as in hearings in open court.

Arbitration procedure does not apply to actions for recovery of land nor, seemingly, to any proceedings other than actions.

Arbitrations other than by 'small claims' procedure

An outside arbitrator may be appointed only on application (Ord 19, r 2(2), (3)) and with consent (Ord 19, r 2(5)(*d*)).

The order for reference has to be served on the arbitrator as well as the parties, but only when such sum for the arbitrator's fees as the registrar determines has been paid into court (Ord 19, r 4). In practice the parties and arbitrator should agree his remuneration in advance. The Terms Nos 1–8 listed as applying to 'small claims' procedure all apply where an outside arbitrator is appointed, except for the powers under Ord 17 exercisable by a registrar on a pre-trial review (see notes on 'Pre-Trial Review').

The outside arbitrator cannot increase the reference to include other matters (Ord 19, r 3).

An outside arbitrator's fees may be justified in those cases where an expert's adjudication is required.

Setting aside the award

Application to set aside must be made to the judge (s 64(4) of the 1984 Act) save under Term No 5 when it may be made to the arbitrator himself.

The application must be on notice, should give the grounds, and be served within fourteen days after the day on which the award was entered as a judgment (Ord 37, r 7).

Awards can usually be set aside only for an error of law on the face of the award or for misconduct on the arbitrator's part (*Meyer* v *Leanse* [1958] 2 QB 371; [1958] 3 All ER 213; and *Leung* v *Garbett* [1980] 2 All ER 436).

Costs

Save for costs on summons and for enforcing the award (or such costs as are directed by the arbitrator to have been incurred through unreasonable conduct), no solicitor's charges as between party and party are allowed in those arbitration proceedings which have been referred because the sum claimed or amount involved did not exceed £500 (Ord 19, r 6). In any other case, solicitor's charges as between party and party are allowable.

References for enquiry and report

The judge has power under s 65(1) of the 1984 Act to refer to the registrar or to a referee (N 280) for enquiry and report:

(a)   any proceedings which require any prolonged examination of documents or any scientific or local investigation which cannot, in the opinion of the judge, conveniently be made before him;

(b)   any proceedings where the question in dispute consists wholly or in part of matters of account;

(c)   with the consent of the parties, any other proceedings;

(d)   subject to any right to have particular cases tried with a jury, any question arising in any proceedings.

A judge may, after deciding or reserving any question of liability, refer to the registrar any mere matter of account which is in dispute. He may then, after deciding the question of liability, give judgment on the registrar's report (s 65(4)).

A registrar may make an order (N 280) referring any question to a referee for enquiry and report if the sum claimed or amount involved does not exceed £1000, or in any other case with the consent of the parties (Ord 19, r 8). Such an order may be made on application on notice by any party before the hearing under Ord 13, r 1; or on application by any party at the hearing; or at any stage of the proceedings by the court of its own motion (Ord 19, r 7). Ord 19, r 9 applies to the conduct of the reference.

It may well be necessary at the time of ordering a reference to a referee to agree the limits of his remuneration and to undertake to make payment thereof when called upon; the registrar is required when the report is filed to fix the remuneration of the referee, unless it has been agreed (Ord 19, r 9(g)(ii)).

Reference to the European Court

An order referring a question to the European Court may be made by a judge only before or at the trial or hearing of any action or matter either of his own motion or on the application of any party. When an order has been made, the registrar sends a copy of it to the Senior Master of the Supreme Court, Queen's Bench Division, for transmission to the registrar of the European Court. Order 19, r 11 applies.

Chapter 14

Non-attendance of Plaintiff: Discontinuance

Non-attendance of plaintiff, or failure to prove his case

If the plaintiff does not appear on the return day, or does not attend by an admissible affidavit, the proceedings may be struck out or, if the defendant appears, the court may proceed in the plaintiff's absence. If proceedings are struck out and the defendant attends, costs may be awarded against the plaintiff (N 290) (Ord 21, r 1(1), (2)). The action may be restored for hearing on application or of the court's own motion (Ord 21, r 1(3)).

If the plaintiff appears but fails to prove his case to the satisfaction of the court, the court may nonsuit him or give judgment for the defendant (N 289) (Ord 21, r 2(1)). A power to nonsuit is peculiar now to the county court and is useful where the plaintiff may have a good case but 'his tackle is not in order'. See Ord 21, r 2(2) as to payment of costs before bringing another action where the plaintiff has been nonsuited or struck out.

Discontinuance

If a plaintiff or applicant desires to discontinue wholly or in part any proceedings against all or any of the parties, he must give notice (N 279) to every such party (Ord 18, r 1). Notice must be given also to the court with a certificate that notice has been given to the other parties. If the hearing date is very close, the court office should also be notified by telephone.

After receiving notice of discontinuance a party may, unless the court on the application of a plaintiff otherwise orders, lodge for taxation a bill of costs incurred by him before the receipt of the notice, or, if the proceedings are not wholly discontinued, his costs incurred before the receipt of the notice in relation to the part discontinued (Ord 18, r 2(1)). If the costs allowed on taxation are not paid within fourteen days after taxation upon application (Ord 22, r 5), judgment may be entered for them together with the costs of entering such judgment. If the proceedings are not wholly discontinued, execution may not issue without leave (Ord 18, r 2(2)).

More often, discontinuance follows agreement between the parties and a letter to the court ends the matter. If doubt exists whether any agreement will be carried out, it is advisable to request the court to adjourn the proceedings sine die.

There can be no discontinuance in the High Court with leave, RSC Ord 21, r 3.

Chapter 15

Evidence

Generally, witnesses must give their evidence under examination in open court (Ord 20, r 4).

Affidavits

In chambers, evidence in any proceedings may be given by affidavit unless otherwise provided or ordered, but the court may order the deponent to attend for cross-examination (Ord 20, r 5).

The judge or registrar may also at any time order that at the hearing of any action or matter any particular facts may be proved by affidavit (Ord 20, r 8), or that the affidavit of a witness be read at the hearing on such conditions as he thinks reasonable (Ord 20, r 6). Where a party desires without having first obtained an order to use an affidavit at the hearing, he may not less than fourteen days before the hearing give notice accompanied by a copy of the affidavit to the party against whom it is to be used. Unless that party, not less than seven days before the hearing, gives notice to the other party that he objects to the use of the affidavit, he is to be taken to have consented to the use of it and the affidavit may be used at the hearing unless the court otherwise orders (Ord 20, r 7(1)). In a fixed date action, if the defendant has not delivered a defence within the time limited, or in any action where the defendant does not appear at the pre-trial review (or preliminary arbitration appointment), evidence by affidavit is admissible without notice unless the court otherwise orders (Ord 20, r 7(2); Ord 19, r 5(2); Term No 2).

Form and content of affidavits

See RSC Ord 41 and notes 41/1 and 41/2–8 and CCR Ord 20, r 10.

Witnesses

Order 20, r 12 applies.

Witness summonses (N 20) may issue to compel oral evidence or the production of documents.

The requirements on issue are:

(*a*) request (N 286);

(*b*) any plaint or originating process for receipts to be marked;

(*c*) conduct money, if service by bailiff or by post by court;

(*d*) addressed envelope, if by post;

(*e*) notice of date of hearing.

Conduct money must be sufficient to cover cost of travelling each way and, in addition, a sum of £15.00 for a police officer or £21.50 for anyone else for compensation for loss of time.

The summons must contain the name of one witness only, but may be issued in blank. The summons and copy are drawn by the court.

The summons must be served personally a reasonable time before the hearing (Ord 20, r 12(4)) unless the applicant or his solicitor gives a certificate for postal service (N 219) when the court serves by first class post. If the witness fails to attend, the applicant must be able to prove in enforcement proceedings that the witness was served, or knew of the service in time, and received the conduct money.

Any witness whose attendance in court ought for some sufficient cause to be dispensed with may be ordered (N 21) by the judge or registrar to be examined before an examiner in England or Wales (Ord 20, r 13). The value of this procedure is much diminished by the decision *In the Estate of Wipperman* [1955] P 59; [1953] 1 All ER 764, that an examiner may not include in the deposition any opinion as to the witness's credibility (Ord 20, r 13(5)(*e*); note 39/13/1 in *The Supreme Court Practice*).

For examination of witnesses abroad, s 56 of the 1984 Act applies, and application is by originating summons to a master of the High Court (RSC Ord 39, rr 1, 2).

Whether or not a witness should remain in court during the hearing is at the discretion of the Court (*Moore* v *Registrar of*

Lambeth County Court [1969] 1 All ER 782) but they are usually brought in and remain there unless some application is made.

Entries in bankers' books

See the Bankers' Books Evidence Act 1879 as noted in *The County Court Practice*.

Entries in Land Register

Leave to search the register may be granted in actions or matters pending in the Court under s 112(3) of the Land Registration Act 1925 as amended. (*Note:* the Land Registration Rules 1967 (SI 1967 No 761 (L 5)) were revoked by the Administration of Justice Act 1982 s 67(2) and s 75).

Expert evidence

Except by order or leave of the court or where all parties agree, no expert evidence (which includes medical evidence) may be adduced at the trial or hearing (Ord 20, rr 27, 28). Application for leave is usually made at the pre-trial review.

Hearsay

Hearsay evidence is not generally admissible but exceptions are afforded by common law and by the Civil Evidence Act 1968. The latter is activated by Rules of Court. Thereunder in the county court, Ord 20, r 15 enables notice to be given of intention to give evidence at the trial pursuant to s 2 of the Act whensoever, for reasons to be given in the notice, a witness cannot be called: see Ord 20, rr 14–24 and notes thereunder in *The County Court Practice*.

There are detailed rules relating to documentary evidence, experts' reports, experts, and evidence in general contained in Ord 20 and the copious notes thereunder, and the general law, and reference should be made to *The County Court Practice* and to the standard text books.

The strict rules of evidence do not apply in arbitrations (Ord 19, r 5(2), Term 3), but, of course, the registrar or other arbitrator may feel that he should give less weight to evidence which is hearsay than to evidence which is direct.

Viewing

This is in the judge's discretion (Ord 21, r 6(1)) with opportunity for the parties to be present.

Chapter 16

Judgments and Orders

Order 22 applies.

In general the court draws up judgments and final orders and orders for directions under Ord 13, r 2 and Ord 17, r 1(*a*), and serves them under Ord 7, r 1 on every party against whom judgment was given or the order made (Ord 22, r 1(1), (2)). Service is presumed in favour of the party in whose favour the judgment or order was made (Ord 22, r 1(2).

For forms of final judgments see N 24–36, N 289–291.

Where judgment is given in a default action (Ord 9, r 6(1)) for payment forthwith, it need not be drawn up or served unless payment is to be made to the plaintiff or his solicitor, or the plaintiff has abandoned part of his claim without amending his particulars of claim and serving the defendant, or where the judgment is interlocutory (N 17) (Ord 22, r 1(3)).

Judgments for money secured by a charge and orders on appeal to a county court are served on all parties (Ord 22, r 1(4)).

Solicitors should remember to inform their clients of judgments and orders made against them at once.

Money judgments

The court may order payment in one sum forthwith or on a fixed day (s 71(1)(*a*) of the 1984 Act). If no date is fixed, payment is fourteen days from judgment or order (Ord 22, r 2(1)). Costs, where taxation takes place after the date for payment specified in the judgment or order, are payable fourteen days after taxation (Ord 22, r 2(2)). The court may order instalment payments (s 71(1)(*b*) of the 1984 Act) or suspend payment altogether (s 71(2)).

Interlocutory judgments and assessment of damages

Order 22, r 6 applies.

If at the pre-trial review the defendant does not appear and has not delivered an admission or defence and the plaintiff produces evidence as to the amount of his damages, then judgment may be entered for them (Ord 17, r 2(2)), but if evidence is not then produced the court may enter a judgment for unliquidated damages and thereafter, unless the court has itself fixed a date for assessment of such damages, the plaintiff may apply for such assessment on seven days' notice to the defendant (Ord 22, r 6(1)). The Registrar has jurisdiction to hear and determine the amount of the damages where the amount involved does not exceed £1000 (Ord 21, r 5). The form of judgment is N 34.

Recovery of land

The order for possession must not in general be postponed to a date later than fourteen days from judgment unless this would cause exceptional hardship, when up to six weeks may be allowed (s 89(1) of the Housing Act 1980) but this is subject to qualifications (s 89(2)) examples of which are those cases under the Rent Act 1977 where the court may only order possession if reasonable, possession actions by mortgagees, and by lessors for forfeiture for non payment of rent, when any order for possession must be for not less than four weeks (s 138(3) of the 1984 Act).

Regulated tenancy, mandatory case

Where a possession order is made in respect of a 'regulated tenancy' of residential property in a mandatory case (Cases 11–20), the court is empowered to grant only a maximum of fourteen days and has no other discretion: Rent Act 1977, Sched 15, Pt II and s 89 of the Housing Act 1980.

Regulated tenancy, discretionary case

Where a possession order is made in respect of a 'regulated tenancy' of residential property in a discretionary case (Cases 1–10), the court may stay or suspend execution, or postpone the date of possession for such periods as it thinks fit but it must (unless there is exceptional hardship) impose conditions as to payment of rent (or mesne profits) and arrears: s 100 of the Rent Act 1977; s 75(1)–(3) of the Housing Act 1980.

Secured tenancy (public sector tenants)

Where the tenant occupies the premises permanently and as his principal home (Housing Act 1985, ss 79–82) and where possession is ordered on grounds 1–8 or 12–16 (which includes non-payment of rent) contained in Parts I and III of Sched 2 of the Housing Act 1985, the provisions are similar to those for regulated tenancies, discretionary cases (above).

Restricted contracts

Where the landlord of a dwellinghouse is a 'residential landlord' within the meaning of s 12 of the Rent Act 1977, the tenant is not a protected tenant as defined in s 1 of that Act, though he will be a person occupying under a 'restricted contract' (s 20 of the Rent Act 1977). A letting by a resident landlord entered into after the commencement of s 69 of the Housing Act 1980 is thus a 'restricted contract', and the court may postpone the date of any possession for up to three months from the date of the order,pursuant to s 106A of the Rent Act 1977 (as inserted by the Housing Act 1980, s 69(2)).

Protected shorthold tenancy

Protection is given for the duration of the term, which must be for not less than one year and not more than five years. The landlord may obtain possession after the expiry of the term, or before expiry if there is a breach of any obligation of the tenancy or non-payment of rent and a proviso for re-entry or forfeiture therefore is contained in the tenancy agreement (s 52(1) of the Housing Act 1980).

The general rule as to period of postponement of the order for possession, viz s 89(1) of the Act, applies. If the order is on the grounds of arrears of rent it will be in form N 27 and will provide that unless payment of the rent is made before a certain date, the defendant shall give possession.

Agricultural tied cottage

Where a possession order is made of an 'agricultural tied cottage' under s 7 of the Rent (Agriculture) Act 1976, the mandatory and discretionary grounds being similar to those which appertain to 'regulated tenancies', there are like provisions as to postponement of date of any possession order and like provisions as to suspension.

Mortgagee possession actions

Under s 36 of the Administration of Justice Act 1970, where a possession order of a dwellinghouse is made, then if satisfied that the defendant can pay the current instalments and the arrears in a reasonable time (or remedy other defaults), the court has wide powers of suspending a possession order. Possession orders in such mortgagee possession cases are in Form N 31.

The period for which the order is stayed or suspended should be defined: *Royal Trust Co of Canada* v *Markham* [1975] 3 All ER 433.

Forfeiture cases

Section 138 does not affect the court's powers to grant relief on such terms as it thinks fit under s 146(2) of the Law of Property Act 1925, but subject thereto, it provides that where rent arrears have not been paid into court not less than five clear days before the hearing, then if there is a right of re-entry or forfeiture the court must order possession at the expiry of such period, not being less than four weeks from the date of the order, as the court thinks fit, unless within that period the lessee pays into court all the rent in arrears and the costs. There is power to extend the time period before actual possession.

See also 'Relief from forfeiture', Chapter 17. A forfeiture order should be on Form N 27, or where the property or part of it consists of premises subject to the Rent Acts on Form N 27(1) or (2), or if the order is made on breach of covenant, other than covenant to pay rent, on Form N 27 adapted.

Summary procedure: Ord 24

Where an order for possession is made under Ord 24 ('summary procedure' for recovery of land occupied without licence or consent), r 5(4) says that there is nothing which prevents the order for possession being given on a specific date as if the proceedings had been brought by action (r 5(3) and (4). Dicta to the contrary in *McPhail* v *Persons Unknown* [1973] 3 All ER 393 are thought to be applicable only if in the High Court. There is, however, no power to suspend execution of the possession order in proceedings for summary possession (*Swordheath Properties Limited* v *Floydd and Others* [1978] 1 All ER 721). The note to Ord 24 says that with reference to occupiers whose occupation was originally unlawful (otherwise, seemingly, if the occupation started as lawful as with for example, a terminated service occupancy), then the court will normally order 'possession forthwith', but the orders issued by the court (unless the court has fixed a date) will simply state that the plaintiff 'do recover possession'. In such cases, a warrant for possession may be issued immediately if issued within three months after the order was made but (Ord 24, r 6) after three months have elapsed, only with leave.

Mesne profits

The usual order is judgment for arrears of rent to date of termination of the tenancy, and for mesne profits to date of hearing and thereafter mesne profits at a daily rate and (almost invariably calculated by reference to the rent) from the date of hearing until actual possession is given up. The registrar may enter judgment for mesne profits accrued after the hearing on application supported if he so requires, by affidavit.

A judgment or order to do or abstain from doing any act

Such judgment or order should fix a time within which the act is to be done (Ord 22, r 1(3)). It should make clear from what date the time runs (*Van Houten* v *Foodsafe* (1980) 124 SJ 277). The order must either (a) specify the time *after service of the order* within which the act is to be done, or (b) specify some other time for the purpose. For forms of wording to be used in the High Court, which could be adopted in the county court, see heading 'Peremptory orders', below.

Such judgment or order if the final time limit has expired, may be enforced by committal by a judge (Ord 29, r 1(1))—see Chapter 23. Order 29, r 1(3) provides that if the order was injunctive, it should have been served having borne thereon a 'penal notice'—see below.

Form of undertaking

A general form of undertaking is now contained in N 117 and is as follows:

'On the   day of   19   (John Smith) appeared in person/was represented by solicitors/counsel and gave an undertaking to the court promising [terms of undertaking then to be set out]. The court explained to John Smith the meaning of his undertaking and the consequences of failing to keep his promises, and the court accepted his undertaking [and, if so ordered] directed that John Smith should sign the statement overleaf.'

The judge may, or may not, direct the respondent to sign the undertaking. If he does so, the respondent is to sign personally.

The Penal Notice contained in the N 117 for undertakings states:

'you may be sent to prison for contempt of court if you break the promises that you have given to the court. If you do not understand anything in this document or the scope of your undertaking you should speak to your solicitor, or go to a Citizen's Advice Bureau'.

To the respondent's solicitor it states: 'you should send a copy of this undertaking to the respondent for him to keep.'

The person undertaking, if required to sign, states: 'I understand the undertaking that I have given, and that if I break any of my promises to the court I may be sent to prison for contempt.'

An undertaking given by a party in person can usually be enforced as if it were an order of the court: *Gandolfo* v *Gandolfo* [1980] 1 All ER 833.

A copy of the undertaking is served by the court on the person giving the undertaking, by post (Note at end of Form N 117).

Form of peremptory order

The specimens provided for use in the High Court by Practice Direction (QBD) Peremptory Order of 12 May 1986 might safely be adopted in the county court. The Queen's Bench Division Direction says that the wording must be specific, and if prescribing unpleasant consequences unless a particular act is done, the order must make clear the precise period within which the act is to be done, except that unless the court otherwise specifies, no time need be specified in the case of judgments or orders for the payment of money, for possession of land, or the delivery of goods; in those cases, the order, unless some time is specified, may be enforced immediately.

In all other cases outside of those exceptions the order which prescribes unpleasant consequences unless a person does a particular act must make clear the precise time within which the act is to be done (RSC Ord 42, r 2(1)).

Where the person is present or represented the following wording may be used:

Unless by [4 pm on Friday 13 June 19   ] The defendant [serves his list of documents] the defence be struck out and judgment entered for the plaintiff with costs.

If however the party affected is not present or represented, then the following, which has slight variance, *must* be used:

Unless within [14] days of service of this order [then continue as above]

The form of order 'Unless within [14] days from today . . .' can still be used where the party is present or represented, but can lead to argument how the time is to be reckoned, and is not suitable for consent orders,for which the wording 'unless by 4 pm on etc . . .' should be used.

Where by the order a party is first ordered to do the act, and there is then added a clause in the order that in default of so doing specific consequences will follow, the part that directs the act to be done must use one or other of the above forms of wording. Selecting the appropriate form seems to depend on whether or not the party affected is present or represented.

If an order of these types does not fulfil these requirements, a supplementary order should be obtained fixing the time, and until this is done the order cannot be enforced.

Penal notice

Where a judgment or order is enforceable by committal, that is where a person is required to do or abstain from doing an act, then if the order is in the form of an injunction, the court office will itself endorse a penal notice (in form N 77), probably by attachment, rubber stamp, or printed on their form. In other cases, a penal notice may be endorsed on application. Such application may be made at the time when the order is made; if not then applied for, the practice required, at least in some courts, is that the applicant should certify in writing that he has notified the other party of the intended application. The application accompanied by such certificate will then be referred to the registrar, ex parte, who may grant the application. Alternatively he may have sent out a notice of appointment. The precise directions in respect of which the penal notice is sought should be specified by the solicitors when applying for such a penal notice. There is a fee of £10 on such an application.

An extension of time for compliance with the order may be required to be given, at the time of endorsing the penal notice.

The wording of the penal notice in Form N 77 is as given at the foot of the draft injunctions in Chapter 33.

Service of peremptory orders

All orders or judgments to do or abstain from doing any act must generally be personally served (Ord 29, r 1(2)), but there are exceptions (Ord 29, r 1(6) and (7)). Substituted service (N 217) can be allowed (Ord 7, r 8(1)).

As to enforcing discovery and inspection of documents and answers to interrogatories, see Ord 14, rr 10, 11.

The drafting or settling of complicated judgments or deeds

For such orders, the court drafts these and sends them with a notice of appointment before the registrar to all parties not less than seven days before the appointment (Ord 22, r 7(1)–(5); otherwise the court simply prepares the orders and sends them out. Nonetheless the bench will in practice expect consent orders, orders for custody and access and injunctive orders to have been prepared beforehand, and to be put up to the bench for approval. As to settling deeds, reference should be made to Ord 22, r 7(6).

Copies and certificates of judgment

Copies or duplicates of a judgment or order are supplied by the court to any of the parties on payment of a fee (see Table of Fees).

A certificate of a judgment or order (N 293) is supplied to a party on a request by letter stating the reason for which it is required, usually for enforcing the judgment in the High Court or as evidence or for bankruptcy proceedings. The certificate must be signed personally by the registrar (s 12(2) of the 1984 Act).

The request if for the purpose of enforcement shall not be dealt with until after any pending proceedings whether for variation of an instalment order, setting aside, an administration order, or a stay of execution, are determined: Ord 25, r 13.

The form of Certificate of Judgment or Order for user outside the UK is a modified Prescribed Form 110 in Appendix A (Volume 2 of the Supreme Court Practice). For use outside England and Wales, but in the UK modified Prescribed Forms 111 or 112 should be used.

The form of Certificate of a Judgment or Order for use in England and Wales in the county court is N 293.

Where the person applying for a certificate of judgment is not a party, he must state in writing with particulars the purpose for which he requires the certificate of judgment and the capacity in which he applies and must satisfy the registrar that the application may properly be granted. The registrar may refer the application to the judge (Ord 22, r 8(2)).

The form of Certificate of Judgment or Order for the High Court outside of UK is Form 110 in Vol 2 of the *Supreme Court Practice* (duly modified) and outside of England and Wales Forms 111 or 122.

The form of Certificate of a Judgment or Order for use in England and Wales in the county court is N 293.

Registration of judgments

Pursuant to s 73 of the 1984 Act, every judgment for £10 or more inclusive of costs is registered if it is not satisfied or wholly complied with (or if £10 or more is still outstanding) at the expiration of one month from the date of the judgment. If the costs are to be taxed, then the time is reckoned from the date of taxation. The judgment remains on the register for a period of six years.

The register is maintained by Registry Trust Ltd, 173–175, Cleveland Street, London, W1P 5PE (Tel 01 380 0133) where searches must be made.

Fees for searches

1) On a search by an individual who attends the registry.   £1 per name.

2) On a request for any entries against a named person.   £2.

3) For a periodic search listing entries of a specified class.   Enquirers should contact RTL to find the current rate. (The fee may not exceed 50p per entry).

4) For a certified copy of an entry   £2
   against a named person.

There is no prescribed form of search. The following 'form' may be used:

To Registry Trust Ltd,
173–175, Cleveland Street,
London,
W1P 5PE

Request for Postal Search of the Register
Please search the Register for the years 198– to 198– (inclusive) for entries against the undermentioned:
Surname
Forenames
Present Address
Previous Address(es) (if known)

I enclose a fee of £

Signature
Address

Date
The remittance by cheque or postal order for the fee should be made payable to Registry Trust Ltd.

Where a judgment has been set aside or reversed, the county court office sends a certificate to that effect to the registry to cancel any entry if it has been registered.

If a person wishes to have the registration of a judgment noted because the judgment has been satisfied, the party should make a request in writing to the registrar of the county court and on payment of a fee to the court where satisfaction was made (see Table of Fees) the court sends a certificate of satisfaction to the registry. Any money that has been paid direct to the plaintiff is usually required to be 'passed through' the court by the plaintiff. An affidavit from a judgment debtor may be accepted as proof of payment if this matter is disputed. (See the Register of County Court Judgments Regulations 1985 (SI No 1087).)

Payment after judgment

Moneys payable under a judgment or order should be paid into court under Rule 20(1) of the Court Funds Rules 1987. This does not apply to costs nor orders in matrimonial causes. In cases where there has been a judgment for possession of land suspended on payment of rent and arrears by instalments, these are normally ordered to be paid direct to the plaintiff or his agent.

In making payment by post the debtor must send the judgment or order (to identify the plaint number and for receipting) and a self addressed stamped envelope. See also Chapter 5 under 'Fees' as to manner in which payment may be made.

Money paid before judgment, direct to a plaintiff, is credited in the judgment.

County courts now remit moneys which have been paid into court at intervals to judgment creditors or their solicitors without demand and by payable order.

The court has jurisdiction to recall money paid out of court in error (*Gainsborough Mixed Concrete Ltd* v *Duplex Petrol Installations Ltd* [1968] 3 All ER 267).

The registrar may, on application, transfer the action or matter to a court more convenient to the party who is to make payment (Ord 16, r 1(*e*)).

Interest on debt or damages

Interest from the date the cause of action arose until judgment (or until payment before judgment) may be included in the judgment (s 69 of the 1984 Act and Ord 6, r 1A and Ord 9, r 8).

Where judgment is given for a sum which exceeds £200 and represents or includes damages in respect of personal injuries, or in respect of a person's death,the court *must* include in that sum interest on those damages or on such part of them as the court considers appropriate, unless the court is satisfied that there are special reasons why no interest should be given (ibid, s 69).

Appropriate rate

The interest is simple interest only.

The rate of interest is that allowed in the High Court (at the date of issue of the summons) or such rate as the court thinks fit.

Interest on judgments

A county court judgment does not carry interest under the
Judgments Act 1838 (*R* v *Essex County Court Judge* (1887) 18
QBD 704). The Lord Chancellor is empowered under s 74 of
the 1984 Act to order by statutory instrument that county court
judgments shall carry interest but no order has yet been issued.

Chapter 17

Suspension and Variation of Judgments and Orders

In general, courts' judgments and orders once made (subject to setting aside or reversal on appeal) are to be carried out and may be enforced unless provision be made to the contrary, such provision being made under various statutues. Power is, however, given to stay, suspend and vary judgments and orders and to stay and suspend execution.

Where the court has power to stay a judgment, order or execution of any warrant, the registrar may exercise this power (Ord 25, r 8). Such applications should be made to him in the first instance (Ord 13, r 1(1), (6)). There are special provisions as to committals in attachment of earnings and judgment summons' proceedings, see below.

Judgments for payment of money

Section 71(2) of the 1984 Act applies.

Applications to suspend or vary payment of a judgment or order for money (a 'variation order') can be made under Ord 22, r 10 (N 245).

The requirements on application by a *judgment debtor* are:

A form of application with two copies, and if served by post, an addressed envelope. The court sends an accompanying memorandum (N 246).

When the application is made by a defendant in person, it is common practice for the court to send notice to the plaintiff or his solicitor.

The requirements on application by a *judgment creditor* are:

(1) *Ex parte* for a variation order to pay by instalments (where payment in one sum has previously been ordered) or, if instalments

have already been ordered to pay by smaller instalments (Ord 22, r 10(2)):

      (*a*) application in N 294;

      (*b*) plaint note or originating process:

      (*c*) addressed envelope, if by post.

(2) *On notice* if application is being made for payment on an earlier date or by larger instalments than those ordered (Ord 22, r 10(3)):

      (*a*) a form of application with two copies:

      (*b*) plaint note or originating process:

      (*c*) addressed envelope if by post.

The judgment creditor usually serves the application by first class post, but in some courts, the court itself serves by first class post.

All applications for suspension and variation are heard by the registrar even judge's orders, unless the judge has reserved them (Ord 22, r 10(5)).

'Variation orders' (N 35) are drawn and served by the court. They may be varied on subsequent application (Ord 22, rr 1(1), (2), 10(6)).

If each party owes the other money under different judgments set off can be ordered under s 72 of the 1984 Act by application under Ord 22, r 11. The order can be made where the judgments or one of them are in a different county court, or in the High Court.

Where the Crown has a judgment for *taxes* and 'passes through' a sum by way of reduction (made on appeal against assessment or otherwise), this does *not* 'count' as payment of the debt or of any instalment (Ord 42, r 10). Thus payment(s) of the balance remain due on the date(s) previously ordered.

Orders for discovery, inspection and interrogatories

These may be revoked or varied (Ord 14, r 12).

Suspension of warrants of execution

There is general power to stay warrants of execution under s 88 of the 1984 Act. This includes 'foreign warrants' (s 103(5)).

Suspension (order in N 41) may be on terms as to payment of warrant costs and registrar's fees and expenses before suspension.

The court may order part of the goods seized to be sold to cover these (Ord 25, r 8).

Unless the court otherwise directs, the warrant re-issues *on the judgment creditor writing to the court* if the conditions of suspension are not met (Ord 25, r 8(2)(*b*)).

Part warrant

Where a part warrant is suspended on payment of instalments the balance of the judgment or order (unless otherwise directed) is automatically suspended on the same terms (Ord 26, r 11).

Applications are made to the registrar (N 245). The court sends an accompanying memorandum in N 246.

Hire-purchase

(1) In the case of an agreement made on 18 May, 1985 or earlier—

The court has power to vary orders and suspend warrants for delivery of goods made under the Hire-Purchase Act 1965 pursuant to s 39 thereof where a suspended order was made. Where execution of a warrant or variation of a registrar's order is concerned, application is to be made to the registrar, and in the case of variation of a judge's order to the judge (Order 49, r 6; order in Form 32(4)).

(2) In the case of an agreement made on 19 May, 1985 or later—

The court has similar power pursuant to s 130(6), Consumer Credit Act 1974 as read with the alternative Ord 49, r 8.

An application by the debtor, or hirer, for a 'time order', may be made by originating application (Form N 440) in the court in whose district the applicant resides or carries on business (alternative Ord 49, r 4(5)). The application must give the particulars specified in the rule. Application for enforcement orders under s 127 (where the 1974 Act has been infringed in various ways); ss 86(2) and 87(1) (relating to the death of debtor or hirer); ss 92(2) and 126 (relating to land), are all commenced by originating application (alternative Ord 49, r 4(9)–(11)).

Suspension of order for possession of land

See also under 'Recovery of Land', Chapter 16.

Applications to stay or suspend the order or warrant are made to the registrar (Ord 25, r 8). Application to vary the order itself is made to the judge or to the registrar according to who made the possession order.

Effect of application for rehearing, setting aside or appeal

The lodging of an application does not act as a stay of execution unless the court otherwise orders (Ord 37, r 8(2); *Moore* v *Registrar of Lambeth County Court* [1969] 1 WLR 141; [1969] 1 All ER 782). As a matter of practice execution is often not carried out pending the hearing. There may of course be persistent and unmeritorious applications, but no court has power to refuse to accept an application: see *Re P (Wardship: Prohibition on Applications)* (1982) 3 FLR 420, CA at 421C and 423B. However:

  (*a*) in cases concerning the welfare of children conditions may be imposed on the making of applications (ibid); and

  (*b*) where the applicant has failed to attend a previous hearing the court may refuse to hear his renewed application until he has paid the previous costs thrown away, which the court may assess for that purpose (*Thames Investments & Securities plc* v *Benjamin* [1984] 1 WLR 1381).

Some courts in such circumstances will mark the court record so that further applications are brought to the registrar's notice before any action is taken in the court office. The court may in such circumstances give an early hearing or order execution to proceed notwithstanding the application (*Moore* v *Registrar of Lambeth County Court*, above).

Relief from forfeiture for non-payment of rent

A Notice under s 146 of the Law of Property Act 1925 need not have been served and the lessor may rely simply on his right of re–entry, assuming such be contained in the lease or tenancy agreement.

Section 138(1)–(10) of the 1984 Act is applicable whensoever a lessor is proceeding by action to enforce a right of re-entry or forfeiture for non-payment of rent in the County Court.

Provided that the action does not cease under sub s (2) of s 138 (that is, the lessee has *not* paid into court not less than five clear days before the return day all the rent in arrear and the costs of the action) then, if the court is satisfied that the lessor is entitled to enforce the right of re-entry or forfeiture for non-payment of rent, it shall order possession to be given not less than four weeks from the date of the order unless within that period the lessee pays into court all arrears and costs (s 138(3)). The court may extend the period of possession at any time before possession is recovered (s 138(4)). Where the court extends a period at a time when that period has expired and a warrant has been issued, the court is to suspend the warrant for the extended period; if before the expiration of the extended period the lessee pays into court all the rent arrears and all the costs, the court shall cancel the warrant (s 138(9)). The extension of a period fixed shall not be treated as relief from which the lessee is barred if he fails to pay arrears and costs within that period (meaning the period fixed) (s 138(8)).

Where the lessor recovers possession after the making of an order under s 138(3) above, the lessee may at any time within six months from the date on which the lessor has recovered possession, apply for relief; the court may grant the lessee relief, subject to such terms and conditions as it thinks fit (s 138(9A).

Claims may not include mesne profits as they may in the High Court, but are confined to claims for non–payment of rent.

The provisions relating to abatement of the action on payment within five clear days of all arrears of rent and costs is not applicable where in the same action the lessor is claiming re–entry or forfeiture on a ground other than, or as well as for non–payment of rent. In such an action, relief may be given pursuant to s 146(2) of the Law of Property Act 1925.

The jurisdiction to grant relief for breach of covenant other than to pay rent is discretionary, and may be given on terms. Section 146(3), statutory and mandatory liability of lessee for costs if breach waived or relief granted, should be noted.

Service of a notice under s 146(1) for breach of covenant other than for non–payment of rent is essential if a right of re–entry or forfeiture for breach of such covenant is sought to enforced.

In cases of breach of repairing covenants where three years or more of the lease remain unexpired a preliminary application for *leave* under s 1(3) of the Leasehold Property (Repairs) Act 1938 will be necessary before an action for forfeiture may be commenced.

Revocation of committals on attachment of earnings orders

Application for revocation of an order for committal of the debtor under s 23(7) of the Attachment of Earnings Act 1971 must be made to the *judge* ex parte in writing explaining the reason for failure to attend court or refusing to be sworn or to give evidence, and undertaking to comply in future (Ord 27, r 8(2)).

Discharge of committals on judgment summonses

Committals for non-attendance

Application is made to the judge (Ord 28, r 4; Ord 27, r 8(2)–(4)).

Committals otherwise

(*a*) *Payment in full* The court arranges for release (N 345) (Ord 28, r 13).

(*b*) *Request by judgment creditor* Request (N 346) lodged with court and registrar orders discharge (certificate in N 347) (Ord 28, r 14(1)).

(*c*) *If debtor can give reasons why he was unable to pay and ought to be discharged* Application to judge (certificate in N 348) (Ord 28, r 14(2)–(4); Ord 27, r 8(3), (4)).

Discharge from prison of persons committed

For committals under the *Attachment of Earnings Act*, application is to be made to the judge (Ord 27, r 8(2), (3), (4)).

For committals for *breach of order or undertaking*, see Ord 29, r 3 for procedure. If the committal order does not reserve the application to the judge *and* the registrar has the judge's leave (enquire of the court), the application may be made to the registrar (order of discharge is N 83).

Chapter 18

New Trials and Setting Aside of Judgments, Orders and Awards

Both parties present or represented

Where no error of the court is alleged, for example where new evidence becomes available after the hearing which could not previously have been discovered by reasonable diligence, then the judge or registrar has power to order a rehearing: Ord 37, r 1(1) and form N 372.

The application must state the grounds of the application and should be made to the judge or registrar who tried the proceedings and (save with leave) not more than fourteen days after the trial and on not less than seven clear days' notice to the opposite party. Unless otherwise ordered, any money in court is retained until the application has been heard (Ord 37, r 1(6)).

The principles upon which a new trial is granted are set out in notes to Ord 37, r 1 in *The County Court Practice* (no application to jury trials—see Ord 37, r 1(1)).

Judgment or order given in absence of party

Any judgment or order made against a party in his absence may be set aside. The application must be made to the judge if the judgment or order was given or made by the judge and, if not, to the registrar (Ord 37, r 2).

It appears that the application need not necessarily be made to the judge or registrar by whom the judgment or order was made (cf Ord 37, r 1(2)). Furthermore, the judgment court can transfer the application once made to the defendant's court for hearing under Ord 16, r 1(*c*).

Where on an arbitration an award has been made against a party in his absence, the award can be set aside, but, in this instance, by the arbitrator only (Ord 19, r 5(2) (Term 6)).

Judgment in default

Where judgment is entered in default under Ord 9, r 6 the court may on application, or of its own motion, set aside or vary the judgment.

Application must be made on not less than two days' notice. The defendant will have to explain his default and satisfy the court that he has a defence or counterclaim which ought to be heard.

Where the defendant has no defence then, if he is unable to come to an arrangement with the plaintiff as to payment, the court may give him time to pay (Ord 37, r 4).

Irregularity

The court may set aside proceedings, including any step taken in the proceedings and any judgment, order or document therein, on the grounds of non-compliance with the Rules. If it does not, the proceedings are not affected. The application must be made on notice and must state the objections. Such an application shall be refused unless made within a reasonable time and will not be granted where the party applying has taken any step in the proceedings after knowledge of the irregularity. Notice of the hearing must be at least two clear days before the hearing (Ord 37, r 5).

Failure of postal service

Where a summons or other originating process has been served on a defendant by post or insertion in his letter-box under Ord 7, r 10(1)(*b*) or (4)(*a*) or r 13(1)(*b*) or (4) and after judgment has been given or entered it appears to the court that the process did not come to the knowledge of the defendant in time, the court may of its own motion set aside the judgment and may give any direction or make any such order as the court may think just. Where a judgment has been so set aside, the court gives notice to the plaintiff (Ord 37, r 3).

Setting aside arbitrator's award

Application to set aside an award must be made within fourteen days after the award was entered as a judgment.

Grounds must be stated in the application (Ord 37, r 7 and see notes under 'Arbitrations'—Chapter 13). A fee is payable: see Table of Fees.

The court may stay execution pending a hearing under any of the rules in Ord 37 (Ord 37, r 8). Application should be made to the registrar in the first instance (Ord 13, r 1(6)).

Chapter 19

Appeals

Appeals from a registrar's final judgment or order

Any party affected by a judgment or final order of a registrar may, except where he has consented to the terms thereof, appeal to the judge. The appeal must be made on notice stating the grounds and the notice must be *served* within fourteen days of the judgment or final order appealed from. The judge has a wide discretion as to how he deals with the matter for example, setting aside, variation, substituting any other order, remitting for further consideration or new trial (Ord 37, r 6). This rule does not apply to orders in bankruptcy (*Williams on Bankruptcy* should be consulted).

The court may stay execution pending the hearing of the appeal (Ord 37, r 8). Application should be made to the registrar in the first instance (Ord 13, r 1(6)).

For fee payable: see Table of Fees.

Appeals from a registrar's interlocutory order

An appeal lies to the judge and the appeal is disposed of in chambers unless the judge otherwise directs. Such an appeal is made on notice, which is to be filed and served on the opposite party within five days after the order appealed from or such further time as the judge may allow (Ord 13, r 1(10), (11)).

For fee payable: see Table of Fees.

No grounds need be given as an appeal against an interlocutory order is to be heard de novo.

For definition of 'interlocutory', see below.

Appeals from a judge (or jury) to the Court of Appeal

The general provisions are to be found in ss 77 to 82 of the 1984 Act. Section 77(1) gives a right of appeal from the determination of a judge (or jury) to the Court of Appeal. A cross appeal may be brought in respect of any claim or counterclaim, notwithstanding that there could be no such appeal if that claim or counterclaim had been the subject of a separate action (s 77(5)). The right of appeal is limited in a number of ways:

(1)   Section 77(2) and (3) of the 1984 Act: The County Court Appeals Order 1981 provides that without the leave of the judge of the county court or of the Court of Appeal there can be no appeal in the following cases:

(a)   where the claim (or counterclaim, if larger) is for an amount not exceeding one-half of the limit of the jurisdiction of a county court under one or other of the following provisions of the County Courts Act 1984:

s 15 (contract and tort);

s 16 (money recoverable by statute);

s 23 (equity);

s 32 (probate).

Jurisdiction under various enactments as set out in Sched 2 to the 1984 Act

(b)   where the determination sought to be appealed from was made by the judge acting in an appellate capacity. This restriction applies to *all* appeals from registrars and also to appeals to county courts heard by the judge. None of the restrictions apply where the determination sought to be appealed from (i) includes or preserves an injunction, or (ii) relates to the custody of or access to a child.

(2)   By s 77 of the 1984 Act when possession is claimed, there is no appeal on a question of fact if the court could only have granted possession on being satisfied that it was reasonable to do so under one or other of the following:

(a)   s 13(4) of the Landlord and Tenant Act 1954;

(b)   cases III to IX in Sched 4 to the Rent (Agriculture) Act 1976;

(c)   s 98 of the Rent Act 1977 as it applies to cases 1 to 6, 8 and 9 in Sched 15 thereof (or that section as applied by any other enactment);

(d)   s 99 of the Rent Act 1977 as it applies to cases 1 to 6 and 9 in Sched 15 thereof;

(e)   s 84(2)(a) of the Housing Act 1985;

(f)   any other enactment whenever passed (s 77(8)).

Procedure on appeals to the Court of Appeal is governed by RSC Ord 59.

Generally there is no appeal to the Court of Appeal from an interlocutory order or judgment, though there are exceptions, for example in relation to minors and liberty of the subject (see s 18(1)(*h*) of the Supreme Court Act 1981 and RSC Ord 59, r 1 and 1A and note 59/1/25 which exhaustively defines final and interlocutory; and see also *Salter Rex and Co* v *Ghosh* [1971] 2 QB 597 wherein it was held that an order is interlocutory unless made on an application which would have finally determined the proceedings. Order 13, r 1(1) refers to applications authorised by or under under any Act or rule to be made in the course of an action or matter before or after judgment seemingly giving the county court's definition.

The notice of appeal to be served within four weeks from the date on which the county court judgment or order was drawn up pursuant to Ord 22, r 1(1): RSC Ord 59, rr 4, 19(3)(*a*). The county court judge may extend the time (viz beyond four weeks) provided an application is made before the four weeks have expired: RSC Ord 59, r 15(1).

Litigants in person should attend on or write to the Appeal Clerk, Room 136, Royal Courts of Justice, Strand, London WC2A 2LL, enclosing a copy of the judgment or order they wish to appeal. The appeal clerk will inform them of the procedure and supply them with specimen forms.

Where leave of the county court judge is required, application should be made under Ord 13.

The effect of an appeal on the judgment

The lodging of an appeal from the registrar to the judge does not stay execution or other proceedings unless the court otherwise orders (Ord 37, r 8(2)). Application for stay should be made initially to the registrar (Ord 25, r 8).

Similar provisions apply where there is an appeal from the judge to the Court of Appeal (RSC Ord 59, r 19(5)).

Chapter 20

Enforcement of Judgments and Orders

The general order governing enforcement is Ord 25.

Orders 26 to 32 each deal with a different mode of enforcement. In Ords 25 to 29, dealt with below, 'judgment creditor' means a person who has obtained or is entitled to enforce an order and 'debtor' means the person against whom it was given or made (Ord 25, r 1).

Orders 25 to 32 do not apply to the Crown (Ord 42, r 13). For the purpose of obtaining satisfaction of a judgment against the Crown, a certificate in N 293 duly adapted is issued by the court under s 25 of the Crown Proceedings Act 1947.

A county court judgment or order for the payment of a sum in excess of £2000 may be transferred to the High Court for enforcement (see Chapter 12).

General limitations on the issue of warrants of execution, delivery and possession

Leave is required where a change has occurred in the persons entitled to enforce or to those bearing liability under the order by death or otherwise. This applies where assets come after judgment into the hands of executors or administrators, or are in the hands of a receiver appointed by a court—or after the expiration of six years from the date of the judgment or order. Application for leave is usually made ex parte and must be by affidavit (Ord 26, rr 5, 16 and 17).

Such a warrant is valid for twelve months from the date of issue only, but may be renewed on an ex parte application by letter in the first instance. (Ord 26, rr 6, 16 and 17). A note of the renewal is endorsed on the warrant which then retains its priority (Ord 26, r 6).

Execution against goods

The requirements for issue of a warrant of execution are:
(*a*) request (N 323);
(*b*) plaint note or originating process (Ord 25, r 5);
(*c*) fee; see Table of Fees;
(*d*) addressed envelope, if by post.

In addition, if judgment or order of the High Court (or enforceable as such) see Chapter 21.

When the execution is on a judgment or order of the High Court, the warrant is issued in the court for the district in which the execution is to be levied. Notice of issue is sent by the court to the proper officer of the High Court (Ord 26, r 2(3)).

Solicitor's costs are added to the warrant: (see Costs Appendix B).

On receiving the *request* (whether by post or at the counter) the registrar must endorse it with the hour, day, month and year (s 85(3) of the 1984 Act. See also s 103(3)).

If, after issue, the registrar of the court in whose district execution takes place has reason to believe that the debtor is a farmer, he may require to be furnished with an official certificate of the result of a search of the Land Registry dated not more than three days beforehand pursuant to the Agricultural Credits Act 1928. The fee paid for the search is added to the warrant (Ord 26, r 3).

A warrant N 42 may be issued for the whole of the unpaid balance of a money judgment and costs when a judgment debtor can be said to be in default as to any part, though when the order is for payment by instalments it may instead be issued for part of the balance only provided it is for an amount being not less than £50, the amount of one monthly instalment or the amount of four weekly instalments whichever is the greater. No warrant may be issued unless at the time when it is issued the whole or part of an instalment which has already become due remains unpaid and any earlier warrant has expired or been satisfied or abandoned (Ord 26, r 1(2), (3)).

The judgment creditor indicates on the request the amount for which he requests a 'part' warrant to issue. Where a 'part' warrant is issued, the registrar of the court where the warrant is to be executed may direct that a notice (N 326) be sent to the judgment debtor allowing him seven days in which to satisfy the warrant (Ord 26, r 1(4)).

Where judgment is given for a sum payable forthwith or within a certain period and costs to be taxed, the creditor may issue a warrant for the judgment only as soon as it remains unpaid and a further warrant for the costs if unpaid, fourteen days after taxation (Ord 26, r 1(5)).

The court marks the number of the warrant and the fee on the plaint note or originating process.

If the warrant is to issue against only one of two or more judgment debtors, this must be shown clearly on the request.

Where the name or address of a party differs from the name as it appeared in the judgment, and the judgment creditor satisfies the proper officer that the amended name or address is applicable to the person as stated in the judgment, both names must be inserted in the warrant as follows: 'CD of (name and address as given in the request) suing (or sued) as AD of (name and address in the judgment or order)' (Ord 25, r 6).

If the debtor's name is clearly that of the original debtor, such as when the full names are given instead of initials, or additional initials are given, the request is accepted as sufficient. If there is any doubt, an accompanying letter of explanation should be written which can be referred to the registrar personally. The registrar may always require an application to be made on notice to amend the debtor's name.

Leave to issue is required where there is in force an Attachment of Earnings Order (Attachment of Earnings Act 1971, s 8(2)(*b*)). Leave of the judge is sometimes required where a suspended committal order has been made under a judgment summons (Ord 28, r 7(3)).

Execution against a firm

Where a judgment or order is against a firm, execution may issue as follows:

(*a*)　against the property of the firm;

(*b*)　against any person who has admitted in the action or matter that he was a partner when the cause of action arose, or who has been adjudged to be liable as a partner;

(*c*)　against any person who was individually served with the summons as a partner:

　　(i) if the action is a default action and judgment was entered in default of defence or on admission; or

　　(ii) if there was a pre-trial review (or preliminary arbitration appointment) and judgment was then entered, the defendant having entered a defence but having failed to attend; or

(iii) if there was a trial and the person so served failed to appear at the trial.

(Ord 25, r 9(1)(c); Ord 19, r 5(2); Term No 2).

Execution may be issued against a partner who was out of England and Wales when the originating process was issued, provided that he was served with the process as a partner in England or Wales, or under Ord 8 (Ord 25, r 9(2)).

Where a judgment creditor wishes to issue against a partner in any of the above circumstances, the court official should refer to the court file to ensure that execution may issue under (i), (ii) or (iii) of the listed headings.

If the party who has obtained the judgment or order claims to be entitled to issue execution against any other person as a partner, he may apply to the registrar for leave to do so. The application must be served as if a fixed date summons under Ord 7, r 10 not less than three days before the hearing. If the alleged partner does not dispute his liability, leave to enforce may be given. If he disputes liability, directions as to the trial of the issue are given (Ord 25, r 9(3), (4)).

The requirements are:

(a) application and copy for service;

(b) no fee, except if for service by bailiff, then see Table of Fees.

In the case of a High Court judgment (or an order or arbitration award enforceable as such) Ord 25, r 9 does not apply, but the procedure is governed by RSC Ord 81, r 5; CCR Ord 25, r 9(5).

Leave is required for enforcing a judgment between a firm and its members (Ord 25, r 10).

Levy

If the place of levy is not within the district of the court, the warrant is sent to the court for the district in which levy is to be made. That court, known as the 'foreign' court, adds its local number to the warrant. The local number appears in notices sent by the 'foreign' court. When a warrant is sent to a 'foreign' court, its priority is taken from the time of its receipt there, and not from the time of making an application for its issue at the 'home' court (s 103(2) of the 1984 Act), and the 'foreign' registrar must endorse the warrant with the hour, day, month and year of receipt (s 103(3)).

If a warrant has not been executed within one month from the date of issue or receipt, the registrar sends notice (N 317) at the end of each month to the judgment creditor, and also the 'home' court if the warrant has been received from another court, giving the reason (Ord 25, r 7(2)).

When the warrant has been sent to another court for levy any enquiry should be made there. If the enquiry is made by letter, the number of the warrant should be quoted as well as the plaint number. The local number should also be quoted, if known; otherwise an indication should be given as to when it was sent to that other court. By internal directive within the Lord Chancellor's Department every foreign warrant is returned to the home court when:

(a) the full amount for which the warrant issued has been paid: (where the payment was made into court the warrant is not returned until the money has been paid out to the creditor);

(b) the warrant is withdrawn or suspended for more than fourteen days at the request of the creditor;

(c) the warrant is suspended or stayed for more than fourteen days by order of the court;

(d) the bailiff has made a final return. If the warrant should be filed and a notice of non-execution sent to the creditor then the warrant should be returned to the home court.

Note

If a sale of the goods levied has taken place the warrant may either be retained until it is audited or returned to the home court, in which case a photocopy is kept at the foreign court for audit purposes.

Warrants are handed to the bailiff, an officer of the county court, for execution. When the bailiff levies, he hands to the execution debtor, or leaves at the place of levy, a notice of levy (see N 42) (Ord 26, r 7).

A bailiff may not force his way into a judgment debtor's house in order to gain entry to levy, such as by pushing a front door against the resistance of the debtor (*Vaughan* v *McKenzie* [1968] 1 All ER 1154), but once the goods have been levied upon, forcible entry may be effected.

If the goods are saleable, the bailiff usually takes 'walking possession', the judgment debtor signing an agreement (N 42) to this effect. The form need not be signed by the judgment debtor personally (*National Commercial Bank of Scotland Ltd* v*Arcam Demolition & Construction Ltd* [1966] 3 All ER 113) but it is preferable that he should do so. For a description of 'walking possession', see *Lloyds & Scottish Finance Ltd* v *Modern Cars & Caravans (Kingston) Ltd* [1964] 2 All ER 732. For effect of 'walking possession' as regards third persons see *Abingdon RDC* v *O'Gorman* [1968] 3 All ER 79.

If payment is likely to be made, the bailiff may allow a reasonable time for payment and no further fees are payable. If furniture, motor vehicles or any other goods are subject to a hire-purchase agreement, the bailiff asks for such evidence as there may be, eg the HP agreement. If a claim is made to the goods by some other person, such as a wife, a claim in writing (see below) must be given to the bailiff unless it is obvious that the goods do not in fact belong to the debtor.

As to caravans and houseboats, there appears to be no authoritative decision to say whether they may be seized under a warrant of execution whilst used as a dwelling or intermittently as a dwelling, or when they are fixed to the land. If a registrar or bailiff refused to levy on such, a complaint might be made by way of summons (N 366) to the judge under s 124 of the 1984 Act and Ord 34, r 1 when an order might be made for the trial of the issue.

Wearing apparel, bedstead and bedding of the debtor and his family, to the value of £100, and the tools and implements of his trade, to the value of £150 are exempted from levy (s 89 of 1984 Act and Protection from Execution (Prescribed Value) Order 1980 (SI 1980 No 26)).

No possession fee is payable in the case of 'walking possession'. Appraisement is usually made after removal by the auctioneer who acts as broker for the court.

When the goods are removed, the bailiff gives or posts to the execution debtor an inventory (N 332). Notice of sale (N 333) must be given to the debtor not less than four days before the time fixed for the sale (Ord 26, r 12).

As to fees (and expenses) see the Table of Fees.

If a sale does not realise sufficient to cover the costs of levy etc, the execution creditor may be required to pay the deficiency (County Court Fees Order 1982, art 3(3) below).

Warrants of execution may be issued concurrently for execution in one or more districts, but the costs of more than one warrant may not be allowed against the execution debtor except by order of the court (Ord 26, r 4).

Costs of warrants

Money paid into court between the issue of a warrant of execution and its final return is usually treated as payment under the warrant. If costs are not recovered under execution, they may be included in a subsequent warrant of execution, but *cannot* be recovered otherwise (Ord 26, r 9).

Suspension of warrant by judgment creditor

Where an execution creditor requests the bailiff to withdraw from possession, he is deemed to have abandoned the execution and the registrar marks the warrant as withdrawn by request; but if the request is made in consequence of a claim to goods seized, the execution is deemed to be abandoned only in respect of the goods claimed. However, where the request indicates that it is in pursuance of an arrangement between the execution creditor and the execution debtor, the registrar marks the warrant as suspended at the request of the execution creditor and the execution creditor may subsequently have the warrant re-issued (Ord 26, r 10).

The request to suspend a warrant by a judgment creditor is in practice usually given by letter. If the goods have been removed the execution creditor must bear in mind his liability for otherwise unrecovered costs of levy etc (County Court Fees Order 1982, art 3(3)).

Re-issue

A *warrant suspended at the request of the execution creditor* may be re-issued on the application of the creditor to the registrar holding it. If re-issued, priority is reckoned from the time of re-issue (Ord 26, r 10(3)).

A *warrant of execution suspended by the court under Ord 25, r 8* (N 41) may, subject to the directions by the court, be re-issued on the judgment creditor's written request by letter showing that the condition of suspension has not been complied with (Ord 25, r 8(2)(b)).

The court will check the court records to see if instalments have been made and any 'pass through' must be taken into account.

As to 'taxes', note Ord 42, r 10.

The court may allow a request for a warrant of execution to

be amended at any time to show the debtor's amended address or place of levy (Ord 15, r 1(1)(*a*)). It would seem that its priority would date from the time of such amendment. A letter is usually accepted.

Payment

If the warrant has been sent to another court for execution, that court remits the money to the creditor and gives notice to the home court (Ord 25, r 7(4)).

Where 'under an execution (in respect of a judgment) for a sum exceeding £250' goods are sold or money is paid in order to avoid a sale, the money, after deducting costs of executing the warrant, is retained by the court which executed the warrant for a period of fourteen days pursuant to s 34 6(3) of the Insolvency Act 1986, and s 622(3) of the Companies Act 1985; notice (N 330) is sent to the execution creditor and to the home court, if any (Ord 26, r 8(1)).

Money will be remitted automatically (with notice in N 318) after the expiration of the statutory period from a 'foreign' court to the home court (Ord 25, r 7(4)).

The amount of £250 referred to is the amount not of the judgment but of the total sum endorsed on the warrant (including the warrant fee, the costs allowed to the solicitor for issue, and the fee for the certificate if required as to a farmer (*In re Bullen* (1872) LR Ch App 732 and *The County Court Practice*).

Claims to goods taken in execution

Order 33 applies.

A claim in writing to the goods levied upon must be given to the bailiff or filed in the court of the district in which the goods were seized. The claim must state the grounds relied upon, and the claimant's name and address for service. Notice of the claim is then sent to the execution creditor (N 358) and (except where the claim is to the proceeds or value of the goods) a notice to the claimant requiring him to give security (N 359) (Ord 33, r 1).

Within four days after receiving the notice, the execution creditor must give notice to the registrar that he admits or disputes the claim, or requests the registrar to withdraw from possession. If he admits or requests withdrawal in time, he will not be liable to the registrar for fees or expenses incurred after the registrar receives the notice (Ord 33, r 2). Walking possession having been taken and the goods not being removed until the question of admitting the claim is settled, there are usually no further costs. Sometimes, however, it is advisable to enquire from the court whether any costs have already been incurred if a claim is to be admitted.

For claims by a landlord for rent, procedure is set out in s 102 of the 1984 Act. A landlord must give his notice of claim in the same manner as other claimants (Ord 33, r 1).

Interpleader proceedings under execution

If the execution creditor disputes the claim or does not give notice admitting the claim or requesting the registrar to withdraw from possession within the four days, the registrar shall issue interpleader proceedings unless the claim is withdrawn. An interpleader summons to the execution creditor (N 88) and claimant (N 88(1)) is prepared and served on them as if a fixed date summons, not less than fourteen days before the return day (Ord 33, r 4).

The summons should be served on the judgment creditor's solicitors only if he signed the request (Ord 50, r 5(1)). Any money in court is retained pending the hearing. Thereafter the registrar directs how the money is to be disposed of, and if payment is due to the judgment creditor (Ord 25, r 7(4) then applies (Ord 25, r 7(5)). The hearing takes place before the judge on the day fixed.

Notice of a claim for damages by any party must be given to the court and the party against whom the claim is made within eight days after service of the interpleader summons on him (Ord 33, r 5).

Warrants of delivery

Order 26, r 16, applies.

There are two forms of warrant of delivery:

(1) *Warrant of specific delivery* where the person against whom the judgment or order was made is not given the alternative of paying the value of the goods. (The forms are N 46 and 47, in hire-purchase cases where the hirer has defaulted under a suspended order N 32(2)).

(2) *Warrant of delivery to recover the goods or their value* where the option is given of paying their value (N 48).

When a warrant of delivery is issued, the judgment creditor may have execution for any sum of money payable under the judgment or order (including costs) by the warrant of delivery or by a separate warrant (Ord 26, r 16(4)). A judgment or order for specific delivery of goods may be enforced by committal (Ord 26, r 18).

The requirements are as for a warrant of execution: see above.

For fee payable—see Table of Fees.

The maximum fee is charged unless the value is stated in the judgment or request when the fee is calculated on that value. Where money is claimed in addition, that sum is added to the stated value to calculate the fee.

Solicitor's costs (see Costs Appendix B) are added to the warrant if the value of the goods plus the sum of money, if any, for which the warrant issues, exceeds £25. Order 26, rr 1–15 (which apply to warrants of execution against goods) also apply to warrants of delivery, so far as applicable (Ord 26, r 16(5)).

The goods, the subject of the warrant, are normally delivered to the plaintiff or his agent at the address where the goods are. The plaintiff has to supply labour and transport for their removal. The method of giving an appointment varies between courts and enquiry should be made on issue as to how an appointment will be given. A preliminary visit is usually made by the bailiff before an appointment is made.

Where judgment is given for 'return or value' and the goods are returned or a warrant to recover goods or value issues, money paid into court is appropriated first to any sum of money or costs awarded (Ord 22, r 9(3)).

Warrants of possession

Order 26, r 17 applies.

A judgment or order for the recovery of land may be enforced by warrant of possession (N 49 in all cases save under Ord 24, when N 52).

The requirements are:
(*a*)   request (N 325);
(*b*)   plaint note or originating process;

(c)   fee (see Table of Fees);

(d)   addressed envelope, if by post.

When a warrant for possession issues, the judgment creditor may have execution for any sum of money payable under the judgment or order (including costs) by the warrant of possession but two fees are payable in any event. A warrant in summary proceedings may not issue after three months from the date of the order without leave. Application for leave may be made ex parte unless the court otherwise directs (Ord 24, r 6(2)). An appointment has to be made to meet the bailiff at the premises. The practice for obtaining an appointment varies between courts. Usually a bailiff makes a preliminary visit to prepare the party for giving possession, to see if there is likely to be resistance requiring the aid of the police, and to see if there are any children requiring the presence of a welfare officer from the local authority. In the event of homelessness, the defendant may be able to obtain help from the local housing authority pursuant to its functions under Part III of the Housing Act 1985. A warrant may not be issued before the date on which possession is ordered to be given (Ord 24, r 6(3)).

For the purpose of a county court executing a warrant to give possession of any premises, it is not necessary to remove any goods or chattels from the premises (s 111 of the 1984 Act). County court bailiffs do not therefore provide for the removal of the furniture on the premises, and the plaintiff or his agent must make his own arrangements. Locks are sometimes changed by the plaintiff to prevent the defendant re-entering.

The warrant is enforceable against all persons on the premises, whether named therein or not (*R* v *Wandsworth County Court* [1975] 1 WLR 1314; [1975] 3 All ER 390). This decision applies to both N 49 and N 52.

A warrant of restitution can be used to evict trespassers currently in occupation whether or not they have been in occupation at the time of the original summons provided there is a plain and sufficient nexus between the original recovery of possession and the need to effect further recovery (*Wiltshire County Council* v *Frazer* (No 2) [1986] WLR 109, applying *R* v *Wandsworth County Council* (above)).

Persons in occupation of the premises who were not parties to the proceedings may apply to the court to be made parties under Ord 15, r 1(1)(b). The application should be made ex parte to the registrar who will require prima facie evidence that the applicant is entitled not to be evicted. If satisfied he stays execution and gives directions. Such a person who has been evicted may be ordered to be re-admitted by the plaintiff, and application for such order should, it would seem, be made to a judge since the order would be in the form of a mandatory injunction which a registrar may grant only at a final hearing and not thereafter (Ord 13, r 6). The application may be made by a person not named as defendant, *Minet* v *Johnson* (1890) 63 LT 507, CA and (1886–90) All ER 586.

If a person evicted re-enters after being ejected under a warrant of possession, a warrant of restitution may be issued (N 50 in all cases save under Ord 24 when it is N 51). In such cases, an application ex parte to the registrar should be made by the plaintiff and should be supported by evidence of wrongful re-entry (Ord 24, r 6(1) and Ord 26, r 17(4), (5)). If a person evicted thereafter re-enters yet again, application should be made to the judge for an injunction (*Alliance Building Society* v *Austen* [1951] 2 All ER 1068; Ord 26, r 18).

See also in relation to Ord 24, applications by occupiers to be joined as parties: Ord 24, r 4.

Oral examination of debtor as to means—judgment for payment of money

A judgment creditor may apply ex parte for an order that the debtor (or, if a corporation, any officer thereof) be orally examined as to the means and produce any books or documents relevant thereto (Ord 25, rr 3(1). The examination may be ordered to take place before an officer of the court.

Where in the case of an examination as to means the person to be examined does not reside or carry on business within the district of the court, the judgment creditor must first apply ex parte under Ord 25, r 2 to transfer the proceedings to the court for the district in which he resides or carries on business. The application is made by letter stating the purpose of the transfer.

The requirements for application are:

(*a*) application (N 316);
(*b*) plaint note or originating process;
(*c*) fees (see Table of Fees) and travelling expenses (optional);
(*d*) certificate for postal service if required (N 219);
(*e*) addressed envelope, if by post.

The court issues the order (N 37, or N 38 if against an officer of a defendant company).

Before the registrar makes an order for oral examination as to means he may give the debtor an opportunity to file a statement or affidavit as to means (Ord 25, r 3(7)).

A copy of any statement or affidavit filed is to be sent by the court office to the creditor, who may accept it in the place of an examination.

The order for oral examination is served as if it were a default summons (Ord 7, r 10)—see Chapter 7—together with conduct money, that is, travelling expenses, if desired. If service is by solicitor, affidavit of service must be filed. When the order is not served, a new day will be fixed without fee. Rules as to substituted service apply.

For the examination, the court officer uses a standard questionnaire a copy of which can be obtained by the creditor.

If the person required to do so does not attend, the court may fix a further date and issue an order (N 39) containing a notice that if he fails to do so, he may be committed to prison for contempt. The order states at the foot thereof, the debtor's right to require, direct from the judgment creditor, his travelling expenses, the rule itself (Ord 25, r 5 A) stating 'unless paid at the time of the service of the order', though the notice to the debtor is not explicit on this, and omits it. A certificate is to be filed not more than four days before the adjourned hearing that conduct money has been paid, or alternatively that none has been requested (Ord 25, rr 5 (A) and (5) (B)).

A committal order (N 40) may be made, by the judge, on failure to attend after service of the 'N 39', but the restriction on committal is that the debtor shall not be committed for failure to attend the adjourned hearing *unless* where he has made a request therefor, he has in fact been paid conduct money (Ord 25, r 5(*c*)). In practice, in most cases conduct money or travelling expenses will have been paid or tendered when the original order was served.

Examination of debtor under judgment not for money

Order 25, r 4 states, 'where any difficulty arises in . . . the enforcement of the judgment or order 'the court may order' 'the debtor' (sic) to attend to be examined on such questions as may be specified in the order (Ord 25, r 4). For 'debtor' presumably should be read 'party against whom the order was made'

High Court ordering examination in county court

When an order for oral examination is made in the High Court, the examination may be ordered to take place before a registrar or nominated officer of a county court (RSC, Ord 48, r 1(1)). The costs are in the discretion of the registrar in whose court the examination takes place.

Enforcement of such an order is undertaken by the High Court.

Costs on oral examinations

Costs are in the discretion of the registrar. The costs may be added to the judgment, or a separate order may be made for them.

Costs allowable are court fees, travelling expenses (if paid), and solicitor's costs (see Costs Appendix A).

Enforcement of ouster orders

An order under s 1 of the Matrimonial Homes Act 1983 terminating a spouse's right of occupation or prohibiting his exercise of that right, and an order under s 1 of the Domestic Violence and Matrimonial Proceedings Act 1976 excluding a spouse (co-habitee) from the (matrimonial) home should be enforced by warrant of possession in the first instance rather than committal proceedings for breach of the order (*Larkman* v *Lindsell The Times*, 30 November 1985 CA).

Enforcement of county court judgments outside of England and Wales

See p 18 and Sched 6 of the Civil Jurisdiction and Judgments Act 1982. The certificate of judgment will be a modified Form 110 in Appendix A to the RSC (Volume 2 of *The Supreme Court Practice*).

Execution of conveyance, contract, or other document

If the person ordered to execute a document fails to do so, the registrar may under his own or a judge's authority, execute it on his behalf: s 39 of the Supreme Court Act 1981, s 38 of the County Court Act 1984 and CCR Ord 50, r 2.

Chapter 21

Enforcement of High Court Judgments and Awards of Tribunals

Enforcement of High Court judgments and orders

High Court judgments and orders, and also judgments, orders, decrees and awards of other courts or awards of an arbitrator which are enforceable as if they were judgments of the High Court, may be enforced in the appropriate county court, usually that in whose district the debtor resides or carries on business, by execution, attachment of earnings or judgment summons (s 105(1) of the 1984 Act). Order 25, r 11 applies, and the judgment creditor shall file in the appropriate court (with such documents as are required for enforcing a judgment or order of a county court, that is, a request for enforcement) the following documents:

(a) an office copy of the judgment or order or, in the case of a judgment, order, decree or award of a court other than the High Court or an arbitrator such evidence of the judgment, order, decree or award and of its enforceability as a judgment of the High Court as the registrar may require;

(b) an affidavit verifying the amount due under the judgment, order, decree or award (N 321) and

(c) where a writ of execution has been issued to enforce it, a copy of the sheriff's return to the writ.

The fee payable is the county court fee for enforcement.

For enforcement against a firm, Ord 25, r 9 does not apply, but instead RSC Ord 81, r 5.

Enforcement of awards of tribunals

Order 25, r 12 applies.

Where, by any Act or statutory instrument other than the

146

County Court Rules, a sum of money may be recoverable as if it were payable under an order of the county court, enforcement in the county court may be ordered (N 322).

The requirements are:

(a)   affidavit verifying the amount remaining due (none pre-scribed but N 321 could be adapted);

(b)   the award, order or agreement (or duplicate thereof);

(c)   fee (see Table of Fees).

Unless otherwise provided, the application is filed in the court for the district in which the person by whom the sum is payable resides or carries on business.

The application is made ex parte by filing the documents with fee, and the application is heard by the registrar. The award may be enforced thereafter as if it were a county court judgment.

Enforcement of county court judgments in the High Court

A county court judgment if of an amount in excess of £2,000 (SI 1984 Nos 1141 and 1142) may be transferred to the High Court, and may there be enforced as if a judgment of the court: s 106(1), (2) and (4) of the 1984 Act. See also Chapter 16 under 'Copies and certificates of judgments'.

The practice requires lodging with the High Court a certificate (and copy) of the judgment (N 293) stating that it is 'for the purpose of enforcing the judgment (or order, if such be the case) in the High Court'. The Form N 293 must be signed by the county court registrar personally, and the copy must bear a facsimile signature—see s 106 of the 1984 Act. Queen's Bench Division Practice Direction 2DA dated 14 November 1988 requires actual attendance at the Action Department to present the certificate of the judgment, and its provisions are also to apply to District Registries.

The advantage of enforcing in the High Court is that the High Court allows interest on the judgment debt (from the date of issue of the certificate allowing it to be transferred to the High Court). There is no interest on a county court judgment debt. Also the initial fees may be less (eg the High Court fee for writ of fi fa on say £3000 is currently £10.30; county court fee on warrant £38).

Chapter 22

Attachment of Earnings

The Attachment of Earnings Act 1971 and Ord 27 apply.

A county court may make an attachment of earnings order to secure payments under a High Court or a county court maintenance order, payment of a judgment debt of not less than £15 or for the balance under a judgment for a sum of not less than £15 (Ord 27, r 7(6)) or payments under a county court administration order (s 1(2), ibid).

Maintenance orders to which the Act applies are set out in Sched 1 to the 1971 Act, and include orders for periodical or other payments under the Matrimonial Causes Act 1973, Pt II, and certain orders under the Guardianship of Minors Act 1971 and other Acts.

The term 'judgment debt' does not include a maintenance order or an administration order (s 2(c), ibid).

Section 24(1) and Sched 3 to the 1971 Act define attachable earnings and s 24(2) and (3) restricts earnings that may be attached, eg the pay or allowances of members of HM Forces cannot be attached.

Members of HM Forces

Since the coming into effect of ss 59 and 61 of the Armed Forces Act 1971, deduction may be made from servicemen's pay at the discretion of the Defence Council or any officer authorised by them. Cases should not be referred to the Service authorities unless it has been established that the serviceman will not comply with the judgment or order voluntarily. The judgment creditor or his solicitor may then refer the case to the appropriate authority, forwarding a copy of the judgment or order giving particulars of the amount already paid and the amount owing.

Enquiry should be made of The Ministry of Defence, Whitehall, London SW1, in the first instance.

Index

Each county court keeps an index of debtors residing within its district against whom there are in force attachment of earnings orders which have been made by that court or notice of which has been received from another court including a magistrates' court. Any person who has a judgment or order against another person believed to be residing within the district of the court may cause a search to be made in the index. Requirements for search are a request for search (N 336) and an addressed envelope if search is made by post. No fee is payable.

The court issues a certificate in N 336 as to the result of the search (Ord 27, r 2).

Obtaining an attachment of earnings order

Application is made to the court for the district in which the debtor resides (Ord 27, r 3(1)). If the debtor does not reside within England or Wales, or if the creditor does not know where he resides, the application may be made to the court in which the judgment or order was obtained (Ord 27, r 3(2)).

Where the creditor applies for attachment of earnings orders in respect of two or more debtors jointly liable, the application is made to the court for the district in which any of the debtors resides; but if the judgment or order was given or made by any such court, the application must be made to that court (Ord 27, r 3(3)).

In the case of a maintenance order made in a county court, the application must be made to that county court (Ord 27, r 17(2)). A High Court maintenance order may be enforced in the county court designated in the High Court Order (Ord 27, r 17(7)). To enforce an order for divorce costs, the application must be made to the court where the debtor resides (Ord 27 r 3(1)).

The persons who may apply for an attachment of earnings order are the persons to whom payment under the relevant adjudication is required to be made (whether directly or through an officer of any court); in the case of an administration order, any one of the creditors scheduled to the order; or the debtor, where the application is to secure maintenance payments: he may apply on the making of the county court maintenance order or on an order varying that order (s 3(1) of the 1971 Act; Ord 27, r 17(4)).

Where a creditor desires to make an application to a county court other than the county court in which the judgment or order was obtained, he must apply for the transfer of the proceedings to the appropriate court under Ord 25, r 2(1)(c). A letter applying for transfer and stating the defendant's address should be written. No fee is payable. The court sends a certificate of judgment or order (see N 313 for the endorsement) to the named court, and the registrar of that court gives the proceedings a fresh plaint number and sends notice of the transfer to both parties (N 314 and 315).

The requirements for the issue of an application are:

(a) application (N 337);
(b) fee (see Table of Fees).

In addition, if the judgment is of the High Court, or of another court or is an arbitration award enforceable as such;

(c) office copy of judgment or order or other evidence;
(d) affidavit verifying amount due (N 321);
(e) where a writ of execution issued, office copy of sheriff's return (Ord 25, r 11).

In addition, if to enforce a magistrates' court order:

(f) certified copy of order;
(g) affidavit verifying amount due (N 321) or if payments are required to be made to the clerk of the magistrates' court, a certificate by him to the like effect.

If the application is made against a partner in a debtor firm, see Ord 25, r 9 (or RSC Ord 81, r 5 if a High Court judgment).

If a county court debt is involved, the plaint note or originating process is to be produced for receipt of the fee to be endorsed. The name and address of the employer should be stated in the application if known. The application issues for the balance of debt and costs in the case of a judgment debt (s 6(4) of the 1971 Act). The balance may not include the costs of an execution not recovered thereunder (Ord 26, r 9(1)). The figures are completed by the court.

An application under s 32 of the Matrimonial Causes Act 1973 for leave to enforce the payment of arrears under a county court maintenance order, which became due more than twelve months before the application, should be made in that application (Ord 27, r 17(3)).

Unless the debtor himself applies in respect of a maintenance order the debtor must be in default (s 3(3) of the 1971 Act). In the case of an application in respect of a maintenance order (unless the debtor applies) fifteen days must have elapsed since the making of the maintenance order, and an order cannot be made unless the debtor's failure to make payments was due to wilful refusal or culpable neglect (s 3(2) and (5) ibid).

For fees: see Table of Fees.

A date of hearing is fixed on issue (Ord 27, r 4(2)).

Service

The court prepares a notice to the debtor and copy. The form informs the debtor that unless he pays the total sum due into court, he must complete and send a reply to the court office to reach it within eight days after service. Notice of the application (N 55) and a form of reply (N 56) are served on the debtor as if the application were a fixed date summons (Ord 27, r 5).

Service must be effected not less than twenty-one days before the return day (Ord 7, r 10(5)). If by post a further seven days must be allowed (Ord 7, r 10(3)).

If the application is not served, notice of non-service (N 216) is sent to the creditor (Ord 7, rr 6(2), 10(4)).

Unless the debtor pays the balance owing, he must, within eight days after service, file in the court office the form of reply setting out particulars of his expenditure and income and the name and address of his employer, if any. The court sends a copy of the reply to the creditor (Ord 27, r 5(3)). If the debtor does not reply in time and the judgment creditor knows the employer, the court should be asked by letter to request the employer (N 338) to give details of the earnings (Ord 27, r 6).

Order 27, r 7(3) prescribes that where, in the opinion of the registrar, he has sufficient information to enable an attachment of earnings order to be made without the attendance of the parties, the registrar may give notice (N 57) to the parties not less than ten days before the return day that he will make an order in the terms specified in the notice unless either party within five days objects. In case of objection the matter is dealt with on the return day. This procedure does not apply to the enforcement of maintenance orders (Ord 27, r 17(5)). Where a reply is filed by a debtor and he gives the name and address of his employer, the court can still send notice (N 338) to the employer requesting him to file a statement of earnings (Ord 27, r 6).

Such a notice may be sent to an employer if the debtor gives information as to his earnings, but the court doubts the debtor's statement.

If an employer does not send a statement of earnings in compliance with the request, the court may compel him to do so (ss 14(1)(*b*), 23(2)(*c*) of the Attachment of Earnings Act 1971; Ord 27, r 15 as to enforcement).

Hearing

This takes place on the return day unless an order has been made under Ord 27, r 7(3) or the application is not served. The hearing is before a registrar, usually in chambers. On receiving notice of hearing, the creditor, if he does not intend to appear, must file an affidavit of evidence or request the court in writing to proceed in his absence, otherwise the application may be struck out (Ord 27, r 7(5); Ord 21, r 1).

If a reply has been filed, there may be sufficient information for an attachment of earnings order to be made in the debtor's absence. The court may already have requested the employer to file a statement of earnings. If the debtor attends, the court should have the necessary evidence available.

If a reply has not been filed, and the debtor does not attend, a variety of courses are open, thus:

(*a*) if it is desired to obtain from the debtor a statement of earnings, he must (i) be proved to have been served personally with N 55, the form of reply and N 337 or the court must be satisfied that they came to his notice in time for him to have complied with the instructions in N 55 (Ord 27, r 5(2) proviso) and (ii) he must be personally served with N 61 (Ord 27, r 15). In default he commits an offence under ss 14(1) and 23(2)(*c*) of the 1971 Act and may be brought before the judge to be dealt with for that offence;

(*b*) alternatively the court may simply order him to attend at an adjourned hearing (N 58) under s 23(1) of the 1971 Act. Notice of adjournment is given to the creditor, who is then made aware of the progress of the application.

The order (N 58) must be served on the debtor personally not less than five clear days before the day fixed for the adjourned hearing (Ord 27, r 8(1)). The order is usually served by bailiff (no fee). No conduct money is payable. If the debtor attends, the hearing proceeds. If the debtor does not attend, the judge may make an order for him to be imprisoned for not more than fourteen days (s 23(1) of the 1971 Act). Warrant of committal is in N 59. The debtor may apply to the judge ex parte in writing for the revocation of the order. If in custody the debtor applies to the judge ex parte in writing attested by the governor or a principal officer, otherwise by affidavit. The debtor must undertake to attend when so ordered. (See Ord 27, r 8 generally).

Alternatively, if the debtor does not attend, the judge or registrar may order the bailiff to arrest him and bring him to court (N 112). The judge can then require him to complete the form of reply and undertake to attend an adjourned hearing. A copy of the form of reply is sent to the creditor. (See Ord 27, r 5(3) and s 23(1) and (1A) of the 1971 Act.)

Costs

Where costs are allowed, they are the same as those which would be allowed on an interlocutory application. The scale of costs is determined by the amount for which the application was issued (Ord 27, r 9(3)). In the case of a maintenance order the scale of costs is determined by the amount of the arrears due at the issue of the application (Ord 27, r 17(6)). For the amount of solicitors' costs, see Costs Appendix B, Pt III.

In the case of county court maintenance orders, the registrar may refuse leave to enforce under s 32 of the Matrimonial Causes Act 1973. If both parties attend and if they agree, he may adjust the maintenance orders in the light of the evidence available.

Form of order

The form is N 60, or N 65 for maintenance. These must specify the normal deduction rate and a protected earnings rate. 'Normal deduction rate' is defined in s 6(5)(a) of the 1971 Act and is the rate at which the court thinks it reasonable for the debtor's earnings to be applied to meeting hs liability. 'Protected earnings rate' is defined in s 6(5)(*b*) and is the rate below which, having regard to the debtor's resources and needs, the court thinks it reasonable that the earnings actually paid to him should not be reduced. Protected earnings are normally calculated by reference to the rates as amended from time to time of supplementary benefits under the National Insurance Acts and to rent or mortgage payments.

An attachment of earnings order is sent by post to the debtor (or his solicitor) and to the employer unless personal service is asked for (Ord 27, r 10(2); and Ord 7). If the debtor is employed by a corporation which has so requested, the order may be sent to the address given by it. If the order is to enforce a judgment or order of the High Court or a magistrates' court, a copy of the order is sent to the proper officer of those courts (Ord 27, r 10(3)). The order to the debtor states that he must inform the court of any change in employment.

An order may be made, but suspended whilst the debtor himself pays (N 64).

Deductions by the employer from the debtor's earnings are made in accordance with Sched 3 to the 1971 Act. Priority as between orders is set out in this Schedule.

The employer is allowed on each deduction to deduct from the debtor's earnings, in addition, fifty pence towards his administrative costs (s 7(4) and Attachment of Earnings (Employer's Deductions) Order SI 1980 No 558).

The employer is under no liability for non-compliance with the order until seven days have elapsed since the service (s 7(1)). If he does not have the debtor in his employment or if the debtor ceases to be in his employment, he must give notice of the fact to the court within ten days of service of the order or cesser (s 7(2)). If an employer ceases to have the debtor in his employment the order lapses, but the court may direct it to another employer (s 9(4)). There appears to be no provision that the court should notify the judgment creditor if a debtor leaves his employment.

The employer pays the sums deducted from the debtor's earnings to the court and the sums in court are paid out to the creditor under normal procedures. There are no rules which prescribe that the court should notify a creditor when an employer makes no payment into court. The court does not act on its own initiative to enquire from the employer any reason for payments not being received. In such cases, the creditor should write to the court requiring an enquiry to be made, and should request the court to take action where an employer refuses or neglects to give the information required.

Consolidated attachment orders

These orders are made to secure the payment of a number of judgment debts (s 17 of the 1971 Act). Order 27, rr 18–22 apply.

A county court may make a consolidated attachment order:

(a) where two or more attachment of earnings orders are in force to secure the payment of judgment debts by the same debtor; or

(b) where on an application for an attachment of earnings order to secure a judgment debt or for a consolidated attachment order, it appears to the court that an attachment of earnings order is already in force (Ord 27, r 18).

A consolidated attachment order in respect of maintenance orders may be made only in a magistrates' court (s 17(1)).

Consolidated attachment orders (N 66) may be made:

(a) on an application by the judgment debtor (Ord 27, r 19(1)(a) (see below)); or

(b) on an application by a judgment creditor who has obtained or is entitled to apply for an attachment of earnings order (r 19(1)(b)); or

(c) on the request of an employer (r 19(4)); or

(d) by the court of its own motion (see below).

The judgment debtor may apply:

(a) in the proceedings in which any attachment of earnings order is in force; or

(b) on the hearing of an application for an attachment of earnings order (Ord 27, r 19(2)).

The requirements are:

Application (N 244) and copies for service.

Copies of the application are served by post on the judgment creditor in the proceedings and also on any other judgment creditor who has obtained an attachment of earnings order which is still in force, giving not less than two clear days' notice (Ord 27, r 19(2); Ord 13, r 1(2); Ord 27, rr 3, 4, 5, do not apply).

Fees (See Table of Fees) are deducted from payments into court.

A judgment creditor's application must:

(*a*) if the judgment which he seeks to enforce was given 'by the court to which the application is made', be made in accordance with Ord 13, r 1, in the proceedings in which the judgment was obtained (Ord 27, rr 4, 5 do not apply):

(*b*) in any other case, be made by originating application (Ord 27, r 4(1), (5) do not apply—Ord 27, r 19(3)).

If the application is to be made by originating application the requirements are:

(*a*) originating application with copies for service;

(*b*) if service is to be by post, certificate in N 219.

In addition, if on enforcement a High Court judgment:

(*c*) office copy of judgment or order as the case may be;

(*d*) affidavit proving outstanding balance (N 321);

(*e*) where writ of execution issued, office copy of sheriff's return;

(*f*) fee: for service by bailiff, otherwise fee is deducted from payments into court if order is made (see Table of Fees).

The judgment debtor and every person who to the knowledge of the applicant has obtained an attachment of earnings order which is in force to secure a judgment debt is to be made a respondent (r 19(3)). Rules as to originating applications then apply.

An employer to whom two or more attachment of earnings orders are directed to secure the payment of judgment debts by the same debtor may himself by a request in writing ask the court to make a consolidated attachment order. On receipt of such a request, the court must fix a hearing at which the request will be considered and give notice thereof to the debtor and the judgment creditors (Ord 27, r 19(4)).

Where an application is made for an attachment of earnings order and there is another order already in force, the court may of its own motion make a consolidated attachment order after giving all persons concerned an opportunity of being heard (Ord 27, r 20).

Where a consolidated attachment order is already in force, any creditor to whom another judgment debt is owed may apply to the court by whom the order was made for the consolidated attachment order to be extended to secure the payment of his judgment debt. Such an application is to be treated as an application for a consolidated attachment order (Ord 27, r 21, applying rr 19,

20). It would appear that the debtor need not be in arrear for the creditor to be entitled to apply.

Payment into court

Where money is received by the court under a consolidated attachment order, the fee is first deducted.

Fee: see Table of Fees.

The remainder is distributed by way of dividends declared from time to time (Ord 27, r 22). Cheques from employers are usually accepted.

Transfer of attachment orders

Where the court has under consideration consolidating attachment orders, but has not itself made all of the orders, the court may make request of the other courts to transfer their orders (Ord 27, r 14(1)).

An attachment of earnings order may be transferred to another county court if the matter could more conveniently proceed there by reason of the debtor having moved his residence, or for other reasons (Ord 27, r 14(2)). Thereafter the transferee court has the same jurisdiction as if it had made the order (Ord 27, r 14(3)).

Cesser, discharge and variation

In the case of a judgment debt where the whole amount has been paid, the court gives notice to the employer that no further compliance is required (s 12(2) of the 1971 Act).

In the case of a maintenance order where it appears to the court that the total payments made by the debtor (whether under the order or otherwise) exceed the total payments required up to that time by the maintenance order, and the normal deduction rate (or where two or more such orders are in force, the aggregate of such rates) exceeds the rate of payments required by the maintenance order, and no proceedings for the variation or discharge of the attachment of earnings order are pending, then the registrar sends a notice (N 341) to the creditor and to the debtor (s 10(1) and (2), ibid; Ord 27, r 17(9)). The notice informs all parties that unless he applies to the court within fourteen days after the date of the notice for an order discharging or varying the attachment of earnings order, the court will make an order varying the attachment of earnings order by reducing the normal deduction rate to the rate of payments required by the maintenance order or a lower rate. Any party can apply under Ord 13, r 1.

When an attachment of earnings order ceases to have effect on the making of an order of commitment or the issue of a warrant of commitment for the enforcement of the debt, the court gives notice of the cesser to the employer (Ord 27, r 12).

The court may make an order discharging (N 339) or varying an attachment of earnings order (s 9(1) of the 1971 Act) and any party may apply on notice (Ord 13). An attachment of earnings order may be discharged (N 339) by the court of its own motion:

(a) where it appears that the employer or person to whom the order is directed does not have the debtor in his employment (but the court may re-direct the order to another employer if known) (Ord 27, r 13(2), (3));

(b) where the court makes or is notified of another such order which is not to secure a judgment debt or payments under an administration order (r 13(4));

(c) where an administration order is made or an order made for the debtor to produce a list of his creditors with a view to the making of an administration order (r 13(5)) (but the court may vary the order to secure payment under the administration order);

(d) where the court makes a consolidated attachment of earnings order (r 13(6));

(e) where the defendant has been made a bankrupt (r 13(7));

(f) where the court grants leave to issue execution (r 13(8));

(g) where the maintenance order being enforced has ceased to have effect (r 17(10)).

Notice is to be given by the court to the debtor and judgment creditor of the time and place at which the question of any discharge or variation will be considered (Ord 27, r 13(1), (9)).

Other matters

In High Court maintenance orders, where an attachment of earnings order made by the High Court designates the registrar of a county court as the collecting officer, the registrar sends notice (N 340) to the employers (Ord 27, r 17(7)).

If an application is required to determine whether particular payments are earnings, such an application is made in writing to the registrar. He thereupon fixes a date and time for hearing and gives notice to the employer, the debtor and the judgment creditor, and, where applicable, the collecting officer of the magistrates' court (s 16 of the 1971 Act; Ord 27, r 11).

Chapter 23

Judgment Summonses: Committal

Order 28 applies.

Judgment summonses (N 67) are issued pursuant to the Debtors Act 1869, s 5. The Administration of Justice Act 1970, s 11, provides that a judgment summons may be issued in a county court in respect of:

(*a*) a High Court or a county court maintenance order; or

(*b*) a judgment or order of any court for the payment of any taxes, contributions or liabilities specified in Sched 4 to the 1970 Act, which specifies:

    (i) income tax or any other tax or liability recoverable under the Taxes Management Act 1970, s 66;

    (ii) state scheme premiums under Pt III of the Social Security Pensions Act 1975 and Class 1, 2 and 4 and contributions under Pt I of the Social Security Act 1975.

Judgment summonses are in practice rarely issued except in respect of judgments obtained by the Inland Revenue when the collector of taxes has their conduct and attends court, and to enforce orders for maintenance.

The requirements are:

(*a*) request (N 342);

(*b*) plaint note or originating process;

(*c*) fee for issue and if service by bailiff (see Table of Fees);

(*d*) travelling money, if desired;

(*e*) addressed envelope, if by post.

In addition, if on a judgment or order of a court other than a county court:

(*f*) office copy of the judgment or order;

(*g*) affidavit proving amount of debt outstanding (N 321);

160

(*h*) copy of the sheriff's return to writ of execution, if any (Ord 28, r 1; Ord 25, r 11).

If it is desired to enforce judgment against a member of a firm then Ord 25, r 9, or RSC, Ord 81, r 5, apply (see Chapter 20 on 'Enforcement of Judgments and Orders').

The number of the judgment summons is endorsed on the plaint note or originating process with the place, date and time of hearing.

A judgment summons may be issued only in the court for the district in which the debtor resides or carries on business, unless it is issued against joint debtors in which case it may be issued in the court in the district of which any one of the debtors resides or carries on business (Ord 28, r 1).

Transfer of proceedings for a judgment summons

Where a judgment creditor, having obtained judgment in the county court, wishes to issue a judgment summons in another county court having jurisdiction to issue the summons, he may apply ex parte to transfer the proceedings to that court. The application is made by letter and should state the address of the judgment debtor. No fee is payable.

The court sends a certificate of the judgment or order (endorsed with N 313) to that court and the registrar of that court gives the proceedings a fresh plaint number and sends notice to both parties (N 314 and 315) (Ord 25, r 2).

Service

Unless a certificate of postal service (N 219) is filed, a judgment summons must be served personally. Where this is done travelling money may be paid on service (Ord 28, r 2(1), (4). It must be served fourteen days before the hearing date (Ord 28, r 3(1)). If service is otherwise than by the court (when N 68 is endorsed on it) an affidavit of service (N 215) must be filed (Ord 7, r 6).

If the court fails to serve personally or if the summons is returned through the post, notice (N 216) is given to the judgment creditor.

Successive judgment summonses

Where a judgment summons has not been served, successive judgment summonses may be issued within twelve months of the date of the original issue.

Application to re-issue a judgment summons, or to issue a successive judgment summons, is made on filing a fresh request. The time for service may be extended for twelve months at a time (Ord 28, r 3(3); Ord 7, rr 19, 20).

Hearing of a judgment summons

Where a judgment summons has been served by post following a certificate for postal service, no order of committal may be made against the debtor unless he appears at the hearing or the judge is satisfied that the summons came to his knowledge in sufficient time for him to appear at the hearing (Ord 28, r 2(3)). A judgment creditor may appear by affidavit if he does not reside or carry on business within the district of the court. A copy need not be served on the debtor unless the judge otherwise orders (Ord 28, r 5). The judge has power to commit to prison for a term not exceeding six weeks (Debtors Act 1869, s 5).

If the judge is of the opinion that an order of committal ought not to be made, he may make a new order (N 73) for payment of the balance owing (Ord 28, r 8(1)). Any later judgment summons may not include any part of the balance for which the debtor has been imprisoned (Ord 28, r 8(2)). The judge may also make an Attachment of Earnings Order (Attachment of Earnings Act 1971, s 3(4), (5), (6)).

If an order of committal should be made, usually it is suspended on payment within a stated period or by instalments (Ord 28, r 7(1)). Notice of the terms of the order is given to the debtor (N 72).

If the judgment summons is issued for one or some of the instalments due under a judgment, then unless otherwise ordered the judgment itself is suspended during the period of suspension of the committal order. Therefore no execution or attachment of earnings order can issue during suspension (Ord 28, r 7(3)).

Costs

On the hearing of a judgment summons, no costs may be allowed unless a committal order is made or the sum for which the judgment summons issued is paid before the hearing of which the court gives notice (N 242) under Ord 28, r 10.

The scale of costs is determined by the sum for which the judgment summons issued. The costs may be assessed and may include the solicitor's attendance including, by affidavit, costs of service, debtor's travelling expenses and court fee including bailiff service fee. See Costs Appendix B, Pt III, counsel's fee may be allowed in case certified fit for counsel (Ord 28, r 10).

Non-attendance at hearing

If a debtor does not attend the hearing, the judge may adjourn the summons to a specified date and order (N 69) the debtor to attend. The rule prescribing the general procedure is Ord 27, r 8. Travelling money must be paid on service of the order unless it was paid or tendered on service of the summons (Ord 28, r 4(2)).

The order must be served on the debtor personally not less than five clear days before the adjourned hearing. The form of order of committal is N 70. Order 27, r 8 contains the procedure for an application by a debtor for an order of revocation, in N 71, of the committal order, or for the debtor's discharge. Alternatively, if the debtor again fails to attend, the judge may order the bailiff to arrest him and bring him before the judge (N 112).

If a judgment summons is struck out for non-attendance of the judgment creditor, or is adjourned generally an application may be made to restore it to the list for hearing.

Issue of warrant of committal

If an order of committal is made and the debtor makes default, the warrant is issued on the judgment creditor filing:
(a)   request (N 344);
(b)   plaint note or originating process;
(c)   addressed envelope, if by post.
(No fee.)
The warrant is in N 74.

Where two or more debtors are ordered to be committed, a separate warrant of committal must be issued for each debtor. A special endorsement (N 75) is required if the warrant is sent to a foreign court (Ord 28, r 11).

If the warrant is not executed within a month, notice of non-execution (N 317) is given by the court at the end of the month and each month thereafter until execution (Ord 25, r 7(2)).

If the debtor is arrested and conveyed to prison, there is no rule requiring the court to notify the judgment creditor.

Payments recovered must be notified by the court office in accordance with Ord 28, rr 12, 13, to foreign courts (N 335) and to prisons (N 345).

Suspension of commitment

A warrant of committal may be suspended before execution by the judgment creditor. A letter is normally sent to the court for this purpose. If the debtor has been imprisoned the creditor must lodge a request with the court in N 346. The court then sends a certificate to the prison in N 347 (Ord 28, r 14(1)).

If a debtor wishes to apply for a further suspension of a suspended committal order, he may either attend at or write to the court office stating his reasons for his inability to comply with the order. The registrar fixes a day for hearing the application and sends notice to the judgment creditor and to the judgment debtor giving three clear days' notice (Ord 28, r 7(4)). He may suspend execution meanwhile (Ord 28, r 7(5)).

Committal for breach of order or undertaking

Where it sought to enforce an 'unless' or peremptory order, the order must have specified the time after service, or some other time, within which the act is to be done, and must have borne a penal notice (see Chapter 16 under 'A judgment or order to do etc any act').

Order 29 applies and provides that where a person refuses or neglects to comply with the judgment or order within the time fixed or as extended, a judge may enforce it by committal.

The judgment or order must have been served (Ord 29, r 1(2)) endorsed with a penal notice (Ord 29, r 1(3)), save that there can be committal without service if the judge is satisfied in the case of orders to abstain from doing any act that the person against whom the order was made was either present or notified whether by telephone, 'telegram' or otherwise (Ord 29, r (6)).

Committal can be ordered only if the order endorsed with penal notice has been served personally (r 1(2)) or otherwise notified (r 1(6)) *in sufficient time* for the order to be obeyed within the time limited by the order (Ord 29, r 1(2)(*B*)).

The judge is empowered (Ord 29, r 1), though possibly he may wish to exercise such power only in exceptional circumstances, to dispense with service of the judgment or order or the notice to show cause. Where service of the notice to show cause (N 78) is dispensed with and a committal order made, the judge may of his own motion fix a date and time when the person to be committed is to be brought before him or before the court (Ord 29, r 8). The latter is a common practice, a usual order being for committal for fourteen days suspended until the adjourned hearing when, if the respondent appears, and is co-operative, the committal is usually then discharged.

Any judgment or order against a corporation which is wilfully disobeyed may be enforced by committal of the directors or its other officers (Ord 29, r 1(1)).

For committal for non-attendance at oral examinations, see Ord 25, r 3(5); for non-attendance on attachment of earnings hearings, see Ord 27 and Chapter 22 and on judgment summonses see Ord 28 and this chapter above.

When an order enforceable by committal has been made, a notice (N 77) will be endorsed on it by the court automatically if it is in the nature of an injunction, and in any other case on the application of the party for whose benefit the order was made (Ord 29, r 1(3)). See Chapter 16 under penal notice.

A duplicate order is issued for endorsement of service by the bailiff, or to exhibit to an affidavit of service.

Fee: for service by bailiff, see Table of Fees.

Where the party is a corporation, service is to be effected on the director or officer whose committal will be sought in default (Ord 29, r 1(2)(a)) and the judgment creditor must give up-to-date details of officers to the court for that purpose.

The rules as to personal service of the order with a penal notice endorsed do not apply to orders for discovery, inspection of documents and delivery of answers to interrogatories. (See special procedure applicable under Ord 14, rr 10, 11.)

If the person served fails to obey the order or see it is obeyed the court, on the application of the party entitled to enforce it, issues a notice of application (N 78) to show cause why he should not be committed.

The application to commit must set out in the notice itself, if need be in a schedule, sufficient information for the respondent to see the charges against him (*Harmsworth* v *Harmsworth* [1987] 3 All ER 816). There should also be an affidavit in support. The notice of application (N 98) must be served personally (Ord 29, r 1(4)), unless service is dispensed with under Ord 29, r 7. The notice must be served at least two clear days before the hearing of the application (Ord 13, r 1(2)). No fee is payable for service by bailiff (see Table of Fees).

The warrant is addressed in particular to the Prison Governor (N 80). The committal order must be a form N 79 and use its precise wording. All the wording of the form should be included and particulars of the breach or contempt must be given. If service of the original order has been dispensed with under Ord 29, r 1(6) or (7), the form N 79 must be amended accordingly. If the order to commit is suspended, then the words are: 'this order will not be put into force if the said [name] complies with the following terms, namely . . . .' A copy of the order must be served on the 'respondent', either before or at the time of the execution of the warrant, unless the judge otherwise orders (Ord 29, r 1(5)).

Imprisonment must be ordered for a fixed term which may be up to two years (s 14 of the Contempt of Court Act 1981 and the County Courts (Penalties for Contempt) Act 1983). Persons aged 17 but under 21 could be sentenced to serve in a detention centre (Criminal Justice Act 1982, s 9). It was determined in *Saving and Investment Bank Limited* v *Gasco Investments* (1988) 137 NLJ 1088, CA that the committal application is in *civil* proceedings, so possibly imprisonment could be imposed instead of a detention centre on persons aged seventeen though under twenty-one—and the proceedings being *interlocutory*, hearsay evidence is admissible in the affidavits.

Half a morning must often be allowed for the hearing, as committal applications are almost invariably contested with counsel appearing for the respondent.

For enforcing by committal in case of breach of a solicitor's undertaking, see Ord 29, r 2 and N 81 and N 82. A judge may initiate the process of such committal on his own motion, but if committal is requested by the 'judgment creditor' the notice to show cause issues on his application supported by affidavit.

A person arrested under a warrant of committal is imprisoned until he purges his contempt or the period of committal fixed by the court expires. He must if necessary apply for his discharge to the 'home court' by written application attested by the prison governor or an officer of at least the rank of principal officer (no prescribed form). He must serve notice of the application on the party (if any) who caused him to be committed not less than one day before the application is to be heard. This procedure does not apply to applications by the Official Solicitor. If the registrar has the judge's leave the application may be made to him unless the committal order directed otherwise (Ord 29, r 3).

Committal procedure does not apply against the Crown (Ord 42, r 13).

For procedure where an arrest has been made by the police under an order giving power of arrest (under the Domestic Violence Act 1976) see end of Chapter 32.

Committal after arrest

For procedure for committal after arrest by a constable pursuant to a power of arrest attached to an injunction under the Domestic Violence and Matrimonial Proceedings Act, 1976—see Chapter 32.

Fines

The county court judge may fine any witness who having been properly summoned, fails to appear or who refuses to give evidence (s 55 of the 1984 Act), or any person who falsely represents a document to have been issued from the county court (s 136) or any person who assaults any officer of the court or anyone insulting himself, a juror, a witness, or an officer of the court, either while at the court or when going to or from the court, or for interrupting court proceedings, or misbehaving in court (s 118). Fines may also be imposed under s 23 of the Attachment of the Earnings Act 1971, for the various offences specified therein.

For breach of an injunction or undertaking to the court, the county court judge has power to fine as well as, or in lieu of, committal: s 38 of the 1984 Act and RSC Ord 52, rr 1 and 9. In default of payment of a fine, CCR Ord 34, r 3 provides that the proper officer (ie the registrar or chief clerk) shall forthwith report the matter to the judge whose powers are those contained in s 129 of the 1984 Act which provides that payment of 'any fine imposed by any court under this Act' may be enforced by order of the judge either as a judgment debt, or 'in like manner', as payment of a sum (payable) upon conviction by a magistrates' court may be enforced under the Magistrates' Courts Act 1980 (see s 81(1) thereof.

The powers of the county court to fine are subject to a maximum of £500 as provided by s 14(2) of the Contempt of Court Act 1981. A fine should not be imposed without some enquiry as to means.

The judge should not when imposing a fine impose a sentence of imprisonment in default of payment. The view to the contrary in the footnote to s 118 of the Act in the County Court Practice is considered injudicious, if indeed there is jurisdiction for the county court to impose a sentence of imprisonment in default at all. The most convenient and effective course is for the judge simply to direct that the order imposing the fine be sent to the Clerk to the Justices reciting that the fine has been unpaid, and accompanied by the direction of the judge requiring it to be enforced through the magistrates' court.

Chapter 24

Garnishee Proceedings: Charging Orders: Receivers

Garnishee proceedings

Order 30 applies.

Any person who has obtained a judgment or order for the payment of money may start proceedings to obtain a payment to him of the amount of any debt owing or accruing to the judgment debtor from any other person (called the 'garnishee') in England or Wales, or so much thereof as may be sufficient to satisfy the judgment or order and the costs of the garnishee proceedings.

The judgment or order must be for at least £25 for a garnishee order to be made (Ord 30, r 1(1)).

A tribunal award may be so enforced but not a High Court judgment (Ord 30, r 1(1); Ord 25, rr 11, 12).

Where the debt is due from a partnership carrying on business in England or Wales, the debt may be attached even though one or more of the partners resides outside England or Wales (Ord 30, r 14).

Moneys in current and deposit bank accounts with any 'clearing' bank, in National Savings Bank accounts, and in building society accounts may be attached. No garnishee order may reduce the balance in a building society or credit union account below £1 (Ord 30, r 1(5)). Types of debt which have been held to be *not* attachable are a legacy in the hands of an executor unless there has been an account from the executors which would constitute the legacy as a legal debt, money paid into court in an administrative action, money in court under a judgment, a dividend distributable amongst creditors in the hands of an Official Receiver, a debt due to a judgment debtor and another party, money which the judgment debtor and his wife have in a joint banking account (even though he has authority to draw), officer's pay and pension, money in a

169

wife's banking account which is housekeeping money (possibly), money held by a trustee under a strict settlement; if in doubt, reference should be made to *The County Court Practice*, Ord 30 and to *The Supreme Court Practice*, RSC, Ord 49, r 1 and notes thereunder.

Garnishee proceedings may be taken even if the debt owing or accruing from the garnishee exceeds £5,000 (Ord 30, r 1(4)).

Where money in court is due to a judgment debtor the judgment creditor may not take garnishee proceedings in respect thereof, but may apply to the registrar on notice for an order that the money, or so much thereof as may be necessary to satisfy the judgment debt and costs, may be paid to him.

On the filing of the application the registrar must retain the money in court pending the hearing of the application (Ord 30, rr 12, 15). The £25 limit does not apply.

Procedure

Application is made ex parte by filing an affidavit in N 349 giving the information required (Ord 30, r 2).

A creditor's bank manager can discover from a debtor's bank manager if the debtor is creditworthy, ie has some money in current account. Such an enquiry may avoid wasting fees on a pointless application. The actual figure in the account will, of course, not be disclosed.

The requirements are:

(a) the plaint note or originating process must be produced;

(b) fees (see Table of Fees);

(c) addressed envelope if application by post;

The order nisi in N 84 is drawn by the court; a return day is fixed before the registrar. A copy is served (a) on the garnishee in the same manner as a fixed date summons (see Ord 7, r 10) at least fifteen days before the return day and (b) on the judgment debtor at least seven days after service on the garnishee and at least seven days before the return day, pursuant to Ord 7, r 1 (Ord 30, r 3).

When served on the garnishee, the order nisi binds in his hands so much of the debts owing or accruing from him to the judgment debtor as will satisfy the debt due and the costs entered on the order nisi (Ord 30, r 3(2)), but a 'deposit-taking institution' may deduct £30 for administrative expenses before paying into court

(Attachment of Debts (Expenses) Order 1983 (SI 1983 No 1621) (L 22)) and ss 108 and 109 of the 1984 Act (as amended by s 55(2) of the Administration of Justice Act 1985). This is so even if it results in a reduction (or extinction) of the payment into court.

Payment into court is provided for by Ord 30, r 4(1). Notice of payment into court is sent by the court to the judgment creditor in N 350 and to the judgment debtor (N 352).

Where a deposit-taking institution alleges it does not hold any money to the credit of the judgment debtor's account, it should give notice to the court and to the judgment creditor. The proceedings against the garnishee are then stayed subject to Ord 30, r 8, see below (Ord 30, r 5).

Where money is paid into court the registrar may on the return day, after hearing the judgment creditor and/or debtor if they appear, order payment to the creditor, or make such order as appears just (Ord 30, r 6). If there is a dispute, Ord 30, rr 8, 9 applies and the court gives direction as to how the dispute may be determined. If the garnishee resides outside the district of the court and disputes the claim, he may apply ex parte for transfer under Ord 30, r 10. Any costs allowed to the judgment creditor which are not ordered to be paid by the garnishee personally shall, unless otherwise ordered, be retained by the judgment creditor out of the money recovered in priority to the amount due under the judgment or order (Ord 30, r 13).

For costs of hearing, see Costs Appendix B, Pt III. The costs may be ordered to be taxed.

If the garnishee (or judgment debtor) is bankrupted before the money is paid out of court, the trustee in bankruptcy can claim it (*George* v *Tompson's Trustee* [1949] 1 All ER 554).

Charging orders

The Charging Orders Act 1979, s 2 states that a charge may be imposed only on the debtor's beneficial interest under a trust (where the debtor has an interest in land held upon trust for sale, such an interest may be charged (*National Westminster Bank Ltd* v *Stockman* [1981] 1 WLR 67; [1981] 1 All ER 800), on land, on securities which consist of government stock, on other stock not that of a building society, on unit trusts, and on funds in court—the precise descriptions of stock given by the section should be referred to if in doubt.

Charging orders may be made under s 23 of the Partnership Act 1890, (for procedure, see notes to RSC Ord 81, r 10, *The Supreme Court Practice*) and charging orders may also be made under s 73 of the Solicitors Act 1974 upon property recovered or preserved through the instrumentality of the solicitor, (Ord 49, r 18 applies but such charging orders are rare).

Order 31 applies in general.

A county court may make a charging order to enforce payment of a judgment or order:

(*a*) to secure a High Court or county court 'maintenance order' (for definitions, see Sched 1 to the Attachment of Earnings Act 1971);

(*b*) to secure a High Court judgment not exceeding £500 or order or a county court judgment or order (Charging Orders Act 1979, s 1). A county court judgment or order here includes the award of a tribunal (Ord 25, r 12).

Venue

(i) If the order is sought in respect of a fund lodged in court, that court (Ord 31, r 1(1)(*a*)).

(ii) Subject to (i) above, if the judgment or order was made by a county court, that court, unless the action has been transferred under Ord 16, r 1(*d*) or (*e*) or Ord 25, r 2 when it is the transferee court (Ord 31, r 1(1)(*b*)).

(iii) Subject to (i) and (ii) above, the court for the district in which the debtor resides or carries on business, or, if none, in which the judgment creditor resides or carries on business (Ord 31, r 1(1)(*c*)).

Procedure

The application is made ex parte by filing an affidavit;

(*a*) giving the debtor's name and address and those of all known creditors;

(*b*) identifying the subject matter of the intended charge;

(*c*) verifying the debtor's beneficial interest (if the asset is held by a trustee, one of the grounds specified by s 2(1)(*b*) of the 1979 Act must be given and verified);

(*d*) where securities (other than those in court) are to be charged, giving the name and address of the person to be notified to protect the charge;

(*e*) where an interest under a trust is to be charged, giving the names and addresses of known trustees and beneficiaries.

If a High Court order is to be enforced, the affidavit must verify the amount due and an office copy judgment and the sheriff's return (if any) to the writ must be lodged (Ord 31, r 1(2)).

In the case of a county court judgment, the plaint note or originating process must be produced (Ord 25, r 5(*d*)).

An addressed envelope is required if issued by post.

Fee: see Table of Fees.

A spare copy of the affidavit should be provided for service on the debtor. One charging order may be made in respect of more than one judgment (Ord 31, r 1(3)).

Note–If an interest in land is sought to be charged, once the application for the charging order is lodged, at the same time as making the charging order nisi, the court may make an order authorising a search of the land register under s 112(3) (as amended) of the Land Registration Act 1925. An office copy of the proprietorship register should be obtained to verify the interest to be shared.

On issue, the court enters the matter in the records and the papers are placed before the registrar. If he is satisfied the registrar makes a charging order nisi fixing a return day (Ord 31, r 1(4) (N 86).

Service of the charging order nisi by the court

Order 31, r 1(5), (6) and (7) applies.

Pursuant to Ord 7, r 1 service should be effected not less than seven days before the hearing on the following:

(*a*)   the judgment creditor (or his solicitor) and the debtor;

(*b*)   (where funds in court are to be charged) the Accountant-General at the Funds Office;

(*c*)   on the debtor's other creditors and (where a trust is involved) such trustees and beneficiaries as ordered by the registrar;

(*d*)   where securities not in court are to be charged, the body or persons required by RSC Ord 50, r 2(1)(*b*).

In addition, copies of the supporting affidavit are to be served on the debtor and such trustees and beneficiaries as may be ordered by the registrar.

To obtain the full value of the order nisi procedure the judgment creditor should take such additional steps before the debtor learns of the order nisi as will ensure that the debtor is not able on so learning to deal with the property which is the subject of the provisional charge. The court itself does no more than effect service of the order nisi on those persons or bodies listed above. Thus as an example, it will be for the judgment creditor promptly to register the order nisi under the Land Registration Act 1925 or the Land Charges Act 1972. The creditor for such purposes should therefore arrange with the court officer to collect a copy of the order nisi as soon as drawn up.

Making orders absolute

The order will be made absolute on the return day (N 87) or else the court will discharge the order (Ord 31, r 2(1)).

The court must consider the debtor's personal circumstances and also other creditors (s 1(5) of the 1979 Act). Conditions may be imposed (s 3(1)).

If an order absolute is made, the court serves it on:
(a)   the debtor and creditor;
(b)   (where funds in court are charged) the Accountant-General at the Funds Office; and
(c)   where securities not in court are charged, the persons or body required by RSC Ord 50, r 2(1)(b), when a stop notice must be put in the order (Ord 31, r 2(2), (3)). For form of notice, see RSC Ord 50, r 5(3); Form 76 in Appendix A to the RSC.

Variation and discharge of orders

The registrar may vary or discharge his order, but if made by the judge only the judge may vary it. High Court procedure is followed. See note 50/1–9/30 in *The Supreme Court Practice* (Ord 31, r 3(2), (3)). Order 13 applies.

Enforcement by sale

Order 31, r 4 applies.

Proceedings for a judicial sale are commenced by originating application, and are supported by affidavit (and copy):
(a)   identifying the charging order and the property;
(b)   specifying the amount for which the charge was imposed and the outstanding balance;
(c)   verifying the debtor's title to the property;
(d)   identifying prior incumbrances and the amounts due to them;
(e)   giving an estimate of the sale price (Ord 31, r 4(1)). (In the case of land, circumstances may favour either a

sale by auction or a sale by private treaty. Time will be a
factor, as also will be the clearing of the charge and prior
incumbrances, with if possible a credit balance in hand for
the debtor).

An addressed envelope is required if issued by post.

Fee, see Table of Fees.

The order for sale of land is in form N 436.

Venue

(*a*)   County court charging order, the court making the order;

(*b*)   in any other case, the court for the district in which the
debtor resides or carries on business or, if none, in which
the judgment creditor resides or carries on business (Ord
31, r 4(2)).

In case (b) it would appear that the county court jurisdiction
is limited to a charging order where not more than £30,000 is
secured (s 23 of the 1984 Act). A copy of the affidavit is served
on the debtor (Ord 31, r 4(3)).

The registrar, may determine the proceedings (Ord 31, 4(4)).

Notes

(i)   In the case of a charging order on land, the creditor is
not thereby entitled to possession; a charging order has
the effect of an equitable charge created by writing under
hand (s 3(4) of the 1979 Act; *Tennant* v *Trenchard* (1869)
4 Ch 537; *The Supreme Court Practice*, note 50/1–9/9).

(ii)   When the debtor has an interest in a property of which he
is joint owner with a non-debtor, judicial sale may not be
appropriate. However, the question whether an equitable
chargee, for example a bank having a charging order over
the interest of one only of two or more co-owners of land
can ask the court to sell the whole of the land to realise the
share over which he has the charge, has been determined
in *Midland Bank plc* v *Pike and Pike* (FTLR 143). The
chargee is entitled to apply under s 30 of the Law of
Property Act 1925 for an order for the sale of all the
land as 'a person interested' within the meaning of that
section; the chargee's rights are also to apply for an order
for the sale of the co-owners beneficial interest only, or
for the appointment of a receiver of that interest, though
obviously this would not enable the chargee to obtain as
much as he could by sale of the property itself.

(iii) The procedure following a charging order is given in the notes to RSC Ords 50 and 88.

If a sale proceeds, a contract for sale is required, title must be proved, the costs of the proceedings and costs on sale must be provided for, a final account taken, and the proceeds distributed.

The county court has jurisdiction only where the capital value of the land does not exceed £30,000, or in the case of a sale, the purchase money does not exceed that figure (s 23(*d*) of the Act and the Notes thereunder and the County Courts Jurisdiction Order 1981).

Receivers

Order 32 applies.

A general power is given to county courts to appoint a receiver by s 38 of the 1984 Act. The power to appoint a receiver by way of equitable execution in relation to all legal estates and interests in land is given by s 107 of the 1984 Act.

The procedure for appointment is set out in Ord 32, r 1; lengthy notes are given under this rule. The provision of RSC, Ord 32, 30 as to remuneration, accounts, payment into court, default of receivers and directions are applied to the county court by Ord 32, r 3.

Chapter 25

Enforcement of Judgments of English and Welsh County Courts inside and outside the United Kingdom; Maintenance Orders

Order 35 as substituted by r 11 of the County Court (Amendment No 2) Rules 1985 (SI 1985 No 846) sets out the procedure for obtaining certificates of judgments of county courts (excepting orders for maintenance) in England and Wales for enforcement firstly, outside the United Kingdom (under the Foreign Judgments (Reciprocal Enforcement Act) 1933) and, secondly, in other parts of the United Kingdom (under the Civil Jurisdiction and Judgments Act 1982). Note the difference in terminology under the two Acts. *The County Court Practice* sets out the relevant sections of the Act in notes under Ord 35 and the procedure to be followed.

The form of certificate for use outside the United Kingdom is Form 110 in Appendix A to the RSC, Vol 2 of *Supreme Court Practice*). For use in other parts of the United Kingdom modified Forms 111 and 112 are used.

Solicitor's costs for obtaining certificates are added to the balance due under Costs Appendix B, Pt III, item 9(a).

Notes (1) Maintenance orders of courts outside England and Wales are registered in magistrates' courts.

(2) Other judgments of courts outside England and Wales are registered in the High Court (s 18 and sched 6, para 5 of 1982 Act). After registration they may, it seems, be enforced in the county court as are High Court judgments.

Enforcement of county court maintenance orders in other courts

This subject is treated at length in *Rayden on Divorce* and under Ord 36 in *The County Court Practice* to both of which it may be necessary to refer.

Applications for registration in Scotland or Northern Ireland

In this context a 'maintenance order' is as defined in s 16 of the Maintenance Orders Act 1950. This includes orders under the Matrimonial Causes Act 1973 for maintenance pending suit, periodical payments and lump sums, and similar orders for the support of children under the Guardianship of Minors Acts 1971 and 1973.

Application is made to the registrar under Ord 36, r 4. As to later variations of the order by the county court, see Ord 36, r 4. Order 36, r 6 relates to the obtaining of evidence in the county court in relation to an order so registered. Order 36, r 5 governs the registration procedure.

Applications for registration in a magistrates' court in England and Wales

The Maintenance Orders Act 1958 applies.

In this context a 'maintenance order' is as defined in Sched 8 to the Administration of Justice Act 1970 as amended. Interim orders and orders for maintenance pending suit are in practice not generally allowed to be registered. Application is made to the registrar (Ord 36, rr 8, 9). As to later variation of the order by the county court, see Ord 36, r 10. Order 36, r 11 governs the registration procedure.

Registration in the Republic of Ireland and abroad

The Maintenance Orders (Reciprocal Enforcement) Act 1972 applies. See Ord 36, rr 12–20.

Chapter 26

Interpleader Proceedings: Payment into Court by Trustees

Interpleader

Where a person is under a liability for any debt, money or goods, in respect of which he is or expects to be sued by two or more persons making adverse claims thereto, he may apply to the court for relief by way of interpleader (Ord 33, rr 6–12).

The application (N 361) is made in the court where the applicant is being sued or, if he has not been sued (N 360) in the court in which he might be sued (Ord 33, r 6(2)).

The notes in *The Supreme Court Practice* after RSC, Ord 17, r 1, set out the cases where interpleader proceedings are appropriate.

Fees, see Table of Fees. In pending proceedings, there is no fee.

A defendant in an action for wrongful interference with goods, where there are two or more claimants or where there are competing rights, should proceed under Ord 15, r 4(2), (3) (see s 8 of the Torts (Interference with Goods) Act 1977).

For interpleader proceedings under execution, see Chapter 20, 'Enforcement of Judgments and Orders'.

Payment into court by trustees

Order 49, r 20 applies.

Where a person wishes to pay money or securities into court under s 63 of the Trustee Act 1925 (which also applies to a debt or other 'chose' in action under s 136 of the Law of Property Act 1925) he must file an affidavit (N 432) containing the information required by Ord 49, r 20(1) and must pay the money or securities into court in accordance with the rr 14–16 of the Court Funds Rules 1987 or lodge the thing in action in the court office. The costs incurred in the payment into court may be taxed and the amount of the taxed costs retained by the person making the payment (Ord 49, r 20(3)).

The affidavit is first lodged for the registrar to give a direction that the money or security may be accepted. If he gives such a direction payment in is made.

The bill of costs is then lodged and an appointment given for taxation. The usual fees for taxation are payable. The money is invested in accordance with the Court Funds Rules 1987. The proceedings are regarded as under equity jurisdiction and thus the county court has jurisdiction in the case of the Trustee Act 1925 where the money or securities to be paid into court do not exceed in amount or value £30,000, and in the case of s 136 of the Law of Property Act 1925 where the amount or value of the debt or thing in action does not exceed £5,000 (Sched 2 to the 1984 Act).

Fees, see Table of Fees.

Trust money should only be paid into court when it is difficult for trustees to obtain a discharge otherwise. Building societies sometimes pay money into court under s 63 of the Trustee Act 1925 when they have become constructive trustees of surplus money arising out of the sale of a security and the mortgagor cannot be found.

Notice is sent to any person interested in the money or securities paid into court if known (N 433) (Ord 49, r 20(5)). Any application, such as for payment out, may be made to the registrar ex parte in the first instance (Ord 49, r 20(6), (7), (8)) unless the fund has been transferred to the High Court.

Chapter 27

Hire-Purchase Act 1965; Consumer Credit Act 1974; Torts (Interference with Goods) Act 1977

In the case of an agreement made on 18 May 1985 or earlier the Hire-Purchase Act 1965 applies to hire-purchase, conditional sale agreements, and credit sale agreements *where the total price does not exceed £7,500*, but not to those agreements where the hirer or buyer is a corporate body (see also Chapter 2 under 'Hire-Purchase').

If, in an action to enforce a right to recover possession of goods whether or not one-third of the hire-purchase price has been paid, the owner or seller claims any sum due under the agreement or contract of guarantee, a county court has jurisdiction to hear and determine it even if apart from the section the county court would not have jurisdiction to do so (s 49).

The owner (hire-purchase agreement) or seller (conditional sales agreement) may not enforce any right to recover possession of 'protected goods' from the hirer or buyer otherwise than by action (s 34).

Goods are 'protected goods' where:
  (a) the goods have been let under a hire-purchase agreement or agreed to be sold under a conditional sale agreement; and
  (b) one-third of the hire-purchase price has been paid or tendered; and
  (c) the hirer or buyer has not terminated the bailment (s 33).

Procedure

For the procedure under the Hire-Purchase Act 1965, see Ord 49, r 6.

Subject to certain exceptions, all parties to the agreement and any guarantor must be made parties to the action (s 35(2)). Where the hirer or a guarantor has not been served the court may, on the ex parte application of the plaintiff made at or before the hearing, dispense with the requirement that he be made a party to the action (Ord 49, r 6(2)).

The court may make an interlocutory order to protect the goods (s 35(3)). An application for such an order may be heard by the registrar (Ord 49, r 6(4)).

Section 35(4) provides that the court may make:

(a) an order for the specific delivery of all the goods (N 32(1)); or

(b) an order for the specific delivery of all goods and may postpone the operation of the order on payment of the unpaid balance of the hire-purchase price by instalments (N 32(2)); or

(c) an order for the specific delivery of a part of the goods and for the transfer to the hirer of the remainder (N 32(3)).

This applies with appropriate modifications to conditional sale agreements (s 45; Ord 1, r 11).

If the offer of payment in an admission by the hirer is accepted, judgment may be entered before the return day unless there is a guarantor, when it may not be entered before the return day (Ord 49, r 6(5)(a) and (b)). Judgment may not be so entered on the hirer filing an admission unaccompanied by an offer of payment (Ord 49, r 6(5)(c)).

Where the goods have not been returned to the owner during the operation of a postponed order, the court may vary the postponement and conditions or revoke the previous order (ss 38, 39).

Where all the goods have not been recovered under any order made under s 35(4) or s 39(1)(c), and the order has not been complied with or the hirer or guarantor has wrongfully disposed of the goods, the court may revoke the order and make an order for payment of the unpaid hire-purchase price (N 32(5)) (s 42). Applications under ss 38 and 39 (variation of postponed orders, N 32(4)) and s 42 are made to the judge or registrar according to who made the original order (Ord 49, r 6(6)).

Where an order has been made under s 35(4)(*a*) or (*b*), if all the goods have been recovered, or if the court has revoked a postponed order, an application may be made for the payment of a money claim (s 44). The plaintiff applies on notice to the defendant and if the claim has not already been made in the action, particulars of the claim must be given in or annexed to the notice (Ord 49, r 6(8)). In the latter case an additional plaint fee may be payable; see Table of Fees.

Where the owner has begun an action to recover 'protected goods' under s 35, he may not take any step to enforce any payment under the agreement except in that action (s 41).

After the death of the hirer or buyer, s 46 and Sched 3 to the 1965 Act apply. Where a postponed order has been made against a deceased hirer or buyer, notice of application to issue a warrant of delivery must be served on the person in possession of the goods as if the application were a fixed date summons under Ord 7 (Ord 49, r 6(7)).

In the case of an agreement dated 19 May 1985 or later the Consumer Credit Act 1974 applies. The powers of the court are virtually the same as those under the Hire-Purchase Act 1965 and the rules above mentioned—which rules remain in force for agreements made on 18 May 1985 or earlier (the County Court (Amendment) Rules 1985, r 10). For later agreements the substituted or amended rules apply (rr 2–9 and 12, and by the County Court (Forms)(Amendment) Rules 1985, rr 2, 5–10 and 12 (see also r 16 of the latter). *The court has jurisdiction where the credit given under the agreement does not exceed £15,000* (Consumer Credit (Increase of Monetary Limits) Order 1983 [SI 1878 of 1983]). As to definitions see s 189(1) of the 1974 Act. In particular, it should be noted that:

(*a*) 'debtor' means the individual receiving credit under a consumer credit agreement or the person to whom his rights and duties under the agreement have passed . . .

(*b*) 'total price' appears, in substance, to mean the same as 'hire-purchase price' under s 58(1) of the Hire-Purchase Act 1965.

It should be noted that the Consumer Credit Act 1974 does not, in terms, provide for making a postponed order for specific delivery as does s 35(4)(*b*) of the Hire-Purchase Act 1965. The same effect can be obtained by combining a 'time order' (s 129 of the 1974 Act) with a 'return order' under s 133(1) and a suspension thereof under s 135(1)(*b*)(ii).

(Form N 32 (2) as amended is the relevant form of order).

As to exempt agreements (s 16(2) of the 1974 Act) see the Consumer Credit (Exempt Agreements)(No 2) Ord 1985 and the amendments thereto (SIs 1736 and 1918 of 1985 and 2186 of 1986).

Application under s 129(1)(b) by the debtor or hirer for a 'time order'

Such an application is made by originating application (form N 440) to the court in whose district the applicant resides or carries on business. (Alternative Ord 49, r 4(5)). The application must give the particulars specified in the rule. Application for enforcement orders under s 127 (where the 1974 Act has been infringed in various ways); ss 86(2) and 87(1) (relating to the death of debtor or hirer); ss 92(2) and 126 (relating to land) are all commenced by originating application. (Alternative Ord 49, r 4(9)–(11)).

Torts (Interference with Goods) Act 1977

In proceedings for 'wrongful interference', the court may make an order, which may be subject to conditions (s 3(6)), for the specific return of goods, accompanied by an order for payment of damages; or for delivery of goods, but giving the defendant the alternative of paying damages by reference to value (s 3(1), (2)). The court may revoke its order for specific return, and make an order for payment of damages by reference to value in lieu (s 3(4)). All of these provisions are without prejudice to any remedies under the Hire-Purchase Act 1965.

The judge has power to make an interlocutory order for the delivery up to the claimant or to a person appointed by the court of goods which are or may become the subject matter of subsequent proceedings (s 4; Ord 13, r 7(1)(*d*), (2)). An application for such an order may be made in accordance with the same rules which apply to interlocutory injunctions. Where proceedings have been brought in a county court on one of two or more claims for wrongful interference with goods, and these are still pending, any proceedings on another of those claims may, if they could be brought in the High Court, be brought in the same county court notwithstanding that they would otherwise be outside or beyond the jurisdiction of that court (Ord 4, r 6).

Where the plaintiff in an action for 'wrongful interference' with goods is one of two or more persons having an interest in the goods, then, unless he has the written authority of every other such person to sue on the latter's behalf, the particulars of claim must contain particulars of the plaintiff's title and identify every other person who has an interest in the goods; but this does not apply to an accident on land involving a vehicle (Ord 15, r 4(1)).

A defendant to an action for 'wrongful interference' with goods who desires to show that a third party has a better right than the plaintiff may, at any time after service of the summons on the defendant and before any judgment or order is given or made on the plaintiff's claim, apply to the court for directions as to whether any person named in the application (not being a person whose written authority the plaintiff has to sue on his behalf) should be joined as a party (ss 7, 8). Notice of the application must be served on the plaintiff. It must also be served on every person named in the application in accordance with the rules applicable to the service of an ordinary summons (Ord 15, r 4(2)). Where the person named in the application fails to appear or to comply with any direction given by the court on the application, the court may by order deprive him of any right of action (Ord 15, r 4(3)).

Where there are concurrent actions in respect of goods subject to wrongful interference and one of the actions is in the High Court and another in a county court, the High Court may, on the application of the defendant after notice has been given to the claimant in the county court action, order that the county court action be transferred to the High Court and may order security for costs (s 9(4); s 41 of the 1984 Act). The procedure is by way of originating summons under RSC Ord 7 (see note 7/1–7/2 in *The Supreme Court Practice*).

When a bailee is unable to return goods to a bailor, such as when the bailor cannot be traced, the court may authorise a sale of the goods (ss 12, 13; Sched 1).

Chapter 28

Tenancies, Leases and Rentcharges

Landlord and Tenant Acts 1927 and 1954

Order 43 applies to proceedings under these Acts.

The Landlord and Tenant Act 1927, Pt I, relates to compensation for improvements of business premises. Part II includes s 19 which contains provisions relating to covenants not to assign or make improvements etc without consent.

The Landlord and Tenant Act 1954, Pt I (ss 1–22) relates to security of tenure for residential tenants under long leases, enabling them in certain circumstances to obtain statutory tenancies after their leases have expired.

The 1954 Act, Pt II (ss 23–46), relates to security of tenure for business tenants, enabling them in certain circumstances to obtain a new lease after their leases have expired.

Jurisdiction

Under Pt I of the 1954 Act, jurisdiction conferred on the court is exercised by the county court (s 63(1)).

Under Pt II of the 1954 Act and Pt I of the 1927 Act, jurisdiction conferred on the court is exercised:

(*a*) by the county court where the rateable value of the holding does not exceed £5,000;

(*b*) by the High Court, where it exceeds £5,000 (s 63(2) of the 1954 Act).

Such jurisdiction may by agreement in writing between the parties be transferred from the county court to the High Court or from the High Court to a county court specified in the agreement (s 63(3)). Subject to such an agreement an application commenced in the wrong court is valid, but shall be transferred to the correct court (s 63(4)(*a*)). An order for transfer may also be made on the application of a person interested on the grounds that the application should be heard with some other proceedings (s 63(4)(*b*)).

In an application for a declaration that consent to assign has been unreasonably withheld, the county court has the same jurisdiction as the High Court (s 53).

Venue

An originating application may be commenced in the court for the district in which the respondent, or one of the respondents, resides or carries on business, or in which the subject matter of the application is situated (Ord 4, r 8). However, the vires of this rule has been lessened by the Court of Appeal in *Sharma* v *Knight* [1986] 1 WLR 757.

Applications

An application for possession of land under s 13 of the 1954 Act is made by ordinary summons and the particulars of claim must contain the additional matters set out in Ord 43, r 5(2). This section is in Pt I of the Act and the jurisdiction of the county court is not limited by the rateable value of £5,000.

All other proceedings under the Landlord and Tenant Acts 1927 and 1954 are commenced in the county court by originating application.

In all originating applications under Ord 43, the respondent must file an answer within fourteen days after the date of service (Ord 43, r 2(1) and Ord 9, r 18). The originating application most commonly made under the 1954 Act is an application for a new tenancy under s 24. The application must be made (that is, filed) not less than two nor more than four months after the giving of the landlord's notice under s 25, or, as the case may be, after the making of the tenant's request for a new tenancy (s 29(3)). The time may not be extended (*Hodgson* v *Armstrong* [1967] 2 QB 299; [1967] 1 All ER 307). The 'landlord' (as defined by s 44) must be made respondent (Ord 43, r 6(2)).

The requirements are:
  (*a*) originating application (N 397) and copy for each respondent (Ord 43, r 6(1));
  (*b*) request (no prescribed form);
  (*c*) fees (see Table of Fees).

The court gives notice to the respondent of the day of hearing and annexes it to the copy of the originating application for service (Ord

3, r 4). When the court office is closed on the last day for making an application, it may be filed on the next day the office is open (see *Hodgson* v *Armstrong* above and *Riley* v *Euro Stile Holdings* [1985] 1 WLR 1139 and 1406). The time within which service must be effected is within two months of issue unless extended; where reasonable efforts have been made to serve the application and service has not been effected, the registrar may order that the time be extended for a further period not exceeding two months and for successive periods, but the time may not be extended unless application is made within the currency of the preceding period or within such later period as the court may allow (Ord 43, r 6(3); Ord 7, r 20).

The respondent must file an answer in N 400 within fourteen days giving the details required by Ord 43, r 7 with a copy for each of the other parties. The copies are served by the court on the other parties. Any person affected by the proceedings may apply to be made a party (Ord 43, r 14). The final order is in N 401 adapted as required.

Where the court is precluded from making an order for the grant of a new tenancy on any grounds specified in s 30 of the 1954 Act, the order must state all the grounds on which the court is precluded (Ord 43, r 8). An application for a certificate under s 37(4) of the grounds for refusing a new tenancy is made ex parte to the registrar (Ord 43, r 9). A consent order may be made by the registrar under ss 7 and 24 (Ord 43, r 15(1)). An application under s 24A of the 1954 Act to determine an interim rent can be made in pending proceedings under Ord 13, r 1. If the tenant has not commenced proceedings under s 24, an application may be made by originating application.

A joint application under s 38(4) of the 1954 Act to the court to authorise an agreement excluding the provisions of ss 24–28 or for the surrender of a tenancy before its natural expiration is made by originating application under Ord 3, r 4.

Fee: see Table of Fees.

The registrar may make the order (Ord 43, r 15(2)). The order is in form N 404(1). As this is a matter of contentious litigation each party should be represented by a separate solicitor: see Chapter 3.

Leasehold Property (Repairs) Act 1938

This Act restricts the enforcement of repairing covenants in leases for a term of seven years or more of which three years or more remain unexpired. Section 146 of the Law of Property Act 1925 requires a lessor to serve notice containing certain particulars prescribed by the section before commencing proceedings to exercise a right of re-entry for breach of a covenant to repair. Section 146 does not require any notice when the claim is for damages, but such a notice is made necessary by s 1(2) of the 1938 Act. Where a counter-notice is served by a lessee on the lessor under s 1 of the 1938 Act, following the service of such a notice the lessors may not commence proceedings to enforce any right of re-entry or forfeiture or for damages without leave of the court.

The court having jurisdiction is the county court except where the subsequent action would have to be taken in another court: (the County Courts Act 1984, Sched 2, para 6).

The requirements in an application for leave under s 1 are:

(a) originating application and copy for service;
(b) request;
(c) fee: see Table of Fees.

Leasehold Reform Act 1967

This Act enables the tenant of a leasehold house to acquire the freehold or an extended lease of fifty years in certain circumstances where the lease is one granted for a term exceeding twenty-one years at a low rent, that is, a rent not exceeding two-thirds of the rateable value. The tenant must have occupied the house as his residence for the last five years or for periods amounting to five years in the last ten years. The rateable value of the house and premises, broadly speaking, must not be more than £1,500 in the Greater London area and £750 elsewhere where the appropriate day is before 1 April 1973. Where the appropriate day is later and the tenancy was created after 18 February 1966, the rateable values must be not more than £1,000 or £500 respectively (s 1 of the 1967 Act).

As to property consisting of a shop and dwelling accommodation, see *Tandon* v *Trustees of Spurgeons Homes* [1982] 2 WLR 735.

Proceedings under the Leasehold Reform Act 1967 are commenced by originating application. Reference should be made to Ord 3, r 4 and Ord 4, r 8. For precedents, see *McCleary's County Court Precedents*.

The county court has jurisdiction to determine the principal issues under the Act (s 20). Assessment of the price of the freehold, the rent payable under an extended lease and the amount of compensation in default of agreement are determined by the Lands Tribunal (s 21) (Ord 49, r 8(3)).

Payment into court

Where payment is made into court under s 11(4) or s 13(1) or (3) of the Act, Ord 49, r 8(2) applies.

The appropriate court for payment in is the county court for the district in which the property is situated or, if the payment is made by reason of a notice under s 13(3), the court named in the notice.

An affidavit containing information is required by Ord 49, r 8(2)(a).

The court sends notice of payment into court to the landlord and to every person named in the affidavit (N 242). On a subsequent payment into court by the landlord under s 11(4), the landlord files an affidavit and notice is sent to the tenant and persons named in the affidavit (Ord 49, r 8(2)(c)).

If proceedings are taken under ss 17 or 18 for the possession of a house, they should be commenced in the county court for the district in which the house is situated (Ord 4, r 3).

The requirements are:

(a)   originating application and copy for service;

(b)   request;

(c)   fees (see Table of Fees).

Notice (N 8(4)) is served on the respondent with the copy originating application. The respondent must forthwith, after being served, serve a notice of the proceedings in N 426 on every person in occupation of the property or part of it under an immediate or derivative subtenancy (Ord 49, r 8(4)(a)). The respondent must within fourteen days after being served file an answer stating the grounds, if any, on which he intends to oppose the application and giving particulars of every subtenancy, together with a copy for every other party to the proceedings (Ord 49, r 8(4)(b)).

The subtenants may, with leave of the court, appear and be heard in the proceedings (para 3(4) of Sched 2 to the Act).

One of the many applications which may be made under the Act is an application by the landlord under Sched 3, para 4(1) for leave to bring proceedings to enforce a right of re-entry or forfeiture where the tenant has made claim to acquire the freehold or an extended lease.

Rentcharges Act 1977

Payment may be made into court pursuant to the Rentcharges Act 1977, ss 9 and 10, in redemption of certain rentcharges. Payment may be made into a county court where the sum does not exceed its general jurisdiction for recovery of debts, namely £5,000 (s 10(4)).

The money must be paid into the court for the district in which the land affected by the rentcharge or any part of it is situated (Ord 49, r 16). The procedure in Ord 49, r 8(2) could well be adapted. No fee is payable. An application should be made for investment under the Court Funds Rules 1987.

The payment must be made within 28 days of the instructions for redemption (s 10(5)).

Chapter 29

Rent Act 1977; Housing Act 1985; Mobile Homes Act 1983; Agricultural Holdings Act 1948

Rent Act 1977

The Rent Act 1977 came into force on 29 August 1977 and consolidated previous Acts. That part of the Rent Act 1965 which dealt with unlawful eviction and harassment and with special provisions for agricultural employees was replaced by the Protection from Eviction Act 1977. The Rent (Agriculture) Act 1976 affords security of tenure for agricultural and forestry workers housed by employers.

A tenancy under which a dwellinghouse (which may be a house or part of a house) is let as a separate dwelling is a protected tenancy (s 1 of the Rent Act 1977). Section 4 to 16 to the Rent Act 1977 provide for exceptions: a tenancy is not protected if the rateable value of the house on or after 1 April 1973 exceeds £1,500 in London or £750 elsewhere (besides exceeding certain lesser values before that day (s 4)). A tenancy is not protected, inter alia, if it is a 'tenancy at a low rent' (s 5); if it is let with other land (s 6); if the rent includes board or attendance (s 7); in some cases of lettings to students (s 8); if it is a holiday letting (s 9); if it comprises an agricultural holding (s 10) or licensed premises (s 11); if the landlord is resident in the building which is not a purpose-built block of flats (s 12); if the landlord's interest belongs to the Crown (s 13); or if the landlord is a local authority (s 14), a housing association (s 15) or a housing co-operative (s 16). The relevant sections in the Act itself should be consulted.

The jurisdiction of the county court is contained in s 141. The powers conferred under this section include the making of orders for possession where the Act applies. The section also permits a county court to deal with money claims arising out of the Act notwithstanding that the amount of the claim would otherwise be outside its jurisdiction. If a person takes proceedings in the High Court which he could have taken in a county court, he will not be entitled to costs (s 141(4)). There are powers to suspend orders for possession (s 100).

In proceedings under the Rent Act the usual county court procedures apply, but as supplemented by the Rent (County Court Proceedings) Rules 1970 and the Rent Act (County Court Proceedings for Possession) Rules 1981.

Rent (County Court Proceedings) Rules 1970

These Rules apply to matters other than actions for possession.

All the Rent Act forms appended to the Rules need to be amended to refer to the Rent Act 1977.

Applications for leave to distrain. The requirements are:
  (a) originating application (form 6 (Rent Act)) and copy;
  (b) request;
  (c) fee: see Table of Fees.
Notice of hearing is prepared by the court, with copy of the originating application annexed, and is served on the respondent not less than four clear days before the hearing (r 3(4)).

The application is heard by the registrar, normally in chambers.

The order is in Form 7 (Rent Act).

Other applications. Rule 3 applies.

The requirements are:
  (a) originating application and copy for service;
  (b) request;
  (c) fee: see Table of Fees.
A general form of originating application is provided for in the Appendix to the 1970 Rules. Notice of hearing is prepared by the court. Notice of hearing with a copy of the originating application annexed is served on the respondent not less than ten clear days before the hearing. Service may be by post. Any answer, with a copy for the applicant, should be delivered to the court office within eight days of service. The application may be heard by the registrar except that an application under para 3 or 7 of Part I Sched 1 to the Rent Act 1977 must in the first place be heard by the judge. The hearing may take place in court or in chambers.

The Appendix to the Rules contains the forms of order which must be served on all parties.

Proceedings for compensation. Such proceedings under s 102 of the Rent Act 1977 are commenced by plaint and, if the judgment complained of is obtained in a county court, the action must be brought in that court (r 4).

The Rent Act (County Court Proceedings for Possession) Rules 1981

Pursuant to these Rules possession of a dwellinghouse may be recovered under Sched 15 to the Rent Act 1977 in the cases listed below, the proceedings being commenced by an action for possession *or* an originating application.

The requirements (if by originating application) are:

Forms of originating application appended to the Rules, viz:

Cases 11, 12, or 20	Appendix A
Cases 13 to 18 inclusive	Appendix B
Case 19	Appendix C (rr 2 and 3)

For general requirements, see notes on 'Commencement of Proceedings' dealing with originating applications.

The special requirement is an affidavit (with copy) as required by r 4.

Service (Cases 11, 12 and 20) must be at least seven clear days before the return day. In other cases at least fourteen clear days before the return day.

Notes

    (*a*) If 'postal service', seven extra days are required (Ord 7, r 10(3)).

    (*b*) Respondents must be served with copy affidavits and exhibits.

    (*c*) Order 7, r 15 applies to service (rr 4 and 5).

The application may be heard by the judge or registrar in chambers or in open court (r 6).

There are no special requirements where proceedings are commenced by action.

Costs

The scale will be fixed by the court at the trial or by the registrar when taxing (Ord 38, r 4(7)), or the trial court may fix costs (Ord 38, r 19).

Where possession proceedings are taken, the solicitor's costs endorsed on the summons are shown in Costs Appendix B, Pt I. When a suspended order is made where the defendant has taken no steps, the costs to be added are shown under item (*d*) in Pt II of Appendix B.

Where the right to possession is admitted in the defence, no costs of proving any matter which the admission makes unnecessary shall be allowed (Ord 9, r 16(2)).

Housing Act 1985

In the main, where the landlord is a Local Authority or Housing Authority and there is occupation as a home, there is 'a secure tenancy'; see sections 79, 80 and 81.

Part V of the Housing Act 1985 gives a 'secure tenant' the right to acquire a freehold of his house or long lease of his flat, and is extended by SI 1732 of 1987.

The county court has jurisdiction to deal with all matters arising (s 181) save the value of property which is fixed by the district valuer (s 128). Proceedings are commenced by originating application.

Possession proceedings against secure tenants under Part IV are brought in the county courts (s 110) and follow the normal county court procedure.

Attention is drawn to s 83 of the Act whereby secure tenancies are brought to an end by a special procedure without notice to quit. This special procedure does not apply where the secure tenant or his successor have vacated the property, when the common law applies.

Mobile Homes Act 1983

Applications under ss 1 or 2 and paras 4, 5, or 6 of Part I of Sched I are made by originating application (Ord 3, r 4). An answer must be filed within fourteen days and the matter may be dealt with by the registrar in chambers (Ord 49, r 13; Ord 9, r 18).

Agricultural Holdings Act 1948

Many sections of the Act provide for reference to arbitration, including if necessary, and if there is no agreement in writing, a reference to the arbitrator to specify the existing terms. Where the arbitrator is appointed by the parties, his remuneration is to be fixed in default of agreement by the registrar, and the costs of an arbitration are taxed by the registrar. The county court may also be concerned with the enforcement of an order made by the Agricultural Land Tribunal where a condition imposed on the giving of consent to the operation of a notice to quit is claimed to have been breached. The procedure is by way of originating application to the court within the district of which the holding or the larger part thereof is situate (s 94(1) of the Agricultural Holdings Act 1948). The procedure is regulated by Ord 44.

Chapter 30

Adoption; Custodianship; Guardianship of Minors

An adoption order is made by the judge who will have before him the entire adoption file. On the appointment, the applicants, the reporting officer and social welfare officer if required, will all attend. Occasionally, applicants are accompanied by a solicitor, but the court itself by its 'proper officer' will have prepared the case for the judge following the sequence outlined at the end of the chapter, in accordance with the Adoption Rules 1984, utilising the forms appended thereto.

Adoption orders are made under the authority of the Adoption Act 1976 (AA 1976) as read with the Children Act 1975 (CA 1975), both as amended apply. Section 3 of the Children Act 1975 provides that in reaching any decision relating to the adoption of a child, the court or adoption agency shall have regard to all the circumstances, first consideration being given to the need to safeguard and promote the welfare of the child throughout its childhood; and shall so far as practicable ascertain the wishes and feelings of the child regarding the decision and give due consideration to them having regard to its age and understanding. Thus judicial consideration is called for, particularly on questions such as the suitability of a single applicant, or as to whether parental consent should he dispensed with. The latter may well require a full hearing, with representation.

The Adoption Rules 1984 (AR, SI 1984 No 265) apply equally in the High Court. The Rules of the Supreme Court 1965 and the County Court Rules 1981 also apply to adoptions and again equally in the High Court and in the county court in both cases, with necessary modifications: AR, r 3(2), (3). Unless the contrary intention appears, any power may be exercised by the 'proper officer': AR, r 3(4). The 'proper officer' in the county court is the registrar, or in relation to administrative or formal acts, the chief clerk or other officer of the court acting on his behalf (Ord 1, r 3).

The Rules consolidate with amendments earlier rules. Where an application is made under ss 14–16 of the Children Act 1975 by an adoption agency, the machinery provides for freeing a child for adoption so that arrangements can go ahead on the basis that any issue relating to parental consent has been settled. The rules, in Part II, regulate the procedure on such applications. They provide also for the appointment and duties of reporting officers.

If the child is already a ward of court, where it is desired to apply for an order under s 14 of the Children Act 1975 freeing for adoption, it is necessary to obtain leave of the High Court to commence adoption proceedings (*Practice Direction*) (*Family Division*) 1 WLR [1985] 924. Where leave is given, the High Court may direct that the adoption proceedings may then be commenced in the appropriate county court (*Practice Direction* (*Adoption: Ward of Court*) 1 WLR [1986] 933.

Convention adoption orders and orders whereby a child acquires British nationality

Convention adoption orders are orders made in inter-country adoptions, where the adopter and a child are subject to different personal laws. Applications for such orders are made to the High Court: CA 1975, ss 24, 100(1), (2) and (5) and AR rr 27–46. For details see *Rayden on Divorce*.

Straightforward applications to free for adoption (see below) or to adopt, which would result in the child acquiring British nationality, should be heard in the county court. (*Re: N and L (Minors)* [1987] 1 WLR 829). Difficult cases should be transferred to the High Court pursuant to the Practice Direction at [1987] 1 WLR 316. In such cases see also *In re W (a minor)* [1985] 3 WLR 945 at 951H.

Freeing for adoption

Where, on an application by an adoption agency, local authority or approved adoption society, the court is satisfied in the case of each parent or guardian of the child that (a) he/she freely and with full understanding of what is involved agrees generally and unconditionally to the making of an adoption order, or (b) his/her agreement should be dispensed with on a ground specified in s 16 of AA 1976, the court shall make a freeing order in Form 12, freeing the child for adoption: AA 1976, s 18. The purpose of this procedure is to enable the problem of parental consent to be dealt with at an early stage and to avoid natural and adoptive parents coming into possible conflict.

Where the natural parent is a minor no guardian ad litem need be appointed for that parent, where he or she agrees to the freeing or adoption order.

On the making of the freeing order, the parental rights and duties vest in the adoption agency and any obligation to pay maintenance ceases: AA 1976, ss 12 and 18.

As to when the High Court should hear such applications—see last section.

Dispensing with parental consent

This may be dispensed with on the grounds that the parent or guardian:

(a) cannot be found or is incapable of giving agreement;
(b) is withholding agreement unreasonably;
(c) has persistently failed without reasonable cause to discharge the parental duties in relation to the child;
(d) has abandoned or neglected the child;
(e) has persistently ill-treated the child;
(f) has seriously ill-treated the child (this does not apply unless (because of the ill-treatment or for other reasons) the rehabilitation of the child within the household of the parent or guardian is unlikely: AA 1976, s 16(2), (5)).

The mother's consent cannot be given within six weeks of the birth: AA 1976, s 16(4).

The court cannot make a freeing order against a father of an illegitimate child who is not its guardian unless it is satisfied that the father has no intention of applying for custody under s 9 of the Guardianship of Minors Act 1971 or that, if he did so apply, custody would be likely to be refused: AA 1976, s 18(7).

The court, before making a 'freeing order', must satisfy itself that each parent or guardian who can be found has had the opportunity of making a declaration that he prefers not to be involved in future adoption proceedings and any such declaration must be recorded by the court. (See final para to Form 12): AA

1976, s 18(6). Any similar later declaration to the agency obtaining the freeing order must also be registered with the court: AA 1976, s 19(4).

Application for a declaration that the child is free for adoption

Application can be made in the county court in whose district the child is or in whose district is a parent or guardian: AA1976, s 62(2)(*b*).

The requirements on issue of such application are:

(*a*) Originating application in Form 1, with three copies.

(*b*) Request for issue.

(*c*) Fee (See Table of Fees).

(*d*) Three copies of birth certificate (as to which see AR r 11), and any other relevant document mentioned in Form 1.

(*e*) Three copies of the report in writing conveying all relevant matters specified in Sched 2, AR, r 4(1).

(*f*) Where the applicant intends to ask the court to dispense with the consent of a parent or guardian under AA 1976, s 16, three copies of the statement of facts to be relied on. This shall not disclose the identity of the person with whom the child has been placed for adoption if that person so requests: AR, r 7.

(*g*) Where a parent or guardian living outside England and Wales has executed an agreement to the making of an adoption order in Form 2 and in accordance with AR, r 8, that agreement.

Note

Where a document is in a foreign language an authenticated translation should be attached to the document. Further, if a parent or guardian does not read English, translation of court forms may be needed: AR, r 46.

The respondents to the application are to be:

(*a*) Each parent or guardian of the child ('parent' includes a natural father);

(*b*) Any local authority having the power and duties of a parent or guardian of the child under s 10 of the Child Care Act 1980;

(*c*) Any local authority in whom the parental rights and

duties in respect of the child are vested, whether jointly or not, under s 3 of the Child Care Act 1980;

(d) Any voluntary organisation in whom the parental rights and duties in respect of the child are vested, whether jointly or not, under s 64 of the Child Care Act 1980;

(e) Any local authority or voluntary organisation in whose care the child is under s 2 of the Child Care Act 1980, or under or within the meaning of any other enactment; and

(f) Any person liable by virtue of any order or agreement to contribute to the maintenance of the child: AR, r 4(2).

The court may at any time direct that any other person or body, save the child, be made a respondent to the process: AR, r 4(3).

On issue, if it appears that a parent or guardian of the child is willing to agree to the making of an adoption order and is in England or Wales, the proper officer appoints a reporting officer in respect of that parent or guardian and sends to him a copy of the application, any documents attached thereto, and a copy of the report supplied by the applicant under Sched 2 of the AR.

The same person may report as to both parents or guardians. He shall be appointed from the panel established by the local authority under the Reporting Officers (Panels) Regulations 1983 (SI 1983 No 1908 as amended by SI 1986 No 3). He may not be a member of the applicant agency or any respondent body, and must not have been involved in arrangements for the adoption of the child.

The reporting officer reports on and deals with the matters set out in AR, r 5(4) and files his report (which is confidential to the court) with the court. He witnesses any agreement by a parent or guardian, in Form 2, to the making of an adoption order: AR, r 5.

If, on or after issue of the application, it appears that a parent or guardian is not willing to agree to the making of an adoption order, the proper officer appoints a guardian ad litem of the child and sends to him a copy of the application, any documents attached thereto, the statement of facts under s 16(12) of the AA 1976, and the report made under Sched 2 of the AR and thereafter there must be a hearing; this may take place with or without the presence of the guardian ad litem and reporting officer. The guardian may be the same person as the reporting officer in relation to a consenting parent or guardian, and is similarly appointed from the panel. He reports on the matters set out in AR, r 6(6) and files his report (which is confidential) with the court. He attends the hearing unless the court otherwise orders: AR, r 6.

On issue the proper officer further fixes a date for hearing before the judge and serves notice in Form 3 on all the parties and on the reporting officer and guardian ad litem. If postal service is used, an extra seven days must be allowed (Ord 7, r 10(3)). In addition, he serves a copy of the application, the report under Sched 2, and the statement of facts to dispense with consent, on the reporting officer and on the guardian: AR, rr 7 and 9. In addition, where a request to dispense under AA 1976, s 16(2) has been made, he so informs the parent or guardian concerned, and serves a copy of the statement of facts relied on, on that person: AR, r 7.

At the hearing, which is in camera (AA 1976, s 64), any person served with Form 3 may attend and the guardian or a representative of the applicant agency and the child must attend, unless the attendance respectively of the guardian and the child have been dispensed with by the court. The reporting officer attends only if requested by the court. If the person(s) with whom the child has been placed for adoption ask(s) that his (their) identity remain confidential, the hearing shall be arranged to achieve this: AR, rr 6, 7 and 10.

Any local authority, adopting agency, or other body may appear at the hearing by an authorised member or employee: AR, r 10(2).

The parental rights of an adoption agency in whose favour a freeing order was made may be transferred by the court to another agency pursuant to AA 1976, s 21, and on application in Form 5: AR, r 13.

Unless a former parent or guardian made a declaration (in Form 2, para 6) under AA 1976, s 10(6) that he wished not to be involved in the adoption, the agency who obtained the freeing order (or the agency to whom the rights thereunder have been transferred) must keep him informed of the making of any adoption order or placement for adoption. Further, within one year and fourteen days from the making of the freeing order, they must (unless they have previously notified an adoption or placement) notify him whether an adoption order has been made, and if not whether the child is living with a person with whom he has been placed for adoption. Any subsequent adoption or departure of the child from the home where he was placed must be likewise notified: AA 1976, s 19.

Revocation of freeing order

If after one year from the freeing order no adoption order is made and the child has ceased to live with a person with whom he has been placed for adoption, the former parent or guardian may apply to revoke the freeing order, and to resume parental rights and duties: AA 1976, s 20. Application is made in Form 4, and is served on the other parent or guardian, the adoption agency in whom the rights and duties under the freeing order are currently vested, any person liable by order or agreement to pay maintenance for the child and any person made a party by the court under AR, r 4(3): AR, r 12(2). The proper officer lists the application before the judge and gives notice of the date to the parties. He appoints a guardian from the panel to whom he sends the application; documents attached thereto and the date of hearing. The guardian investigates the case for revoking the freeing order and reports to the court to whom the report is confidential. He attends the hearing unless released by the court: AR rr 6(6)–(11) and 12(4).

If a revoking order is made the parental rights and duties revert in the persons or bodies in whom they were vested prior to the freeing order being made, and any obligation to pay maintenance revives: AA 1976, s 20(3). If the application is dismissed, pursuant to AA 1976, s 20(4) no further application to revoke the freeing order can be made unless special leave is given: CA 1975, s 16(4) and (5).

Adoption order

Problems may arise under CA 1975, ss 10(3) and 11(4) where a step-parent and natural parent (or a single step-parent) seek to adopt a child of a dissolved marriage. The judge hearing the adoption application may consider an order under s 42 of the Matrimonial Causes Act 1973 more appropriate and dismiss the application. The divorce court judge may then opine that an adoption order should have been made. Thus the applications in the alternative are best heard by one judge. Application may also be made in any divorce county court which has made a declaration about the child under s 41 of the Matrimonial Causes Act 1973: Ord 47, r 7.

Save in the most exceptional case, access to the natural parent would not be imposed without the adopter's agreement and in any event such a term would not be imposed save when it was clearly in the best interest of the child to have further contact with a member of the natural family (see *In re C (a minor)* (1988) *The Times* 26 February, HL).

Applicants and child

A married couple may apply for an adoption where each has attained the age of twenty-one; one of them must be domiciled in the United Kingdom, the Channel Islands or Isle of Man: CA 1975, s 10(1), (2), and the applicant's permanent home must be in England or Wales (*In re Y (Minors)* (Adoption Jurisdiction) [1985] 3 WLR 601).

One person may apply for an adoption order where he or she has attained the age of twenty-one and is domiciled in the United Kingdom, the Channel Islands or the Isle of Man. The person must either not be married, or if married (a) the spouse cannot be found, or (b) the spouses are separated and the separation is likely to be permanent, or (c) the spouse is incapable of making an application because of ill-health (physical or mental).

An adoption order may not be made on the application of the mother or father alone unless the court is satisfied that the other natural parent is dead, or cannot be found, or there is some other reason justifying the exclusion of the other natural parent: CA 1975, s 11.

'Child' (to be adopted) means a person who has not attained the age of eighteen: CA 1975, s 107(1). The child must not be, or have been married: CA 1975, s 8(5). The child must have been continuously with the applicants (or one of them) for thirteen weeks where the applicant(s) is/are a parent, step-parent or relative or where the child was placed by an adoption agency in pursuance of a High Court order, or, in any other case, for twelve months: CA 1975, s 9.

At least three months before the anticipated date of the adoption order, the applicants must notify the local authority (usually the Director of Social Services) of their intention to apply, unless the child was placed with them by an adoption agency: CA 1975, s 18. The local authority must investigate the matter and report to the court as to the child's welfare and as to whether there has been a breach of AA 1958, s 29, forbidding payment for adoption placements: CA 1975, s 18.

Where a child is a ward of court the leave of the High Court is required before adoption proceedings are commenced. (*Practice Directions* (Family Division) [1985] 1 WLR 924).

Application for adoption order

Application is made in the county court in whose district the child is: CA 1975, s 100(2). If the proposed adopter wishes to keep his identity confidential the court, on application, will assign him a serial number (AR, r 14).

Requirements on issue of an application for an adoption order

(*a*) Originating application in Form 6 with three copies.

(*b*) Request for issue.

(*c*) Fee (see Table of Fees).

(*d*) Three copies of birth certificate (as to which see AR, r 11) and any other relevant document mentioned in Form 6 including where the applicant intends to ask the court to dispense with the consent of a parent or guardian under s 12(2) of CA 1975, three copies of the statement of facts to be relied on. (Where a serial number has been allocated the statement must not disclose the identity of the applicant.) If executed by a parent or guardian outside England or Wales before issue, any document consenting to the adoption in Form 7, witnessed by the persons referred to in AR r 8(2), (3) or (4).

Note

(1) Where a document is in a foreign language an authenticated translation should be attached to the document. Further, if a parent or guardian does not read English, translations of court forms may be required: AR, r 46.

(2) On receipt of the application the proper officer considers whether the court may be unable to make an order by virtue of AA 1976, ss 24 and 57, or for want of jurisdiction. If so, he refers the matter to the judge: AR, r 16.

(3) The Central Registry of the Family Division in London, although having county court jurisdiction, is not a 'county court' for the purposes of adoption and, therefore, such applications cannot be made to the Central Registry even

if it originally acted as a divorce county court in dissolving the marriage. To avoid conflict, an application for transfer of the adoption application to the High Court (Family Division) may be made on application to the Senior Registrar (Practice Note [1978] 3 All ER 960; [1978] 1 WLR 1456). Lastly, if the adoption application is started in a county court other than the (earlier) divorce county court, and a potential conflict arises, the application may be transferred to the divorce county court: Ord 16, r 1(*a*)).

(4)   If the child holds a foreign passport, a letter from the Immigration Department of the Home Office should be lodged with the court papers to show that the Home Office has no observation on the proposed adoption. (See *In re W (a minor)* [1985] 3 WLR 945 at 951 H). The respondents to the application are the same as those to a freeing application unless the child is free for adoption when the parent or guardian need not be served.

Consent of parent or guardian where child not free for adoption

Where the child is not free for adoption, but it appears that a parent or guardian is willing to consent to adoption and is in England or Wales the proper officer appoints a reporting officer: AR, r 17, whose function is to witness the signature of a natural parent on the form of agreement to adoption and to make a report to the court that the agreement was given freely. Only if application has to be made to dispense with parental consent, or if the court considers that there are special circumstances and the welfare of the child requires it, will the court appoint a guardian ad litem. In the county court the guardian ad litem will be a person chosen from a panel established by regulation under s 103 of the 1975 Act, and he or she will supply a full report to the court. For the preparation and readiness of these reports at least six weeks must be allowed, if not more, so no fixed date is usually given until the reports are actually filed.

If the applicants apply to dispense with the agreement of a parent or guardian under AA 1976, s 16(2), the proper officer shall inform the parent or guardian thereof and send him a copy of the statement of facts relied upon: AR, r 19.

On issue the proper officer further fixes a date for a full hearing before the judge which in practice may be preceded by his directions and serves notice in Form 8 on all the parties, the reporting officer and the guardian ad litem. Where the child was not placed for adoption by an adoption agency the hearing date shall be three months or more after notice was given to the local authority under AA 1976, s 22. If postal service, an extra seven days must be allowed: Ord 7, r 40(3). He sends a copy of the application to the reporting officer, the guardian and (unless the child was placed for adoption by an adoption agency) to the local authority to whom notice was given under CA 1976, s 22: AR, r 21.

The adoption agency who placed the child for adoption, or the local authority to whom the proposed adoption was notified under s 22 (ibid) (as the case may be), must submit reports to the court covering the matters mentioned in Sched 2 to the AR within six weeks of receiving Form 8: AR, r 22. The proper officer sends copies of the report to the reporting officer and guardian ad litem.

Such reports are otherwise confidential to the court: AR, r 22.

The hearing takes place in camera: AA 1976, S 64. The judge may not make an adoption order unless the applicant has attended in person. Where there are joint applicants, one of the applicants need not attend if he or she verifies the application by affidavit or, if outside the United Kingdom, by declaration attested by a person authorised to administer an oath in the place where the document is executed, a British consular officer, a notary public or, if the person is serving in the regular armed forces of the Crown, by a commissioned officer. The child must attend unless his attendance is dispensed with.

In serial number cases, arrangements must be made by the court so that the applicant(s) are not seen by or identified by any respondent who does not know their identity: AR, r 23.

Where the court refuses to make an adoption order and proposes to make an order under AA 1976, s 26, committing the child to the care of the local authority, AR, r 26, applies.

Where an order is made or refused, notice is served on every respondent by the registrar: AR, r 52(5). The adoption order itself in Form 15 is sent by the court to the Registrar General and sent to the applicant(s) within seven days: AR, r 52(3) and (4). The order directs the Registrar General to make an entry in the adopted children register. Where the adoption order is made by a court sitting in Wales and the child was born in Wales and the adopter so requests, the schedule to the order is drawn up in Welsh and English: AR, r 52(2) and (4).

Interim orders

The court may postpone the determination of the application for an adoption order and make an interim order giving custody of the child to the applicant(s) for a period not exceeding two years by way of a probationary period (Form 14). All requirements must be complied with as to agreements, age of child, the giving of notice to the local authority of the intention to apply for an adoption order, etc. Where the court has made an interim order giving the custody of the child to the applicant for a period of less than two years, the court may by order extend the period but the total period must not exceed two years: AA 1976, s 25. The registrar must not less than one month before the expiration of the period specified in the order fix a time, if no time has previously been fixed, for the further hearing of the application and serve notice of the hearing on all parties and on the guardian ad litem: AR, r 25.

Removal of child abroad

Where a person, who is not domiciled in England or Wales or Scotland, intends to adopt a child under the law of the country in which he is domiciled and for that purpose wishes to remove the child from Great Britain, he may apply for a provisional adoption order authorising the removal and giving to the applicant the custody of the child pending his adoption: AA 1976, s 55. An interim order may not be made. The originating application is in Form 6. The provisions which apply to other adoption orders generally apply, save that where the child was placed for adoption by an adoption agency he must be at least thirty-two weeks old and have been in the applicant's care for twenty-six weeks before the order is made. Evidence of the law of adoption in the country in which the applicant is domiciled is given by affidavit sworn by a person such as is mentioned in s 4(1) of the Civil Evidence Act 1972, that is, a person who is suitably qualified on account of his knowledge and experience. The affidavit is admissable without giving notice to other parties: AR, r 48. The order is in Form 15.

There are restrictions on the removal of a child pending adoption. The court may order the person who has removed the child to return it to the applicant: AA 1976, ss 27–31.

Confidentiality

All information relating to adoption proceedings is confidential and may be disclosed only in the circumstances prescribed in AR, r 53. A copy of an adoption order may be supplied to the Registrar General at his request, to the applicant or one of the applicants and to any other person with the leave of the judge: AR, r 52(8), (10). The Registrar General may furnish certain information as to the original entry in the register of births relating to an adopted person but subject to limitations: AA 1976, s 51.

Amendment and revocation

As to the amendment and revocation of adoption orders, for which there is limited scope, see AR, r 49.

Costs

The judge may make such order as to costs as he thinks fit and, in particular, may order the applicant to pay the out-of-pocket expenses of the reporting officer and guardian ad litem and the expenses incurred by any respondent in attending the hearing, or part of such expenses: AR, r 51.

Custodianship and guardianship of minors

Under s 33 of the Children Act 1975:
Any of the following categories of persons may apply for a custodianship order:

(i) provided they have the consent of the person having legal custody of the child, any relative or step-parent with whom the child has had his home for the three months last preceding the application or any person with whom the child has had his home for the three months preceding the application and a further nine months in total;

(ii whether or not there is consent of the legal guardian, any person with whom the child has had his home for a total period of three years including the three months immediately preceding the application.

Neither the natural mother nor the father of the child may apply.

If an order is made, the right of any other person to custody is suspended. Where the child is the subject of an order under s 41(1) of the Matrimonial Proceedings Act 1973, a step-parent may not apply, and any application for custody where there has been such an order, must be made in the matrimonial suit.

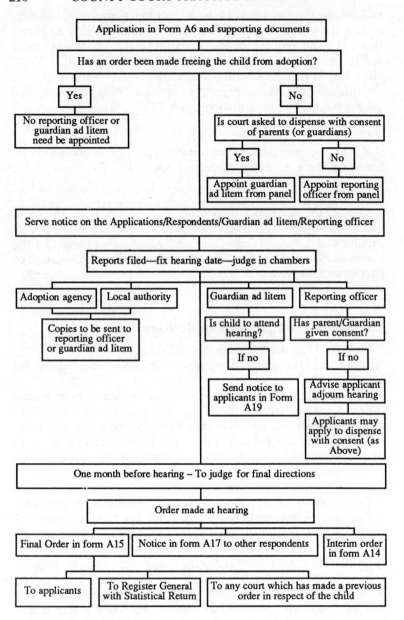

Note: once the applicants have lodged their application the Court itself, through its 'proper officer' takes all remaining steps.

Custodianship

The procedure for applications for custodianship is to be found in RSC Ord 90, Part III, as modified by CCR Ord 47, r 7. Application is made in the county court on form N 114, and any necessary consent can be given in form N 116.

The county court registrar can determine the extent of access and award and vary maintenance in all cases: RSC Ord 90, r 15.

Once a guardianship order has been made and further proceedings under part II of the 1975 Act are pending, applications under the Guardianship Acts must be made in the guardianship proceedings under CCR Ord 13, r 1, (Ord 47, r 6(1)(A).

The form of report in custodianship cases is set out in the Custodianship (Report) Regulations 1985 (SI 1985 No 792). The medical certificate is given in form N 115.

The entire contents of s 33 of the Children Act 1975 should be considered and *The Supreme Court Practice* should be consulted.

Guardianship of minors

The Guardianship of Minors Act 1971 and the Guardianship Act 1973, with Ord 47, r 6 and Ord 3, r 4 apply.

These Acts give the court power to make orders as to custody, access and maintenance regarding a minor and are frequently used today where the parents of the minor are unmarried. They also give power to the court to appoint a guardian of a minor in certain circumstances, such as on the death of a parent.

An application may be made to the county court for the district in which the minor to whom the application relates habitually resides, is in fact residing (if he has no habitual residence) when the application issues and, in certain other special cases, where he has wrongfully left the district in which he habitually resided (Ord 47, r 6). A county court does not have jurisdiction where any respondent resides in Scotland or Northern Ireland unless the originating process can be served on the respondent in England or Wales (s 15(3)). See notes on 'Commencement of proceedings' relating to originating applications.

Service must be effected not less than twenty-one clear days before the return day. Seven further days must be allowed if service is by post (Ord 3, r 4; Ord 7, especially r 10(3)). As to parties, see Ord 47, r 6(1).

The proceedings are heard by the judge in chambers unless the court otherwise directs (Ord 47, r 6(3)).

If the court is making a custody order under the Guardianship of Minors Acts 1971 and 1973, or if an order for custody is made in divorce proceedings, whether or not after decree absolute, then contemporaneously, or subsequently, an application may be made for an interlocutory injunction for non-molestation in support of the custody order: *In re W (a minor)* [1981] 3 All ER 401, CA, and see also *Rayden on Divorce* under 'Injunctions and Committals'.

Chapter 31

Family Disputes

Law Reform (Husband and Wife) Act 1962

Section 1(2) of the Act provides that in an action in tort brought by one party to the marriage against the other during the subsistence of the marriage, the court may stay the action if it appears that no substantial benefit would accrue to either party from the continuation of the proceedings, or if the question in issue could be more conveniently disposed of in an application under s 17 of the Married Women's Property Act 1882.

The power of the court to stay the action may be exercised by the registrar if the action is to be heard by the judge, at any time before the hearing, or if the action is to be heard by the registrar, at any stage of the proceedings. The court must, after a defence has been filed or, in a fixed date action, when the time for filing a defence has expired, consider whether the power to stay the action should be exercised and must fix a day for preliminary consideration under Ord 17 (Ord 47, r 3(2)).

In the case of a default action, judgment may not be entered save by leave of the registrar on application on notice (Ord 47, r 3(3), (4)).

Matrimonial Causes Act 1973

A number of county courts have jurisdiction in matrimonial causes, and in a number of these matrimonial causes trials of undefended suits may be heard. They are shown in the directory in the county court practice as 'divorce' or 'divorce trial' courts. The procedure is governed by the Matrimonial Causes Rules 1977 which incorporate the 1981 Rules (MCR 3, 2(7)). For further detail reference should be made to *Rayden on Divorce*.

Law of Property Act 1925, s 30

The section enables an application to be made to the court by 'any person interested' for a vesting or other order where trustees refuse to sell.

Notes

(a) *Where the parties are co-habitees*, and there is no express trust, the contributions or mortgage repayments, or the particular circumstances, may raise an equity, and a trust may be implied; if a party then seeks an order for sale and a declaration as to division of the proceeds, an originating application can be issued, quoting therein s 30 of the Law of Property Act 1925, in which an order is sought directing the trustees of the property to give effect to the trust.

(b) *Where the parties are engaged to be married*, application can be made under s 17 of the Married Women's Property Act 1882 (below).

Married Women's Property Act 1882, s 17

In any question between husband and wife as to the title to or possession of property, either party may apply to the judge or registrar who may make such order with respect to the property in dispute as he thinks fit (Married Women's Property Act 1882, s 17)(Ord 47, r 2(4)).

A county court has concurrent jurisdiction with the High Court irrespective of the value of the property.

For general requirements, see notes on 'Commencement of Proceedings' relating to originating applications.

For special requirements, see Ord 47, r 2.

Notice to the respondent and any mortgagee is given by the court in N 8(3) with a copy of the application attached.

The respondent must file an answer and a copy for each other party within fourteen days after the day of service (Ord 47, r 2(3); Ord 9, r 18). The registrar sends the copy of the answers to the other parties.

The first hearing is usually for giving directions. For form of order for selling a house, see *Re Draper's Conveyance* [1967] 3 All ER 853. If heard by the registrar, an appeal from the registrar lies to a judge. The powers under s 17 of the Married Women's Property Act 1882 apply to formerly engaged couples (s 2(2) of the

Law Reform (Miscellaneous Provisions) Act 1970) and to disputes between formerly married couples if the application is made within three years from decree absolute or decree of nullity (s 39 of the Matrimonial Proceedings and Property Act 1970). This should only be necessary where the applicant has failed to apply in time for a property adjustment order (s 28(3) of the Matrimonial Causes Act 1973; *Rayden on Divorce*). Where a sale of property is sought in divorce proceedings, the previous need to apply under s 17 of the Married Women's Property Act 1882 is obviated by s 24A of the Matrimonial Causes Act 1973.

Inheritance (Provision for Family and Dependants) Act 1975

The county court has jurisdiction under the Inheritance (Provision for Family and Dependants) Act 1975 and s 36 of the Matrimonial Causes Act 1973, where the value of the deceased's net estate does not exceed £30,000: s 25 of the 1984 Act and s 36(3) of the Matrimonial Causes Act 1973.

Section 1 of the 1975 Act enables an application to be made for an order for reasonable financial provision to be made out of a deceased's estate.

Section 1 of the Act also allows such an application to be made by:

(*a*)   the wife or husband of the deceased;

(*b*)   a former wife or husband who has not remarried;

(*c*)   a child of the deceased;

(*d*)   a person treated by the deceased as a child of the family; and

(*e*)   any person being maintained by the deceased immediately before his death.

Section 36 of the Matrimonial Causes Act 1973 enables a party to a maintenance agreement to apply for an alteration of a continuing agreement after the death of the other party. Application must be made within six months from the first grant of representation unless the court permits a later application.

Where proceedings under either the Matrimonial Causes Act 1973 or the Inheritance (Provision for Family and Dependants) Act 1975 are commenced in the High Court and it appears to the court that a county court would have jurisdiction, the High Court may order the proceedings to be transferred to a convenient county court (RSC, Ord 99, r 11; MCR, r 105). In the case of an application under the 1973 Act, the transfer is to a divorce county court.

Procedure in the county court is regulated by Ord 48. Application is made in the court for the district in which the deceased resided at his death or, if he was not then resident within England or Wales, in the court for the district in which the respondent or one of the respondents resides or carries on business or the estate is situated or, in any case, in the court for the district in which the applicant resides or carries on business.

For general requirements, see notes on 'Commencement of Proceedings' relating to originating applications.

Special requirements are:

(a)   the originating application in N 423 (for financial provision) or N 424 (for alteration of maintenance agreement) must give the details required by Ord 48, r 2(1) or 2(2);

(b)   official copy of grant of representation and of every testamentary document admitted to proof;

(c)   in cases under s 36 of the 1973 Act, a copy of the agreement to which the application relates.

Notice with a copy of the application annexed is served. Every respondent must file an answer giving the prescribed details within twenty-one days after service, with copies thereof to be sent by the court to every other party (Ord 48, r 5).

The registrar may hear the application in chambers (Ord 48, r 7). Application for an interim order may be made on notice under Ord 13, r 1 (Ord 48, r 6). The court may order other parties to be added (Ord 48, r 4).

The court may transfer the proceedings to the High Court (Ord 48, r 9).

The personal representatives must produce at the hearing of an application under the Inheritance (Provision for Family and Dependants) Act of 1975 the probate or letters of administration. If an order or an interim order is made, a sealed copy of the order is sent by the court to the principal Registry of the Family Division at Somerset House, Strand, London WC2R 1LP. With the order is sent the probate or letters of administration so that a memorandum of the order may be endorsed thereon or permanently annexed thereto. The probate of letters of administration is returned after the memorandum has been made (Ord 48, r 8).

Chapter 32

Domestic Violence and Matrimonial Proceedings Act 1976: Non-Molestation of Spouse or Co-Habitee, and Matrimonial Homes Act 1983; Ouster of Spouse

The Domestic Violence and Matrimonial Proceedings Act 1976

This Act provides (s 1) that on an application by a party to a marriage, a county court has power to grant an injunction (whether or not any other relief is sought in the proceedings):

    (*a*) restraining the other party to the marriage from molesting the applicant;

    (*b*) restraining the other party from molesting a child living with the applicant;

    (*c*) excluding the other party from the matrimonial home or a part of the matrimonial home or from a specified area in which the matrimonial home is included;

    (*d*) requiring the other party to permit the applicant to enter and remain in the matrimonial home or a part of the matrimonial home.

This section also applies where a man and women are living with each other in the same household as husband and wife (s 1(2)).

Where the judge grants an injunction to a party to a marriage containing a provision:

    (*a*) restraining the other party to the marriage from using violence against the applicant;

    (*b*) restraining the other party from using violence against a child living with the applicant; or

(c)   excluding the other party from the matrimonial home
       or from a specified area in which the matrimonial home
       is included the judge may, if he is satisfied both that the
       other party has caused actual bodily harm to the applicant
       or child concerned, and that he is likely to do so again,
       attach a power of arrest to the injunction (s 2(1)).

Procedure

Ord 47, r 8 applies (see also 'Commencement of Proceedings',
Chapter 5 'Originating Applications').

Special requirements

Ord 13, r 6(3):
(a)   if interim injunction applied for ex parte affidavit in
       support and a copy for service;
(b)   if interim injunction applied for on notice, then notice
       of application and copy for service;
(c)   except in case of urgency, draft injunction to submit
       to judge (Ord 13, r 6(6)—(but most courts have their
       own proforma for draft order and themselves write up
       the draft for signature by the judge, and also prepare the
       final sealed order).
       If power of arrest is granted it must be added to the order.
(d)   On the issue of the proceedings, a return day should
       be fixed to allow for service on the respondent not less
       than four days before that date (Ord 47, r 8(3)). Order 7,
       r 10(3) adds a further seven days if postal service is used.
       The application will be heard by the judge in chambers
       unless otherwise ordered (Ord 47, r 8(4)).
(e)   If a power of arrest is attached to the injunction a copy
       of the injunction is delivered by the court to the officer
       in charge of the police station for the applicant's address
       (Ord 47, r 8(5)).
       Any change in the order must be notified by the court to
       the officer in charge of the police station (Ord 47, r 8(6)).
       Fee: see Table of Fees.

Form of order

See Chapter 33, 'Injunctions'. There is no power under the
Domestic Violence Act to order a party to discharge rent, mortgage
or other liabilities—see instead the Matrimonial Homes Act. The

time for which a non-molestation order is to extend should always co-incide with the period for which the power of arrest is to run. A period of three months is usual. See also under Chapter 33.

Undertakings

The power of arrest cannot be attached to an undertaking, though a Penal Notice will be endorsed.

The Matrimonial Homes Act 1983

Section 1(1) of this Act provides that where one spouse is legally entitled to occupy the matrimonial home and the other spouse is not, the latter has, if in occupation, a right with the leave of the court to enter into and occupy the home.

Section 9(1) provides for the court to control occupation where both parties have a legal estate in the property.

Section 1(2) of the MHA provides that the court may make an order:

 (*a*) declaring, enforcing, restricting or terminating rights of occupation, or

 (*b*) prohibiting, suspending or restricting the exercise by either spouse of the right to occupy the dwellinghouse, or

 (*c*) requiring either spouse to permit the exercise by the other of that right.

In addition, the court may make an order in relation to a part of the home only and may order either spouse to discharge obligations to meet liabilities for rent, mortgage, etc or for repairs (see s 1(3)).

Procedure

Order 47, r 4 applies (see also Chapter 5, 'Commencement of Proceedings'—'Originating applications').

If there are matrimonial proceedings within the meaning of s 32 of the Matrimonial and Family Proceedings Act 1984 (viz suits for judicial separation, divorce or nullity) or an application under s 17 of the Married Women's Property Act 1882 pending in a county court between the parties, the application must be made under Ord 13, in those proceedings (Ord 47, r 4(4) and (7)).

Special points

Where the application is for an order terminating the respondent's rights of occupation and it appears to the registrar, on the ex parte application of the applicant, that the respondent is not in occupation of the dwelling house to which the application relates and his whereabouts cannot after reasonable enquiries be ascertained, the registrar may dispense with service of the application on the respondent and hear and determine the application (Ord 47, r 4(5)).

Note Return date to be not less than twenty-one days after issue. Application could be made to abridge time limit. Fee: see Table of Fees.

Hearing

The applications are heard and determined in chambers unless the court otherwise directs (Ord 47, r 4(1)). They can be heard by the judge or registrar (Ord 47, r 4(2)) save that a judge only may make an ouster order (ibid). An application to remove a Matrimonial Homes Act caution, notice etc, from the Land Register may be heard by a registrar.

Form of order

The order should so far as practicable be in the form laid down in s 1(2): per Lord Brandon in *Richards* v *Richards* [1983] 2 All ER 807.

The court may make an order in relation to a part of the home only, and may also order either spouse to discharge obligations to meet liabilities for rent, mortgage etc, or for repairs (s 1(3)).

Choice of the Domestic Violence Act, the Matrimonial Homes Act or a combination

The choice will depend on the status of the applicants (viz are they spouses in a subsisting marriage or co-habitees), the remedy desired, the case which can be proved in accordance with established or statutory criteria, and, to a degree, on the permanency or relative permanency of the order likely to be made, and on its urgency. The Abstract below may afford some guide.

Applications where they are necessary to be made under both the Domestic Violence Act and the Matrimonial Homes Act (eg by a spouse seeking an ouster order under MHA and a non-molestation order under the Domestic Violence Act) must be made in separate applications because there is no provision in Ord 5 ('Causes of action and parties') for ongoing applications (by which such applications are commenced) to be made jointly in one matter. In making the decision as to whether the application is proper to be made under the Domestic Violence Act or the Matrimonial Homes Act, it will be noted that the rules distinguish venue (see Abstract below) under the two Acts and provide for different periods to be given for the respective return dates. The application of the rules appears to vary widely in different courts and when proceeding in a court with which the applicant is not familiar, inquiry should be made.

Committal after arrest

The respondent must be brought before a judge by the police if they have arrested him under the power of arrest (see Domestic Violence Act s 2(3), (4) and (5)). Arrest may be effected albeit the order has not been served. The police and the court will notify the applicant and her solicitor of the place of hearing. The hearing will take place within twenty-four hours before a judge, but not necessarily a judge at the original court, as there may be none available. Copies of the police statement taken from the applicant, and respondent if at all, will be available and oral evidence, including that of witnesses, will be heard, making generally for an extensive hearing, particularly as the judge invariably ensures that the respondent has legal aid and is represented, as the respondent's committal to prison will be in issue. The judge approves the grant of legal representation under reg 19 of the Legal Advice and Assistance Regulations (No 2) 1980. The applicant and her solicitor or counsel and the arresting officer will all attend the hearing. Evidence at such a hearing will be oral and on oath, and Ord 29, r 1(4) does not apply thereto.

Although the male gender is referred to, non-molestation orders with power of arrest, may of course be made against either a male or female party.

Abstract

Statute	Status of applicant	Ex-parte or inter-partes	Case to be made out	Criteria	Remedy	Likely duration of order	Venue
Domestic Violence and Matrimonial Proceedings Act 1976.	(a) Spouse, whether residing with other spouse or not. (b) A cohabitee (who may be a divorcee after decree absolute) living in the same household as husband and wife.	Ex-parte if urgent but if for ouster, only if necessary for protection. If inter-partes, minimum of four days' notice required. (two days if in 'matrimonial proceedings').	Fear of violence.	Basically, the DVA was to provide a remedy for 'battered women' and the order to be made is intended as a short-term basis of dealing with the problem. *Spindlow* v *Spindlow* [1978] 3 WLR 777. Violence is not a pre-requisite to granting an ouster injunction if primary need is a home for the children.	(a) A non-molestation order, and (b) If the other party has caused actual bodily harm to the applicant or child and the judge considers he is likely to do so again, a power of arrest: (s 2(1)). (c) An ouster where the parties are cohabitees (which may be granted irrespective of any right of property): *David* v *Johnson* [1978] 2 WLR 553, HL. BUT, in the case of married couples applications for ouster injunctions can now only be made under the Matrimonial Homes Act 1983 (per *Richards v Richards*	'Up to three months is likely to suffice': Practice Direction of President of Family Division, [1978] 1 WLR 1123. *Freeman v Collins* [1983] NLJ 1000, CA. If local authority is re-housing, an ouster of only one month may be appropriate.	Any county court, not necessarily a divorce county court, for the district where the property is situate (spouse or co-habitee), or where the applicant resides (spouse).

| Matrimonial Homes Act 1983 ss 1 and 9. | Spouse of a subsisting marriage (viz not after decree absolute). | Inter-partes with return date not less than twenty-one days after issue. (two days if in 'matrimonial proceedings'). | As in 'criteria'. | The particular criteria for the granting of an ouster injunction is as laid down in s 1(3) of the Matrimonial Homes Act 1983 (per Lord Hailsham in *Richards v Richards* (above), viz 'On an application for an order under this section, the court may make such order as it thinks just and reasonable having regard to the conduct of the spouses in relation to each other and otherwise to their respective needs and financial resources, to the needs of any children and to all the circumstances of the case . . .' | (above)), and must be made by way of a separate application. | An ouster order, but the court's powers are confined to regulating occupation, not ownership. If a non-molestation order is required, application must be made under the DVA. | Orders under this section may, in so far as they have a continuing effect, be limited so as to have effect for a period specified in the order (s 1(4)). The normal 'rule' is that these ouster orders should last for three months. Longer periods can be ordered, see *Fairweather v Kolosine* (1983) 133 NLJ 785, CA, fifteen years. | County court for the district in which the applicant or respondent resides or the matrimonial home is situated (Ord 47, r 8(2)). |

Chapter 33

Injunctions

Injunctions, being orders which if disobeyed can result in committal to prison, need to be drafted with great care.

The general procedure as to making application for them is contained in Ord 13; r 6, and is dealt with in Chapter 10 under 'Injunctions before and at trial'.

Notes on drafting

1   Any injunction must be endorsed with a penal notice in N 77 by the court (Ord 29, r 1(3)). This should be in block capitals on the front of the injunction (N 16).

2   The time within which a mandatory injunction is to be obeyed must be clearly stated (Ord 22, r 3). 'Forthwith' or 'forthwith on service' is sufficient where proper (but see also Chapter 16 under 'a judgment . . . to do any act').

3   In general no committal may be ordered for breach of a mandatory injunction to do an act within a certain time, unless the injunction endorsed with penal notice in N 77 was served before that time expired (Ord 29, r 1(2)(*b*)), but for exceptions see again Chapter 16. Injunctions may need updating by the judge from time to time if service is delayed.

4   The injunction should be complete in itself, so that the defendant knows what he must, or must not, do. Thus, if he is to be excluded from visiting an office the address should be stated in detail, not as 'the address in the particulars of claim'. He may, for example, have been served with an injunction before the claim was issued (Ord 13, r 6(4)).

5   The order should be enforceable in practice. (Thus as an example, it may be impracticable in a small town to order

the defendant not to come within a mile of the address, though equally it may be possible in a large city.)

6 Apart from costs, other orders, eg granting custody, should be in a separate document. Failure to observe this practice has often resulted in such orders being unintentionally cancelled or lapsing with the injunction.

7 The mandatory (or positive) part of an order should be clearly separated from the prohibitory (or negative) part. This is especially important in the case of an interim injunction granted ex parte. Thus a prohibition from returning to an address in an ex parte order should be included in the negative portion which usually runs until the court further hears the matter.

8 Where a power of arrest is attached to an injunction under the Domestic Violence and Matrimonial Proceedings Act 1976, the power of arrest and the injunction should cease at the same time; otherwise confusion and false arrest can result. If there is need, the injunction can be renewed, preferably by making a fresh injunction (Practice Direction of 21 July 1978, [1978] 1 WLR 1123). The power of arrest can only attach to a non-molestation order, viz not to 'an ouster'.

A sample form of interim injunction for domestic violence and a general form are provided below.

9 If an injunction is made, the court office will prepare the engrossment for sealing, and the judge will sign it; the draft should have been prepared and submitted by the solicitors, but where, as is now often the case, the court has its own proforma, a draft from the solicitors is not called for.

10 It is inappropriate in matrimonial and children's matters concerning personal conduct for an undertaking as to damages to be given: Practice Direction (Family Division [1974] 2 All ER 400). Save in the Chancery Division, such undertakings as to damages are not given where in lieu of an Injunction a party for any purpose undertakes.

In the Snodgrass County Court

Case No:
or
8—D

IN THE MATTER OF The Domestic Violence and Matrimonial Proceedings Act 1976

BETWEEN   Applicant
AND   Respondent

Interim Injunction

UPON HEARING [Counsel etc]

IT IS ORDERED THAT the respondent in this matter whether by himself, his servants, agents or otherwise do
[mandatory or positive orders eg 'vacate 6 Green Park, Blueships'— the time and date limited must be clearly stated]

AND IT IS FURTHER ORDERED THAT the respondent in this action, by himself, his servants, agents or otherwise be restrained from [negative or prohibitory orders eg 'returning to 6 Green Park, Blueships' or 'molesting the applicant']
until the day after the day upon which this matter shall be heard, or until further order, or until   the   day of   19 at o'clock when this court will consider whether this order shall be further continued.

AND the judge being satisfied that the respondent has caused actual bodily harm to the applicant [or the child concerned] and being of opinion that he is likely to do so again, a power of arrest is attached to this injunction whereby any constable may arrest without warrant a person whom he has reasonable cause for suspecting of being in breach of the injunction as mentioned in Section 2(3) of the Domestic Violence and Matrimonial Proceedings Act 1976.

This order and power of arrest expire(s) on the   day of 19–
Liberty to apply/restore

AND IT IS FURTHER ORDERED (provision as to costs).

To   (the Respondent) of

TAKE NOTICE THAT unless you obey the directions contained in this order you will be guilty of contempt of court, and will be liable to be committed to prison.

Dated this   day of   19

Judge

Address all communications to the Chief Clerk AND QUOTE THE ABOVE NO. OF MATTER

The court office at

is open from 10 am to 4 pm Monday to Friday.

In the Snodgrass County Court   Case No:
BETWEEN   Plaintiff
AND   Defendant

Interim Injunction
The plaintiff undertaking by his counsel [or solicitor] to abide by
any order this court may make for the payment of damages in case
this court shall hereafter find that the defendant has sustained any
loss or damage by reason of this order IT IS ORDERED THAT
the defendant in this action whether by himself, his servants, agents
or otherwise do
[mandatory or positive orders eg 'admit the plaintiff to the
1st floor flat at 9 Updown Lane, Pittdown and return the keys
thereof to the plaintiff'—the time and date limited must be clearly
stated]

AND IT IS FURTHER ORDERED THAT the defendant in this
action by himself, his servants, agents or otherwise be restrained
from [negative or prohibitory orders eg 'breaching the plaintiffs'
quiet enjoyment of the said flat']
until the day after the day upon which this action shall be heard,
or until further order, or until   the   day of   19   upon
which day this court will consider whether this order shall be
further continued.

To   (the Respondent) of

TAKE NOTICE THAT unless you obey the directions contained
in this order you will be guilty of contempt of court, and will be
liable to be committed to prison.

Dated this   day of   19

Judge

Address all communications to the Chief Clerk AND QUOTE
THE ABOVE CASE NUMBER

The court office at

is open from 10 am to 4 pm Monday to Friday.

Chapter 34

Solicitors: Discrimination

Solicitors Act 1974

No action may be brought by a solicitor to recover costs due to him, whether for contentious or non-contentious business, before the expiration of one month from the date on which a bill in due form is delivered to his client (s 69(1), (2) of the 1974 Act).

As to county court jurisdiction to enforce and set aside agreements, under ss 62 and 63 of the Solicitors Act 1974, if not more than £50 is payable, see s 61(6), ibid.

Where a bill of costs relates wholly or partly to contentious business done in a county court and the amount does not exceed £5,000, any county court in which any part of the business was done has jurisdiction under ss 69, 70, 71 of the act (s 69(3), ibid).

An application under the Act is made by originating application and determined by a registrar (Ord 49, r 18).

Fees, see Table of Fees.

Where an order has been made for the taxation of the costs as between solicitor and client, the solicitor must lodge his bill within fourteen days of the order (Ord 38, rr 21(6), 20(1)).

Thereupon, the court sends notice of the appointment for taxation to the applicant and any other party entitled to be heard. Notice must be not less than fourteen clear days (Ord 38, rr 21(5), 20(2)(a)).

Sex Discrimination Act 1975

Proceedings under the Act are governed by Ord 49, r 17. The Act and the rule should be studied in *The County Court Practice*.

Race Relations Act 1976

The Lord Chancellor designates certain county courts for the purposes of the Act (s 67); see the Civil Courts Order 1983 (SI 1983 No 713) (as amended).

The proceedings for making complaints and for taking proceedings are to be found in the Act, and as to proceedings only, in Ord 49, r 17. Both may be studied in *The County Court Practice*.

Chapter 35

Miscellaneous

Insolvency

The courts having jurisdiction in insolvency are the High Court and certain county courts (s 117 of the Insolvency Act 1986). The directory at the end of *The County Court Practice* shows which courts exercise insolvency ('bankruptcy') jurisdiction. For procedure see *Williams on Bankruptcy* and *Insolvency* by S Frieze (Longman) 1989.

For Deeds of Arrangement see *Williams on Bankruptcy* and *The County Court Practice*.

Companies

Those county courts shown as having jurisdiction in 'bankruptcy' also have jurisdiction in company matters. Reference should be made to *Palmer on Company Law* for detail on company proceedings.

It should be noted that procedure and practice in 'Insolvency' and 'Companies' is not governed by the County Court Rules but by the Acts and Rules specific to those subjects.

Bills of sale

The Bills of Sale Act (1878) Amendment Act 1882, the Act of 1878 and the Bills of Sale (Local Registration) Rules 1960 apply.

A register of bills of sale is kept in county courts outside the 'London Bankruptcy District' of those bills of sale made, that is, granted, by persons residing in its district or if the goods are situated within its district. For the London Bankruptcy District see

RSC, Ord 95 and notes in *The Supreme Court Practice*. Copies of the bills of sale may be inspected by the public. There is no fee for searching the index in the county court, though there is a fee payable in the High Court.

Certified bailiffs

The Law of Distress Amendment Acts of 1888 and 1895 and the Distress for Rent Rules 1983 apply.

No person may act as a bailiff to levy any distress for rent unless he is authorised to act as a bailiff by a certificate in writing under the hand of a county court judge or, subject to rules made under the Act, a registrar (s 7 of the 1888 Act).

Certificates may be general or specific. A general certificate, which may be granted only by a judge, authorises the bailiff named in it to levy at any place in England or Wales. A special certificate is granted by a judge or registrar for a particular distress. A certificate may not be granted to an officer of a county court.

A certificate otherwise may be granted to any applicant who satisfies the court that he is a fit and proper person to hold it, who does not carry on the business of buying debts, and who gives an undertaking that he will not levy distress at any premises in respect of which he is regularly employed in person to collect a weekly rent. He shall be required to give security (ibid rr 7–10).

A general certificate remains in effect until the following 1 February and may be renewed for a successive period of twelve months.

A special certificate, unless directed, is effective for one month from issue.

Fees, on application for certificate or its renewal, see Table of Fees.

A table of fees, charges and expenses chargeable by a certificated bailiff appears as Appendix 1 to the Distress for Rent Rules 1983 (see *The County Court Practice*).

Application for a certificate is made in Form 3 in the 1983 Rules.

Administration orders

Order 39 applies.

Where the whole indebtedness of a judgment debtor does not exceed £5,000, the court, in whose district he resides or carries on business, may make an administration order in respect of his debts. The order provides for the debtor to pay these in full or to such extent as under the circumstances appears to the court to be practicable. The debtor pays instalments into court. There must be at least one judgment debt.

Sections 112–117 of the 1984 Act apply.

The debtor files a request (N 92) which is supplied by the court. This form lists the debtor's creditors and the amount of each debt and sets out his means (Ord 39, r 2(1)).

On an oral examination under Ord 25, r 3, if a debtor furnishes on oath a list of his creditors with amounts owing and details of his resources (N 93) the court may proceed as if a request had been filed (Ord 39, r 2(2)).

An administration order may be made under the Attachment of Earnings Act 1971, s 4 on an application for an attachment of earnings order where the court orders the debtor to furnish a list of his creditors (in N 93) with amounts owing. Unless otherwise directed the debtor must file the list within fourteen days (Ord 39, r 2(3)). An attachment of earnings order may also be made to secure payment under an administration order on the application of a scheduled creditor (Attachment of Earnings Act 1971, s 3(1) (b)) or of the court's own motion on review of an order (Ord 39, r 14(1)(d)). Notice of hearing of an application for an administration order is sent to the creditors (N 373). The application may be heard by the registrar. The order (N 94) is administered and enforced by the chief clerk or other officer of the court (Ord 39, r 13).

After an administration order has been made, dividends are declared from time to time and distributed to the creditors (Ord 39, r 17 (N 377).

The order may be reviewed and on the review it may be varied, suspended or revoked (Ord 39, rr 13(3), (4), 14). See N 374 and 95.

Chapter 36

Costs: Administration of Funds: Time

Order 38 applies and incorporates RSC Ord 62, Pt II: rules 12, 14, 15, 16, 24 and 26 to 28 thereof and para 1(2) of Appendix 2 thereto.

Bases of costs

These were substantially altered by rr 8, 9, 12 and 15 of the County Court (Amendment) Rules 1986 [SI 1986 No 636 (L3)]. But where the judgment, order or event giving rise to an immediate taxation of costs occurred before 28 April, 1986 the old bases of taxation apply for which see the previous edition of this book. The new figures for witness fees and in costs Appendix A do not apply to anything done before that date. However, where costs fall to be fixed or assessed under Appendices B or C the new rates apply whenever the proceedings began (ibid r 24).

Costs are now awarded and taxed in both the High Court and county court on the 'standard' or 'indemnity basis' but in the county court solicitors' charges are confined to the scales which are retained in Appendix A to Ord 38 (Ord 38, rr 3, 4 and 5); witness fees are limited by Ord 38, rr 13, 14 and 15 and interpreters' fees by r 16.

Subject to these specific rules, the two bases of costs are as follows.

(a) the standard basis

On this basis, a reasonable amount is to be allowed in respect of all costs reasonably incurred, any doubt as to the reasonableness of incurrence or amount being resolved in favour of the payer.

(b) the indemnity basis

On this basis all costs are allowed unless they are of an unreasonable amount or have been unreasonably incurred, any doubt being resolved in favour of the payee.

If neither basis is specified, costs are taxed on the standard basis. (Ord 38, r 19A and RSC Ord 62, r 12).

The standard basis

The standard basis applies (unless otherwise ordered):
- (a) where one party to a proceedings is ordered to pay another party's costs;
- (b) where an order is made for payment of costs out of any fund (including the Legal Aid Fund) or;;
- (c) where no order for costs is required—the court may order the indemnity basis in any of these cases (Ord 38, r 1(3) and RSC Ord 62, r 3(3) and (4)). No order is required where a payment into court is accepted and in the other cases set out in RSC Ord 62, r 5 (Ord 38, r 1(3)).

The indemnity basis

The indemnity basis applies (unless otherwise ordered):
- (a) to the costs of a trustee or personal representative (RSC Ord 62, r 14(1));
- (b) to a solicitor's bill to his own client (save for a Legal Aid taxation) RSC Ord 62, r 15(1));
- (c) to the costs of a minor or patient (RSC Ord 62, r 16) (Ord 38, r 19A).

Discretion

Costs are in the discretion of the court (ord 38, r 1(2)). If the court, in the exercise of its discretion sees fit to make any order as to the costs of any proceedings the court shall follow the event except where it appears to the court that some other order should be made as to the whole or any part of the costs (Ord 38, r 1(3) and RSC Ord 62, r 3(2) and (3)).

In particular, the court may award a specific proportion of taxed costs from or up to a specified stage of the proceedings or a specified sum (Ord 38, r 1(3) and RSC Ord 62, r 7(4)).

The court in exercising its discretion as to costs shall consider, or take into account:

(*a*)   any offer of contribution brought to its attention in accordance with Ord 12, r 7;

(*b*)   any payment of money into court and the amount of such payment;

(Where the defendant pays into court the same or a larger sum than the plaintiff recovers in respect of this claim including any interest which may be awarded pursuant to s 69 of the 1984 Act under the judgment, the plaintiff recovers costs until payment in, on the scale appropriate to the amount recovered, and the defendant recovers costs from the date of payment in, on the scale appropriate to the sum claimed and similarly, where it is the plaintiff who makes payment into court in satisfaction of a counterclaim, reversing the references to plaintiff and defendant);

(*c*)   a written offer, for example, to consent in specific terms to an injunction or declaration, provided that the court shall not take such an offer into account if, at the time it was made, the party making it could have protected his position as to costs by means of a payment into court (Ord 38, r 1(3) and RSC Ord 62, r 9(*d*) and Ord 11, r 10);

(*d*)   in the case of an assisted person, the effect of s 8(1)(*e*) of the Legal Aid Act 1974. The discretion of the court to award costs against an assisted person is limited by the section to the amount (if any) which is reasonable for him to pay having regard to all the circumstances, including the means of all the parties, and of their conduct in connection with the dispute. Before the amount of any costs which might be awarded against an assisted person can be decided, his means must be determined (Reg 117 of the Legal Aid (General Regulations) 1980). Regulations 118 to 125 set out the criteria and procedure for determining means in such circumstances. Regulation 126 provides protection in respect of costs for next friends or guardians of assisted minor or patient—and see 'Legal Aid Costs' below.

Stage of proceedings at which costs to be taxed

Generally the costs of any proceedings shall not be taxed until the conclusion of the cause or matter in which the proceedings arise. However, if it appears to the court when making an order for costs that all or any part of the costs ought to be taxed at an earlier stage it may order accordingly unless the person against whom the order for costs is made is a legally aided person (Ord 13, r 1(9)) and RSC Ord 62, r 8(1) and (3).

In an action in which provisional damages are awarded under RSC Ord 29, Part II the conclusion of the cause or matter is construed as a reference to the conclusion of the proceedings in which the provisional damages are awarded, notwithstanding the possibility that the plaintiff may claim further damages at a future date.

Lastly, where it appears to a taxing officer on application that there is no likelihood of any further order being made in a cause or matter he may tax forthwith the costs of any interlocutory proceedings which have taken place (Ord 38, r 1(3) and RSC Ord 62, r 8)

Liability for costs

In determining where the costs shall lie, the court makes orders in one or other of the following standard forms:

Term	Effect
'Costs' (the party entitled is designated)	(a) Where this order is made in interlocutory proceedings, the party in whose favour it is made shall be entitled to his costs in respect of those proceedings whatever the outcome of the cause or matter in which the proceedings arise; and (b) where this order is made at the conclusion of a cause or matter, the party in whose favour it is made shall be entitled to have his costs taxed forthwith.
'Costs reserved'	The party in whose favour an order for costs is made at the conclusion of the cause or matter in which the proceedings arise shall be entitled to his costs

'Costs in any event' (the party entitled is designated)

'Costs in the cause' or 'costs in application'

'Plaintiff's costs in the cause' or 'Defendant's costs in the cause'

'Costs thrown away' (the party entitled is designated)

of the proceedings in respect of which this order is made unless the court orders otherwise.

This order has the same effect as an order for 'costs' made in interlocutory proceedings;

The party in whose favour an order for costs is made at the conclusion of the cause or matter in which the proceedings arise shall be entitled to his costs of the proceedings in respect of which such an order is made.

The plaintiff or defendant, as the case may be, shall be entitled to his costs of the proceedings in respect of which such an order is made if judgment is given in his favour in the cause or matter in which the proceedings arise, but he shall not be liable to pay the costs of any other party in respect of those proceedings if judgment is given in favour of any other party or parties in the cause or matter in question.

Where proceedings, or any part of them, have been ineffective, or have been subsequently set aside, the party in whose favour this order is made shall be entitled to his costs of those proceedings, or that part of the proceedings, in respect of which it is made (Ord 38, r 1(3) and RSC Ord 62, r 3(6)).

Costs on claim and counterclaim

(i) where the claim succeeds and the counterclaim fails, or vice versa, judgment is entered for the plaintiff (or defendant) on both claim and counterclaim with a likely order for costs on claim and on counterclaim on the appropriate scale or scales;

(ii) where the claim and the counterclaim are both wholly, or both partially, successful, or where both fail, there should generally be two judgments with, if appropriate, a final set-off as to damages and two orders for costs, with a final set-off after taxation. The registrar on taxation will then treat the claim as if it stood alone, and allow as costs of the counterclaim only the amount by which the costs have been increased by reason of the counterclaim.

Giving two separate judgments in favour of the plaintiff and the defendant respectively and making two orders for costs may, however, be unjust for cases where the issues on the claim and the counterclaim are substantially the same or 'are very much interlocked', or wherever the counterclaim is a set-off. For example, this might apply in a road collision case, where often the only different issues are the damages themselves as claimed by the respective parties. In these cases, the principles in *Medway Oil and Storage Co* v *Continental Contractors* [1929] AC 88 apply and the plaintiff will be allowed the full costs of proving the common issues as to liability, and as to his damages, whilst the defendant will be allowed only the costs of proving his damages. For instance, a defendant may be given a net judgment in his favour where he is awarded 50 per cent of, say, £6,000 on his counterclaim, and the plaintiff 50 per cent of, say, £2,000 on his claim, which, on set-off, provides for a net judgment of £2,000 in favour of the defendant. In such a case it may be put to the court that it should exercise its discretion as to costs with consideration for the results of the order so as to avoid an incongruous outcome, and that an order might properly be made so that costs are awarded to the party who in effect succeeds after a set-off is made in respect of the damages. The scale applicable would then be the scale appropriate to the net balance recovered; in the example given above, costs for the defendant on scale 2 on his net judgment of £2,000.

An unsuccessful defendant may be ordered to pay the costs of a successful co-defendant direct (a 'Sanderson order' from the case *Sanderson* v *Blyth Theatre Co* [1903] 2 KB 533, CA). Again, the court may order that plaintiff to pay the successful defendant's costs, and to add such costs to his own, all to be paid by the unsuccessful co-defendant (a 'Bullock order' from

Bullock v *London General Omnibus Co* [1907] 1 KB 264, CA).
Such orders are in the discretion of the court.

Legal aid taxation

The court has no power to refuse to make an order for
legal aid taxation (Legal Aid Act 1974, s 10(1) and 2 A).

Solicitor's charges and disbursements

In the county court these are subject to the limitations of
Ord 38, r 3(1).

Money claims

(i) Scales applicable to money claims

Sum of Money	Scale
Exceeding £25 but not exceeding £100	Lower scale
Exceeding £100 but not exceeding £500	Scale 1
Exceeding £500 but not exceeding £3,000	Scale 2
Exceeding £3,000	Scale 3

No party and party costs may be ordered in actions for money
only where the judgment does not exceed £25 unless the judge or
registrar certifies that a difficult question of law or complexity of
fact is involved; he may then certify costs to be on such scale as
he thinks fit (Ord 38, rr 3(4) and 4(6)).

(ii) Determination of scale in money claims

The scale of costs in an action for money only is determined
as follows:

(a) the costs of the plaintiff, by the amount recovered or
accepted;

(b) the costs of the defendant, by the amount claimed;

(c) the costs of a third party, by the amount claimed against
him;

(d) the costs payable by a third party, by the amount
recovered against him (Ord 38, r 4(1), (2)).

Counterclaims

Where in an action for recovery of money only there is a counterclaim for money only, then the scale is determined as follows:

(*a*) the costs of the defendant, by the amount recovered;

(*b*) the costs of the plaintiff, by the amount claimed (Ord 38, r 4(3)).

Actions transferred from the High Court

If at the date of transfer the amount in dispute is less than the original claim, the defendants' costs in the county court are determined by the amount remaining in dispute (Ord 38, r 4(4)).

Garnishee proceedings

Substitute 'judgment creditor' for 'plaintiff' and 'judgment debtor' for 'defendant' in (ii) (*a*) and (*b*) above (Ord 38, r 4(5)).

Certificate as to complexity

If in any proceedings, whatever the amount claimed, the trial court gives a certificate as to a difficult question of law or exceptional complexity of facts, then the court may award costs on such scale as it thinks fit (Ord 38, r 4(6)).

Determination of costs in certain other claims

In claims arising in non-money, mixed, equity and admiralty proceedings and in claims where the title to a hereditament is in question and in possession proceedings the scale is fixed by the trial court or the registrar on taxation (Ord 38, r 4(7)).

Companies Acts and insolvency

Special rules apply to costs in proceedings under the Companies Acts and in insolvency.

Costs in cases referred to arbitration

Where in proceedings the sum claimed (or involved) does not exceed £500 and there has been an automatic reference to arbitration (Ord 19, r 2(3)) which has not been revoked (Ord 19, r 2(4)), then no solicitor's charges are allowed save:

(*a*) solicitor's fixed costs on summons (see below);

(*b*) costs of enforcement;

(*c*) costs certified by the arbitrator as having been incurred by unreasonable conduct in relation to the proceedings or claim (Ord 19, r 6).

This rule does not exclude proper disbursements and witnesses' allowances and fees.

Where the amount recovered or claimed exceeds £500 solicitor's charges are allowable in the normal way (Ord 19, r 5(2); Term No 8).

Discontinued proceedings

The scale is determined by the registrar on taxation according to the amount claimed.

Court fees

These are allowable whatever the nature of the proceedings, but plaint fees are recoverable appropriate only to the sum recovered (Ord 38, r 3(5)).

The scale items

(*a*) The registrar on taxation has a discretion of what to allow within the range up to the maximum specified bearing in mind the principles applied in the Supreme Court for similar items. Such principles also apply where no amount is specified in the scale.

(*b*) If the trial court at the hearing or on application on notice served within fourteen days thereof so certifies, or if the trial court has not directed to the contrary, then if the registrar on taxation considers that from the nature of the case or its conduct the costs allowed on taxation may be inadequate, he may on taxation exceed the maximum on any item except item 5 but must have regard to the maximum for the item in the next higher scale (if any) (Ord 38, r 9).

In exercising his discretion, the taxing officer shall have regard to all the relevant circumstances, and in particular to:

(*a*) the complexity of the item or of the cause or matter in which it arises and the difficulty or novelty of the question involved;

(*b*) the skill, specialised knowledge and responsibility required of, and the time and labour expended by, the solicitor or counsel;

(*c*) the number and importance of the documents (however brief) prepared or perused;

(*d*) the place and circumstances in which the business involved is transacted;

(*e*) the importance of the cause or matter to the client;

(*f*) where money or property is involved, its amount or value;

(*g*) any other fees and allowances payable to the solicitor or counsel in respect of other items in the same cause or matter but only where work done in relation to those items has reduced the work which would otherwise have been necessary in relation to the item in question (Ord 38, r 5 and RSC Ord 62, Appendix 2, para 1(2)).

Disallowances and allowances against successful party

(*a*) Any scale item may be disallowed by the trial court (Ord 38, r 6).

(*b*) The cost of proving any admitted matter once properly admitted shall be disallowed (Ord 9, r 16(2); Ord 20, r 1).

(*c*) Failure to admit documents or facts or requiring proof thereof, or to comply with a notice to admit facts after service of a 'Notice to admit' results in the cost of proof being borne by the party failing to admit or requiring proof, unless the court otherwise orders (Ord 20, rr 2 and 3).

(*d*) In collision actions, the costs of preparing a plan other than a sketch plan shall be disallowed unless the court authorised this before trial or the registrar is satisfied on taxation that it was reasonable (Ord 38, r 10).

(*e*) The costs of amending any summons or pleading without leave or where leave is required fall on the party so amending (Ord 38, r 1(3) and RSC Ord 62, r 6(5)).

(*f*) The costs of any application to extend time shall be

borne by the party making the application (Ord 38, r 1(3) and RSC Ord 62, r 6(6)).

(g) Misconduct or neglect in the conduct of any proceedings. Where it appears to the court that anything has been done, or that any omission has been made, unreasonably or improperly by or on behalf of any party, the court may order that the costs of that party in respect of the act or omission, as the case may be, shall not be allowed and that any costs occasioned by it to any other party shall be paid by him to that other party. Instead of making such an order the court may refer the matter to a registrar, in which case he shall deal with the matter under RSC Ord 62, r 28(1); (Ord 38, r 1(3) and RSC Ord 62, r 10)).

Special matters

(a) Costs of inspection under Ord 21, r 6. These are to be paid by the plaintiff and then become 'costs in the proceedings' unless the trial court otherwise orders (Ord 38, r 11).

(b) Non scale items. Reasonable costs are allowed, by comparison with the nearest scale item, if any (Ord 38, r 12(1)).

(c) Conveyancing costs. The sums usually chargeable are to be allowed (Ord 38, r 12(2)).

(d) Interpreters. Fees allowable as witness of fact (Ord 38, r 13) or if the trial court so orders as an expert witness (Ord 38, rr 14, 16(1). (This does not apply to interpreters employed under s 3 of the Welsh Courts Act 1942, Ord 38, r 16(2)).

Costs of litigants in person

Order 38, r 17 applies.

Rules as to the costs of litigants in person are prescribed under the Litigants in Person (Costs and Expenses) Act 1975.

Generally the litigant is treated as if he were a solicitor conducting the case (Ord 38, r 17(1)).

A litigant in person may not be allowed more than £6.50 an hour in respect of the time spent by him in doing any work to which the costs relate if he has not suffered pecuniary loss, and the amount allowed in respect of any work done by the litigant must not in any case exceed two-thirds of the sum which would have been allowed to a solicitor acting for him (Ord 38, r 17(4) and RSC Ord 62, r 18(3)).

Fixed costs in Appendix B are not allowed to litigants in person (Ord 38, r 17(2)).

Costs on Lower Scale are assessed without taxation (Ord 38, r 19(1)). Where costs are on Scales 1, 2 or 3 the costs are assessed without taxation, unless the court otherwise orders (Ord 38, rr 17(3), 19(1)). Costs are assessed under Costs Appendix C.

If the litigant is allowed a charge for attending court to conduct his own case, he is not entitled to a witness allowance in addition (Ord 38, r 17(5)).

'Litigant in person' does not include a practising solicitor acting for himself who may be awarded costs as a solicitor on the record acting in the proceedings.

Witness fees

For witnesses of fact or producing documents (including a party), the maximum is £15 for a police officer or £21.50 for any other person unless the registrar on taxation or assessment thinks this inadequate (Ord 38, r 13).

In addition to his witness fee, any witness's actual travelling and hotel expenses may be allowed (Ord 38, r 15(1)). If called in more than one case, witness fees and expenses may be apportioned (Ord 38, r 15(2)). Any witness's fees and expenses may be allowed if his attendance was necessary, even though he was not called (Ord 38, r 15(3)).

Expert witnesses

For attending court, not less than £21.50 or more than £43 (or £85 on Scale 3) and a qualifying fee, or for a necessary report where no qualifying fee is allowed, of not more than £20.50 (£41 on Scale 3) (Ord 38, r 14(1)).

The trial court (or the registrar on taxation in the absence of a contrary direction by the trial court) may direct that the upper limits shall not apply (Ord 38, r 14(2), (3)).

Restrictions on counsel's fees

Unless the court so orders at the hearing, no counsel's fees are allowed on interlocutory applications or where a defendant to a money claim only, neither delivers a defence nor attends the hearing (Ord 38, r 8(1), (2)). However, in such cases, solicitor's charges may be allowed as if the solicitor and not counsel had conducted the case as advocate (Ord 38, r 8(3)).

Fees of more than one one counsel are allowed only if the court so orders at the hearing (Ord 38, r 8(1)).

Value-added tax

In addition to the amount of costs allowed to a party on taxation or assessment in respect of the supply of goods or services on which value added tax is chargeable, there may be allowed as a disbursement a sum equivalent to value-added tax at the appropriate rate on that amount in so far as the tax is not deductible as input tax by that party (Ord 38, r 7). This does not apply to fixed costs.

Fixed costs

Costs Appendix B, Pt I shows the solicitor's charges to be entered on the summons on issue. Where the case is not covered, the words 'to be taxed' are to be inserted on the summons (Ord 38, r 18).

Costs Appendix B, Pt II shows the sum for solicitor's charges to be added to the summons costs when judgment is entered in cases where broadly there is no defence and the question of mode of payment only is in issue (Ord 38, r 18(1)).

Assessed costs

Solicitor's charges may be assessed within the amounts given in Costs Appendix C. No court fee is payable on the assessment of costs. The following provisions apply:

(a) All costs awarded or payable on the Lower Scale are assessed.

(b) Costs on Scales 1, 2 and 3 may be assessed at the request of the party entitled to taxation (Ord 38, r 19(1)).

(c) Costs on interlocutory applications on Scales 1, 2 and 3, not included in the general costs, may be assessed without taxation unless the court otherwise orders (Ord 38, r 19(3); but see Ord 13, r 1(9)).

(d) The court may ask for details of the sums claimed to be lodged before assessment (Ord 38, r 19(4)). Practitioners may always volunteer details by letter addressed to the court and this often ensures that disbursements are not overlooked.

(e) Litigants in person costs. When these are assessed the Costs Appendix C figures are adjusted (see 'Costs of litigants in person' above).

Agreed costs

Judgment may be entered for costs agreed (Ord 38, r 19(5)). A letter signed by both sides should be lodged. No fee.

Taxation of costs 'inter partes'

(a) The bill (with copy for the 'party entitled to be heard on taxation' and with all necessary papers and vouchers) must be lodged within three months after the order (or event) entitling the party to tax (Ord 38, r 20(1)). It should follow Costs Appendix A.

(Note that a 'party entitled to be heard on taxation' includes not only a party to the proceedings, but a person who has given notice to the party applying for taxation and to the court that he has a financial interest in the taxation or a person so entitled under a registrar's direction. (Ord 38, r 20(4)). Such persons will include those liable as third parties and under 'Sanderson' orders to indemnify defendants and those liable to indemnify plaintiffs under 'Bullock' orders).

(b) The court sends a copy of the bill to anyone entitled to be heard with a notice requiring him to say within fourteen days if he wishes to be heard (form N 252, Ord 38, r 20(2)).

(c) (i) If this person so asks to be heard on taxation the court fixes a taxation and gives not less than 7 days notice to all relevant persons (in form N 254, Ord 38, r 20(3)). The registrar taxes the bill on that date.

(ii) If this person does not so ask, the registrar provisionally taxes the bill and the proper officer notifies the party lodging the bill in form N 253 of the figures allowed and requires that party to give notice within fourteen days if he requires a taxation (Ord 38, r 20(3A)). If notice is so given a taxation is given to that party on not less than seven days' notice (Ord 38, r 3B).

After taxation is complete the solicitor lodging the bill should total it at the court office. A certificate of the amount allowed is issued by the court on payment of the taxing fee (see Table of Fees) and judgment entered. Note, however, the special position as to taxed costs after payment into court (Ord 11, rr 2(3)(*a*), and 3(5)(*a*)) and on discontinuance (Ord 18, r 2(1)) where a request for judgment for the taxed costs to be entered in default of payment within fourteen days after taxation must be lodged.

Counsel's fees

Before the court issues a certificate of the amount allowed, except in legal aid cases, counsel's receipted fee sheet must be produced (Appendix A, item 12, note 3.)

Taxation as between solicitor and his client

The provisions given hereunder apply equally to:
(*a*) costs payable to a solicitor by his own client (usually on an indemnity basis);
(*b*) costs payable to a solicitor out of the legal aid fund (standard basis); and
(*c*) costs payable to a trustee or personal representative out of a fund (indemnity basis) (Ord 38, r 21(1)).

Scales are determined by reference to the amount claimed (Order 38, r 21(2)), but the court ordering the taxation may, after allowing the solicitor to make representations, fix the scale and exercise discretion, grant any certificate, and give directions (Ord 38, r 21(3)).

On taxation, the registrar is not bound by any cost ruling between party and party and he may unless a contrary order has been made exercise the court's powers under Ord 38, r 21(3). However, he may not exceed the maximum of the item on the scale ordered (Ord 38, r 21(4)).

If, when taxing a solicitor's bill against his own client (not Legal Aid) more than one-fifth is disallowed, the solicitor pays the costs of taxation, otherwise the client does. This does not apply where the solicitor asked for taxation and his client fails to attend the taxation nor if otherwise ordered (s 70(9) of the Solicitors Act 1974; Ord 38, r 21(7)).

Where the bill is payable by a client, on receipt of the bill the court gives not less than fourteen days' notice of an appointment to tax to the solicitor and client (Ord 38, r 21(5A)). However, if the bill is payable out of the Legal Aid Fund then, unless a party and party taxation is required or the registrar directs a taxation, the registrar provisionally taxes the bill and the court sends to the solicitor a note of the sum he has provisionally allowed together with a notice requiring the solicitor to inform the court within fourteen days, if he wishes to be heard (Ord 38, r 21(5A)). If he does so inform the court, he will be given not less than seven clear days' notice of an appointment to tax (Ord 38, r 21(5A)).

If taxation is ordered under the Solicitors Act 1974, the bill must be lodged with the court within fourteen days of the order (Order 38, r 21(6)).

Section 9 of the Legal Aid Act 1974

Where a legally-aided party:
(a) has been awarded damages and/or
(b) has recovered or preserved any property in the proceedings the damages and/or property are subject to a charge in favour of the Law Society for that party's solicitor's costs (less any sum paid by that party or recovered from another party) save where the property is exempt under reg 96 of the Legal Aid (General) Regulations 1980 (s 9 of the Legal Aid Act 1974).

Such a legally-aided party (and one paying a contribution towards his costs under s 8(1)(c) of the 1974 Act) has a financial interest in the outcome of the taxation. He may give notice to his solicitor and the court that he has such an interest or the registrar may direct that he is entitled to be heard on taxation. Thereupon the procedure set out above under 'Taxation of costs inter partes' (Ord 38, rr 21(5A) and 20) applies.

Taxation by third parties

The Solicitors Act 1974 s 74 (1) enables third parties to apply for taxation of costs for which they may be liable, for example a mortgagor who may be liable for a mortgagee's costs under a provision in the mortgage deed. The originating application is supported by affidavit and directions are likely before a full hearing, costs being reserved depending on the results finally of the registrar's certificate certifying what costs if any are payable. The application under the section is to be made within fourteen days of delivery (or notification) of the bill.

Legal aid

A solicitor may not lodge a bill for taxation until the work for which the certificate was granted has been completed or the certificate has been discharged or revoked. The area committee may make payment on account of disbursements and counsel's fees from time to time (para 25 of the Legal Aid Scheme 1980).

Disallowance of a solicitor's costs payable from the Legal Aid Fund

See reg 104 of the Legal Aid (General) Regulations 1980.

Taxation of costs awarded by tribunals

See Ord 38, r 22.

Objections and review

The procedure is set out in Ord 38, r 24.

Any party dissatisfied with the taxation of any costs by the registrar may apply to him to reconsider the taxation within fourteen days after taxation. The application must be made on notice. Order 7 applies. No fee. The notice must specify the items in respect of which the application is made and the grounds and reasons for the objections (Ord 38, r 24(1), (2)). On receiving the request, the registrar must reconsider and notify each party of the result and the reasons for his decision (r 24(3)). Any party who is dissatisfied with the registrar's decision on his reconsideration may apply to the judge for a 'review' on notice. Order 13, r 1 applies. Fee: see Table of Fees. The application must be filed within fourteen days of the registrar's reconsideration. The application must specify the items in respect of which the application is made and the grounds and reasons for the review. The judge may, without any application of any party, appoint two assessors to sit with him, one of whom must be a registrar. (See Ord 38, r 24(6)–(8) as to procedure generally.)

Where a party has legal aid, bringing in (ie raising) objections or a request for reconsideration, requires the authority of the appropriate legal aid area committee (Legal Aid (General) Regulations 1980, reg 107) and the authority of the Council of the Law Society to extend the certificate to enable proceedings for a review by a judge (reg 108).

Persons under disability

Costs payable to the plaintiff's solicitors are taxed on an indemnity basis and the solicitor may not lawfully charge more than the amount allowed (Ord 10, r 11(4)–(6), Ord 38, r 19A and RSC Ord 62, r 16).

Reference to costs in instructions to counsel

Counsel, or the solicitor advocate, should come into court instructed to consider asking for orders on the following matters (because even though the registrar has very wide powers when conducting the taxation (see Ord 38, r 21(4)) if not dealt with at the hearing there may be difficulties):

1 Interlocutory hearings
  (a) A certificate for counsel or for more than one counsel (Ord 38, r 8(1)):
  (b) that interpreters be paid as if expert witnesses (Ord 38, r 16).

2 Final hearings
  (a) A certificate for more than one counsel (Ord 38, r 8(1));
  (b) that reserved costs should be dealt with specifically in the final order, otherwise they will be allowed on taxation against the losing party (Ord 38, r 1(3) and RSC Ord 62, r 3(6));
  (c) a certificate of difficult law or exceptionally complex fact where a money claim only is in issue (Ord 38, r 4(6));
  (d) that interpreters be paid as if expert witnesses (Ord 38, r 16).
      For definition of interlocutory see Chapter 19.

Liability of a solicitor for costs

Order 38, r 1(3) and RSC Ord 62, rr 11 and 28 apply.

By RSC Ord 62, rr 11 and 28 wide powers are given to impose personal liability on the solicitor in respect of costs unreasonably or improperly incurred, and these rules are applied in the county court.

Misconduct in the proceedings leading to taxation or in the taxation proceedings

The registrar has wide powers to deal with misconduct or delay in taxing (Ord 38, r 19A and RSC Ord 62, rr 28, 10(1) and 11(1)(*a*)).

Costs of taxation

The party liable to pay the costs of proceedings may make an offer of a specific sum in satisfaction of the costs 'without prejudice save as to the costs of taxation' within fourteen days after delivery of the bill of costs. This may be brought to the attention of the registrar after he has taxed the bill and he can take it into account in dealing with the costs of and the fee payable for taxation. The provision does not apply where the person entitled to costs is a legally aided party (Ord 38, r 19A and RSC Ord 62, r 27).

Administration of funds

See the Court Fund Rules 1987.

Legal aid costs

Payment to solicitors

Solicitors may now await issue of pro-formas by their Legal Aid Area Committees periodically for completion.

Costs awarded against legally aided litigants

An assisted person cannot be ordered to pay costs exceeding the 'amount which is reasonable for him to pay having regard to all the circumstances' including the means of the parties and their connections with the dispute (s 8(1)(*e*) of the Legal Aid Act 1974) but the usual order against an unsuccessful legally aided litigant is for the successful party's costs 'such order not to be enforced without the leave of the court'—and see above, under 'Discretion'.

Payment to successful opponents of legally aided litigants out of public funds

The Legal Aid Act 1974 ss 13 and 14 applies and the court may make an order for payment out of public funds but only if satisfied that such is just and equitable and that the unassisted party will suffer severe financial hardship unless such an order is made. The procedure is contained in regs 127 to 135 of the Legal Aid (General) Regulations 1980.

Time

Computation

Order 1, r 9 should be referred to. Important provisions are as follows:

(*a*) Where the act is required to be done not less than a specified period before a specified date, the period starts immediately after the date on which the act is done and ends immediately before the specified date.

(*b*) Where the act is required to be done within a specified period after or from a specified date, the period starts immediately after that date.

(*c*) Where, apart from the above provisions, the period in question, being a period of three days or less, would include a day on which the court office is closed, that day shall be excluded.

(*d*) Where the time fixed for doing an act in the court office expires on a day on which the office is closed, and for that reason the act cannot be done on that day, the act shall be in time if done on the next day on which the office is open.

Note that any order or judgment requiring a person to do an act (other than to pay money) shall state the time within which the act is to be done (Ord 22, r 3).

This involves two elements:

(*a*) specifying the length of time involved, and

(b)   specifying the date from which time runs. If it is the date of the order the word 'hereafter' should be used; if the date of service the words 'after service of this order' and if any other date it should be stated and 'thereafter' used. (See *Hitachi Sales (UK) Ltd* v *Mitsui Osk Lines Ltd*, (1986) *The Times* 16 April)—and see 'judgment or order to do etc any act'—Chapter 16.

Extension or abridgement of time

Times laid down in the 1981 Rules, or by any judgment, order or direction, may be extended or abridged by consent or by the court on application. Extension may be retrospective (Ord 13, r 4).

A *statutory* time limit cannot be extended, eg the court cannot extend the tenant's time specified in s 29(3) of the Landlord and Tenant Act 1954 for applying for a new tenancy under s 24. But see *Hodgson* v *Armstrong* [1967] 2 QB 299; [1967] 1 All ER 307 and *Riley* v *Eurostile Holdings* [1985] 1 WLR 1139 and 1406 where the court office was closed on the relevant day.

Appendix I

Costs
(CCR, Appendices A–C)

Appendix A
Higher Scales of Costs

Item No		Scale 1 £ 100–500	Scale 2 £ 500–3,000	Scale 3 £ 3,000 +
	PART I			
	PREPARATION OF DOCUMENTS			
	The following items shall not apply to any action or matter to which Part II applies.			
1	*Institution of Proceedings*: Preparing, issuing, filing and service of particulars of claim or originating application, petition, or request for entry of appeal to a county court, or particulars of counterclaim, or third-party notice; preparing preliminary act or pleading in Admiralty action.	*For all Scales* 6·24		
	Note 1 Except where item 14 or Note 2 below applies, no profit charges for service of any process are to be allowed.			
	Note 2 Where a solicitor properly makes use of a process server, the process server's charges are to be shown as a disbursement.			
2	*Interlocutory proceedings*: Preparing, issuing, filing and service of any documents in connection with interlocutory proceedings, including any application or notice of application or notice of interlocutory appeal.	*For all Scales* 6·23		
	(continued overleaf)			

255

Item No		Scale 1 £ 100–500	Scale 2 £ 500–3,000	Scale 3 £ 3,000 +
	Note 1 This item applies to an arbitration, inquiry or reference.			
	Note 2 Interpleader proceedings are to be treated as an application to which this item refers.			
3	*Other Documents:* Preparing (including where necessary filing, serving or delivering to all parties) any documents not otherwise provided for, including–			
	(*a*) any document to obtain an order for substituted service;			
	(*b*) pleadings (other than pleadings instituting proceedings), defence or counterclaim thereto, particulars of pleadings, requests for such particulars, interrogatories, affidavits and lists of documents, notice to produce, admit or inspect documents, and amendments to any documents;			
	(*c*) any other affidavit;			
	(*d*) any brief to counsel or case to counsel to advise in writing or in conference;			
	(*e*) any instructions to counsel to settle any document except where an allowance for the preparation of that document is recoverable under item 1, 2 or 3–			
	for first five A4 pages		*For all Scales* 4·10 per page	
	for each A4 page thereafter		(or proportionately) 2·80 per page (or proportionately)	
	Note 1 Items 1, 2 and 3 include engrossing and one copy for service and are only to be allowed where the document is signed by the solicitor or his clerk duly authorised in that behalf. Any additional copies required are to be charged under item 4. Item 3(*d*) and (*e*) include copy for counsel where counsel's fee is allowed. Preparation of proofs of evidence is to be charged under item 6 and not this item.			

Item No		Scale 1 £ 100–500	Scale 2 £ 500–3,000	Scale 3 £ 3,000 +
	Note 2 Item 3 is not to be allowed for preparing a request for summons etc or a notice of acceptance or non-acceptance of an admission and proposal as to time of payment.			
4	*Copy documents:*			
	(*a*) Typed top copy– (i) A5 (quarto) (ii) A4 (foolscap) (iii) A3 (brief)	*For all Scales* 0·52 per page 0·88 per page 1·20 per page		
	(*b*) Photographic, printed and carbon copies– (i) A5 and A4 (ii) A3	0·18 per page 0·34 per page		
	Note 1 Where the construction of documents is in issue, the costs of copies supplied for the use of the judge are to be allowed.			
	Note 2 Copy documents required to be exhibited to an affidavit are to be charged under item 4 and the collating time is to be charged under item 6, note 2(*a*)(ix).			
	PART II			
5	BLOCK ALLOWANCE			
	In any action for damages for personal injuries, or for the cost of repairs to collision-damaged vehicles, and in any other action or matter as the party entitled to receive the costs may elect, a block allowance shall be made in place of the items prescribed in Part I unless, in any such case, the taxing officer otherwise directs.	*For all Scales* 10·63		
	Note 1 No profit charges for service of any process are to be allowed except (*a*) where item 14 applies or (*b*) where a solicitor properly makes use of a process server, in which case the process server's charges are to be shown as a disbursement.			

(continued overleaf)

Item No		Scale 1 £ 100–500	Scale 2 £ 500–3,000	Scale 3 £ 3,000 +

Note 2 In an action (other than one relating to personal injuries or collision-damage) where a party has elected to insert a block allowance, no application may be made on taxation for an allowance in excess of the permitted maximum.

Note 3 If an action for damages for personal injuries or for collision-damage is of such unusual weight that the block allowance would be wholly inappropriate, an application should be made to the taxing officer for leave to deliver an extended bill. This application may generally be made ex parte, and before the bill is drawn, by letter setting out the grounds, although the taxing officer may require the applicant to attend him before giving his decision. The lodging of a bill in extended form will in itself be accepted as an application for leave but there is no right of election in personal injuries and collision-damage cases and, should leave be refused, no extra costs will be allowed on taxation for drawing the rejected bill. Leave will normally be granted only where it is clearly shown that there are unusual circumstances which would make the use of the block allowance wholly inappropriate or unfair.

Note 4 In cases other than for personal injuries or collision-damage the lodging of a bill which includes a block allowance will generally be taken as a sufficient election. Since the taxing officer may of his own motion refuse to accept the election, with or without affording the elector the right to be heard, a preliminary application may, if so desired, be made to him ex parte by letter in any case of real doubt or difficulty.

Item No		Scale 1 £ 100–500	Scale 2 £ 500–3,000	Scale 3 £ 3,000 +

PART III

6   PREPARATION FOR TRIAL

	Scale 1	Scale 2	Scale 3
Instructions for trial or hearing of action or matter, whatever the mode of trial or hearing, or for the hearing of any appeal.	such sum as is fair and reasonable not exceeding 348	such sum as is fair and reasonable not exceeding 892	Discretionary

Note 1 This item applies to an arbitration, inquiry or reference, but may only be allowed once in the same proceedings.

Note 2 This item is intended to cover–

(a) the doing of any work not otherwise provided for and which was properly done in preparing for a trial, hearing or appeal, or before a settlement of the matters in dispute, including–

   (i) *The Client*: taking instruction to sue, defend, counterclaim, appeal or oppose etc; attending upon and corresponding with client;

   (ii) *Witnesses:* interviewing and corresponding with witnesses and potential witnesses, taking and preparing proofs of evidence and, where appropriate, arranging attendance at court, including issue of witness summons;

   (iii) *Expert evidence:* obtaining and considering reports or advice from experts and plans, photographs and models; where appropriate arranging their attendance at court, including issue of witness summons;

   (iv) *Inspections:* inspecting any property or place material to the proceedings;

   (v) *Searches and inquiries*: making searches in the Public Record Office and elsewhere for relevant documents; searches in the Companies

(continued overleaf)

Item No		Scale 1 £ 100–500	Scale 2 £ 500–3,000	Scale 3 £ 3,000 +
	Registration Office and similar matters;			
	(vi) *Special damages:* obtaining details of special damages and making or obtaining any relevant calculations;			
	(vii) *Other parties:* attending upon and corresponding with other parties or their solicitors;			
	(viii) *Discovery:* perusing, considering or collating documents for affidavit or list of documents; attending to inspect or produce for inspection any documents required to be produced or inspected by order of the court or otherwise;			
	(ix) *Documents:* consideration of pleadings, affidavits, cases and instructions to and advice from counsel, any law involved and any other relevant documents, including collating;			
	(x) *Negotiations:* work done in connection with negotiations with a view to settlement;			
	(xi) *Agency:* correspondence with and attendance upon or other work done by London or other agents;			
	(xii) *Notices:* preparation and service of miscellaneous notices, including notices to witnesses to attend court;			
	(*b*) the general care and conduct of the proceedings.			

The sums sought under each subparagraph (i) to (xii) of paragraph (*a*) should be shown separately against each item followed by the total of all items under paragraph (*a*); the sum charged under paragraph (*b*) should be shown separately; and the total of the items under (*a*) and (*b*) should then follow.

Item No		Scale 1 £ 100–500	Scale 2 £ 500–3,000	Scale 3 £ 3,000 +

Note 3 This item should be prefaced by a brief narrative indicating the issues, the status of the fee earners concerned and the expense rates claimed. The narrative should be followed by a statement in two parts–

    (i) setting out the breakdown of the work done in relation to the relevant sub-paragraph of note 2(*a*); and

    (ii) a statement in relation to care and conduct under note 2(*b*) referring to the relevant factors relied upon; the sum claimed for care and conduct should be expressed as a separate monetary amount as well as a percentage of the work figure.

Note 4 Telephone calls will be allowed as a time charge if, but only if, they stand in the place of an attendance whereby material progress has been made and the time has been recorded or can otherwise be established. A notional conversion into a time charge of letters and routine telephone calls will not be accepted.

Note 5 Where an action is settled before delivery of the brief, the costs of all work reasonably and properly (but not prematurely) done are allowable, and the taxing officer, having regard to the circumstances of each case, must decide whether the work was reasonable and proper and that the time for doing it had arrived.

Note to Parts III, IV and VI. Where in the opinion of the taxing officer, it would have been reasonable to employ a solicitor carrying on business nearer to any relevant place, he shall not allow under Parts III, IV and VI more than he would have allowed to such a solicitor.

(continued overleaf)

Item No		Scale 1 £ 100–500	Scale 2 £ 500–3,000	Scale 3 £ 3,000 +
	PART IV ATTENDANCES			
7	*Lodging:* To lodge papers, when proceedings transferred to county court, including preparation of all necessary documents.		5·75	9·90
8	*Counsel:* Attending counsel in conference including attending to appoint the conference, for each half hour or part thereof.		*For all Scales* 10·00	
9	*Interlocutory attendances etc:* Attending at court, or in chambers, on an interlocutory or any other application to judge or registrar in the course of or relating to the proceedings including time travelling thereto–			
		not exceeding	not exceeding	not exceeding
	(*a*) without counsel	25	71·00	88·00
	(*b*) with counsel	5–6·12	6·19	6·25
	Note 1 This item applies to further consideration pursuant to Ord 23, r 3.			
	Note 2 This item applies to an arbitration, inquiry or reference.			
	Note 3 Interpleader proceedings are to be treated as an application to which this item refers.			
10	*Examination:* On examination of witness under Ord 25, r 3, or RSC Ord 26, r 5, as applied by Ord 14, r 11, for each half-hour or part thereof.			
	Note. This item is allowable where any responsible representative of the solicitor attends.		*For all Scales* 3–9	
11	*Trial or hearing:* Attending the trial or hearing, or hearing of an appeal from an interlocutory or final order or judgment, or to hear a deferred judgment, or where trial is adjourned for want of time or on payment of costs of the day, including time travelling thereto, per day or part of a day.			

Item No		Scale 1 £ 100–500	Scale 2 £ 500–3,000	Scale 3 £ 3,000 +
		not exceeding	not exceeding	not exceeding
	(a) without counsel	43·00	105	152
	(b) with counsel	6·14	6·52	6·76

Note 1 An attendance on the examination of a witness under Ord 20, r 13, is to be treated as an attendance to which this item relates.

Note 2 This item applies to an arbitration, inquiry or reference. If the reference or inquiry was directed at the trial and began on the same day, this item is only to be allowed once in respect of that day.

Note to Part IV: Attendances in court or at chambers or on counsel in conference should appear with a note of the time engaged.

PART V

COUNSEL'S FEES

Item No		Scale 1	Scale 2	Scale 3
12	(a) With brief on trial or on hearing	24–85	30–198	Discretionary
	(b) Where the trial or hearing is continued after the first day or is adjourned for want of time, or on payment of costs of the day or on examination of witness under Ord 20, r 13, for each day or part of a day	⁓ 12–44	15–160	Discretionary
	(c) With brief on further consideration pursuant to Ord 23, r 3, or to hear a deferred judgment; with brief on application in the course of or relating to proceedings: with brief on examination of witness under Ord 25, r 3, or RSC Ord 26, r 5, as applied by Ord 14, r 11; with brief on hearing or judgment summons	9–35	11–49	13–65
	(d) Where there is no local Bar in the court town or within twenty-five miles thereof, if in the opinion of the registrar the maximum fee allowable with the brief is insufficient, a further fee may be allowed, not exceeding for each day on which the trial or hearing takes place			

FOR ALL SCALES
17

(continued overleaf)

Item No	Scale 1 £ 100–500	Scale 2 £ 500–3,000	Scale 3 £ 3,000 +

Note 1 For the purpose of this sub-item there shall be deemed to be a local Bar only in such places as may from time to time be specified in a certificate of the General Council of the Bar published in their Annual Statement.

The General Council of the Bar has certified that the following towns have a Local Bar, viz:– Birmingham, Bournemouth, Bradford, Brighton, Bristol, Cambridge, Cardiff, Chester, Chichester, Colchester, Derby, Exeter, Guildford, Hull, Ipswich, Leeds, Leicester, Liverpool, Manchester, Middlesborough, Newcastle-on-Tyne, Newport, Norwich, Northampton, Nottingham, Plymouth, Preston, Sheffield, Southampton, Swansea.

If counsel has more than one brief on the same day in the same court, that is not a fact to be taken into consideration: *Isaacs* v *Issacs* [1955] P 333, [1955] 2 All ER 811.

Note 2 This sub-item is not allowed in any court within twenty-five miles of Charing Cross.

(e) On conference in chambers or elsewhere: for each half-hour or part thereof	5	9	13
and for leading counsel:	6	15·50	24
(f) For settling any document including particulars of claim, defence, interrogatories and answer	5·50–9·50	9·50–25	11–35
(g) For advising in writing including advising on liability and quantum	4–10·50	10·50–30	12–60

Note 3 Fees to counsel are not to be allowed unless the payment of them is vouched by the signature of counsel or the head of chambers.

Note 4 This item applies to an arbitration, inquiry or reference, but a fee reflecting preparation for trial is only to be allowed once in the same proceedings. If the reference or inquiry was directed at the trial and the reference or inquiry began on the same day, a fee for attending court or attending in chambers is only to be allowed once in respect of that day.

Item No		Scale 1 £ 100–500	Scale 2 £ 500–3,000	Scale 3 £ 3,000 +

Order 50, r 6 provides that where a pleading or other document is settled by counsel it shall be signed by him. Counsel's signature to the draft is sufficient, but counsel's name should appear on the document filed.

PART VI

TAXATION OF COSTS

13   (a) *Taxation:* Preparing bill of costs and copies and attending to lodge; attending taxation; vouching and completing bill; paying taxing fee and lodging certificate or order.   7–18·25   7–51·25   7–65·50

(b) *Review:* Preparing and delivering objections to decision of taxing officer on taxation, or any answers to objections, including copies for service and lodging, considering opponent's objections or answers, if any; preparing for and attending hearing of review.   7·00   7–18·50   7–26·50

Note: This item includes travelling time.

PART VII

SERVICE OUT OF THE JURISDICTION

14   Service of process out of England and Wales, to include drawing, copying, attending to swear and file all affidavits and to obtain order and the fees paid for oaths, such sum as the registrar thinks reasonable.

Appendix B

Fixed Costs

Directions

1 The Tables in this Part of this Appendix show the amount to be entered on the summons (or garnishee order nisi) in respect of solicitors' charges–

    (*a*) in an action for the recovery of a debt or liquidated demand (other than a rent action), for the purpose only of Ord 11, r 2(2) or 3(4), Ord 19, r 6, and Part II of this Appendix; or

    (*b*) in garnishee proceedings, for the purpose only of Ord 30, r 4; or

    (*c*) in an action for the recovery of property, including land, with or without a claim for a sum of money, for the purpose of Part II of this Appendix or of fixing the amount which the plaintiff may receive in respect of solicitors' charges without taxation in the event of the defendant giving up possession and paying the amount claimed, if any, and costs; or

    (*d*) in a rent action, for the purpose of Part II of this Appendix and of fixing the amount which the plaintiff may receive in respect of solicitors' charges without taxation in the event of the defendant paying the amount claimed in sufficient time to prevent the plaintiff's attendance at the hearing.

2 In addition to the amount entered in accordance with the relevant Table the appropriate court fees shall be entered on the summons.

3 In the Tables the expression 'claim' means–

    (*a*) the sum of money claimed, or

    (*b*) in relation to an action for the recovery of land (with or without a claim for a sum of money), a sum exceeding £600 but not exceeding £2,000;

    (*c*) in relation to an action for the recovery of property other than money or land, the value of the property claimed or, in the case of goods supplied under a hire-purchase agreement, the unpaid balance of the total price.

4 The Tables do not apply where the summons is to be served out of England and Wales or where substituted service is ordered.

TABLES OF FIXED COSTS

TABLE I
Where claim exceeds £25 but does not exceed £250

	Amount of charges £
(*a*) Where service is not by solicitor	19·00
(*b*) Where service is by solicitor	20·50

TABLE II
Where claim exceeds £250 but does not exceed £600

	Amount of charges £
(*a*) Where service is not by solicitor	25·00
(*b*) Where service is by solicitor	29·00

TABLE III
Where claim exceeds £600 but does not exceed £2,000

	Amount of charges £
(*a*) Where service is not by solicitor	42·00
(*b*) Where service is by solicitor	46·00

TABLE IV
Where claim exceeds £2,000

	Amount of charges £
(*a*) Where service is not by solicitor	46·00
(*b*) Where service is by solicitor	50·00

PART II
JUDGMENTS
Directions

Where an amount in respect of solicitors' charges has been entered on the summons under Part I of this Appendix and judgment is entered or given in the circumstances mentioned in one of the paragraphs in column 1 of the following Table, the amount to be included in the judgment in respect of the plaintiff's solicitors' charges shall, subject to Ord 38, r 3(4), be the amount entered on the summons together with the amount shown in column 2 of the Table under the sum of money by reference to which the amount entered on the summons was fixed.

Where judgment is entered or given for a sum less than the amount claimed or for the delivery of goods of which the value or the balance of the hire purchase price is a sum less than the amount claimed, the foregoing paragraph shall, unless the court otherwise directs, have effect as if the amount entered on the summons had been fixed by reference to that sum.

(continued overleaf)

APPENDIX I

Fixed Costs on Judgments

Column 1	Column 2 Sum of money		
	A Exceeding £25 but not exceeding £600	B Exceeding £600 but not exceeding £3,000	C Exceeding £3,000
(a) Where judgment is entered in a default action in default of defence	7·00	12·50	14·00
(b) Where judgment is entered on the defendant's admission and the plaintiff's acceptance of his proposal as to mode of payment	16·50	25·00	28·50
(c) Where judgment is entered on an admission delivered by the defendant and the court's decision is given as to the date of payment or instalments by which payment is to be made	15·50	31·50	37·00
(d) Where judgment is given in a fixed date action for– (i) delivery of goods; or (ii) possession of land suspended on payment of arrears of rent, whether claimed or not, in addition to current rent, and the defendant has neither delivered a defence, admission or counterclaim, nor otherwise denied liability	23·00	34·50	43·00

Column 1	Exceeding £500 but not exceeding £3,000	Exceeding £3,000
(e) Where summary judgment is given under Ord 9, r 14	£ 54	£ 62

The following Table shows the amount to be allowed in respect of solicitors' charges in the circumstances mentioned.

	Amount to be allowed
1 For making or opposing an application in the course of or relating to the proceedings where the costs are on lower scale	£7·50
2 For making or opposing an application for a rehearing or to set aside a judgment where the costs are on lower scale	£7·50
3 For filing a request for the issue of a warrant of execution for a sum exceeding £25	£1·25
4 For service of any document required to be served personally (other than an application for an attachment of earnings order or a judgment summons unless allowed under Ord 27, r 9(1)(*a*), or Ord 28, r 10(2)(*a*)(i)), including copy and preparation of certificate of service	£4·80
5 For substituted service, including attendances, making appointments to serve summons, preparing and attending to swear and file affidavits and to obtain order, and the fees paid for oaths	£15·20
6 For each attendance on the hearing of an application for an attachment of earnings order or a judgment summons where costs are allowed under Ord 27, r 9, or Ord 28, r 10	£5·00
7 For the costs of the judgment creditor when allowed in garnishee proceedings or an application under Ord 30, r 12 –	
(*a*) where the money recovered is less than £52	one half of the amount recovered
(*b*) where the money recovered is not less than £52	£28·00
8 For the costs of the judgment creditor when allowed on an application for a charging order	£28·00
9 For obtaining or registering a certificate of judgment where costs are allowed under Ord 35, r 5(3)(d).	£4·80

Appendix C

Assessment of Costs

1 The following Table shows the amount which, pursuant to Ord 38, r 19, may be allowed where costs are to be assessed without taxation. The amount includes the fee for counsel where applicable.

2 In addition to the amount shown in the Table there may be allowed, where appropriate –
   (i) court fees,
   (ii) allowances to witnesses.

Column 1 Scale	*Column* 2 Amount of Charges
Lower Scale	£35–53·50
Scale 1	£39–£99
Scale 2	£60–£369
Scale 3	£88–£445

Fees
(County Court Fees Order 1982)
SI 1982 No 1706
[As amended 1983, 1984, 1985 and 1986]

SCHEDULE 1

FEES

1. The fee payable on entering a plaint or any other originating process includes:

(a) the examination and filing of the application, petition, request or other process or any amendment to it;

(b) the preparation and issue of any summons or other originating document and of any second or subsequent successive summons or origination document together with any notice of hearing;

(c) except where Fee No 2 applies, the service by the court of the summons, application, petition or request and any notice of hearing;

(d) the examination and filing of any affidavit in support of or in opposition to an application;

(e) the issue of an interlocutory application except where a fee is specifically prescribed;

(f) except where otherwise provided, the trial or hearing of any action, originating application, petition or appeal and of any interlocutory application in the course of the proceeding together with the drawing, entering, sealing and issue of the judgment, order or certificate given or made thereon, and the service of the judgment, order or certificate by post.

2. Where any claim, counter-claim, originating application, notice of application or petition is amended and the fees paid before amendment are less than those which would have been payable if the document as amended had been so drawn in the first instance, the party amending the document shall pay the difference.

3. Fee No 1 (ii) shall not be payable on an originating application for the taxation of a solicitor's bill of costs.

4. Where value added tax is chargeable in respect of the provision of any service for which a fee is prescribed by this Schedule, there shall be payable in addition to that fee the amount of the value added tax.

5. In relation to an action for the recovery of goods under a hire-purchase agreement 'value' in this Schedule means the unpaid balance of the total price at the date of the issue of the relevant process.

Col 1 *No and description of fee*	Col 2 *Amount of fee*	Col 3 *Method of charging fee*
1. COMMENCEMENT OF PROCEEDINGS (i) On entering a plaint for the recovery of a sum of money or the delivery of goods. Where the sum claimed or the value of the goods — .... does not exceed £300 ..	10p for every £1 or part thereof claimed. Minimum fee £7	1.(i) Where a sum of money is claimed as an alternative to a claim for another sum of money or to the delivery of goods this fee is to be calculated on the greater sum of money or the value of the goods, whichever is the greater. Where a sum of money is claimed (whether by way of interest or otherwise) in addition to another sum of money or to the delivery of goods then for the purpose of calculating this fee the additional sum is to be added to the sum on which this fee would otherwise be calculated.
Exceeds £300 but does not exceed £500	£37	
Exceeds £500 or is not limited to a particular amount..................	£43	On a claim for delivery of goods it shall be the duty of the plaintiff to estimate the value of the goods and the amount so estimated shall be entered in the request. If the value appears subsequently to the court to have been under-estimated, the plaintiff shall pay the difference between the amount paid by him on entering the plaint and the fee which would have been payable if the estimate had been correct.
(ii) On the commencement of proceedings for any other remedy or relief (other than an order freeing a child for adoption or an adoption order) whether by plaint, originating application, notice of application, petition, appeal or otherwise	£30	1. (ii) Where such a claim is joined with a claim for a sum of money then this fee or Fee No 1 (i) calculated on the sum of money claimed is payable whichever is the greater. Where two or more such claims are joined in the same proceedings the maximum fee payable is £40.

Col 1 *No and description of fee*	Col 2 *Amount of fee*	Col 3 *Method of charging fee*
		On delivery of a counter-claim which exceeds the amount of the claim there shall be paid the amount by which the fee calculated on the amount of the counter-claim exceeds the fee paid by the plaintiff or applicant.
2. SERVICE On request for service by bailiff of any document except– (a) an order in Form N69; (b) an interpleader summons under an execution; (c) an originating application for an adoption order; (d) an order made under s 23 of the Attachment of Earnings Act 1971; (e) an order made under Ord 25, r 3 (4);	£5	Fee No 2 is payable in respect of each person to be served, but in respect of a document not requiring personal service only one fee is payable in respect of two or more persons to be served at the same address. This fee is not payable where service is to effected by post pursuant to Ord 7, r 10 (2).
2A APPEALS ETC (i) On giving notice of an appeal to the judge from the registrar	£10	
(ii) On an application to the judge to set aside the award of an arbitrator	£10	
3. TAXATION (i) On the taxation of costs of expenses	For every £1 or part thereof allowed, 5p	3. (i) No fee is payable where costs are allowed without taxation pursuant to Ord 38, r 18 or 19.

Note.—The Lord Chancellor has directed (1) that in any case where a party has been awarded a proportion only of his costs, this fee should be calculated on the amount allowed on taxation as the party's costs in the action or matter, and not on the proportion of those costs which he is entitled to recover from the other party: (2) that where the costs of an assisted person fall to be taxed between party and party and between solicitor and client, the taxing fee attributable to purely solicitor and client items should be the difference between the taxing fee payable on the party and party items of the bill and the taxing fee payable on the total of the bill: it should be noted that, in view of this direction, there may be cases in which less than the minimum taxing fee will be payable.

Col 1 *No and description of fee*	Col 2 *Amount of fee*	Col 3 *Method of charging fee*
(ii) On an application to the judge to review a taxation......................	£10	3. (ii) The registrar may in any case before taxation require a deposit of the amount of fees which would be payable if the bill or the expenses were allowed by him at the full amount thereof. This fee is not payable if, in an action by a solicitor for costs, the judge refers the bill to the registrar under s 70 of the Act.

4. ENFORCEMENT
    On an application for enforcement of a judgment or order of a county court or through a county court;
(i) By the issue of a warrant of delivery or of execution against goods except a warrant to enforce payment of a court fee or an order for payment of a fine ....
	For every £1 or part thereof of the amount for which the warrant issues, 15p
	Minimum fee £5
	Maximum fee £38
		4. (i) On a warrant of delivery:–
		    (a) the maximum fee is payable unless the value is stated in the judgment or in the request and in that case the fee is to be calculated on that value or the greater value if more than one.
		    (b) where a sum of money is claimed in addition (whether by way of interest or otherwise) then, for the purpose of calculating this fee the sum of money is to be added to the sum on which the fee would otherwise be calculated.

(ii) By an application for an order for the attendance of a judgment debtor or any other person under Ord 25, rr 3 or 4	£12	
(iii) By entering garnishee proceedings ..	£12	
(iv) By the issue of a warrant of possession ...	£25	
(v) By an application for an order charging the land or securities of a judgment debtor	£5	4. (iv) Where the recovery of a sum of money, other than this fee, is sought in addition, the appropriate

Col 1 No and description of fee	Col 2 Amount of fee	Col 3 Method of charging fee
		fee under Fee 4 [i] is also payable.
(vi) By the issue of a judgment summons......	£10	
(vii) By an application for an attachment of earnings order (other than a consolidated attachment of earnings order) to secure payment of a judgment debt..........................		4. (vii) This fee is payable for each defendant against whom an order is sought. Fee No 4 (vii) is not payable where an attachment of earnings order is made on the hearing of a judgment summons.
(viii) On a consolidated attachment of earnings order under Ord 27, r 18, or on an administration order made under s 112 of the Act or s 4 of the Attachment of Earnings Act 1971 ...	10p for every £1 or part thereof Minimum fee £5 Maximum fee £40 For every £1 of the money paid into court in respect of debts due to creditors, 5p	
4A TRIBUNAL AWARDS ETC On an application for the recovery of an award under Ord 25, r 12	£10	
5. SALE		5. (i) This fee to include the reasonable expenses of feeding and caring for any animals.
(i) For removing or taking steps to remove goods to a place of deposit	The reasonable expenses thereof	
(ii) For advertising a sale by public auction pursuant to s 97 of the Act..........................	The reasonable expenses thereof	
(iii) For the appraisement of goods	5p in the £ of the appraised value	
(iv) For the sale of goods (including advertisements, catalogues, sale and commission and delivery of goods) ..	15p in the £ on the amount realised by the sale or such other sum as the register may be considered to be justified in the circumstances.	
(v) Where no sale takes place by reason of an execution being withdrawn satisfied or stopped	(a) 10p in the £1 on the value of the goods seized, the value to be the appraised value where the goods have been appraised or such other sum as the	

Col 1 No and description of fee	Col 2 Amount of fee	Col 3 Method of charging fee
	registrar may consider to be justified in the circumstances and in addition; (b) any sum payable under Fee 5 (i), (ii) or (iii)	
6. COPIES OF DOCUMENTS For a copy of any document, or for examining a plain copy and marking it as an office copy, per page; (a) Typewritten .... (b) Carbon or photographic.........	 50p 25p	6. This fee is payable whether or not the copy is issued as an office copy.
7. REGISTRY OF COUNTY COURT JUDGMENTS On a request to cancel the registration of judgment which has been satisfied	 £1	This fee is to be paid to the county court in which satisfaction was made.
8. ADMIRALTY ACTIONS (i) For a warrant of arrest of a ship or goods including the execution thereof or the issue of a warrant of execution where the ship or goods are not under arrest (including the execution thereof)..................... (ii) On a bail bond ...... (iii) On the sale of a ship or goods .... (iv) For keeping possession of a ship or goods where the registrar employs:— (a) a possession man (b) a shipkeeper	 £10 £2 For every £5 or part thereof of the price, 5p For every day, £10 The reasonable expenses of the shipkeeper employed.	

Index